Tradition and Transition:
The international Imperative
in Higher Education

Publication Series
Center for International Higher Education

Philip G. Altbach. *Comparative Higher Education: Knowledge, the University and Development*, 1997, reprinted 2006. (Commercial edition published by Ablex Publishers. Asian edition published by the Comparative Education Research Centre, University of Hong Kong. Japanese-language translation published by the Tamagawa University Press, Tokyo, Japan. Chinese-language translation published by the People's Education Press, Beijing, China.)

Philip G. Altbach, ed. *Private Prometheus: Private Higher Education and Development in the 21st Century*, 1999. (Commercial edition published by Greenwood Publishers, Westport, CT. Spanish-language translation published by Centro de Estudios Sobre la Universidad, UNAM, Mexico. Japanese-language translation published by the Tamagawa University Press, Tokyo, Japan.)

Philip G. Altbach and Patti McGill Peterson, eds. *Higher Education in the 21st Century: Global Challenge and National Response*, 1999. (Published in cooperation with the Institute of International Education, New York. Spanish-language translation published by Editorial Biblos, Buenos Aires, Argentina.)

Philip G. Altbach and David Engberg. *Higher Education: A Worldwide Inventory of Centers and Programs*, 2000. (Commercial edition published by Oryx Publishers, Phoenix, AZ.)

Philip G. Altbach, ed. *The Changing Academic Workplace: Comparative Perspectives*, 2000. (Also published as a special theme issue of Higher Education, vol. 41, no. 1–2, January/March, 2001.)

Philip G. Altbach and V. Selvaratnam, eds. *From Dependence to Autonomy: The Development of Asian Universities*, 2002. (Commercial edition published by Kluwer Academic Publishers, Dordrecht, Netherlands. Japanese-language edition published by Tamagawa University Press, Tokyo, Japan. Chinese-language edition published in Taiwan. Asian paperback edition published by De La Salle University Press, Manila, Philippines.)

Philip G. Altbach and Yoshikazu Ogawa, eds. *Higher Education in Japan: Reform and Change in the 21st Century*, 2002. (Also published as a special theme issue of *Higher Education 43, no. 1*, January 2002.)

Philip G. Altbach, ed. *The Decline of the Guru: The Academic Profession in Developing and Middle-Income Countries*, 2002. (Commercial edition published by Palgrave Publishers, New York and London. Spanish-language translation published by the

Universidad Metropolitana Autonoma, Mexico City.)

Glenda Kruss and Andre Kraak, eds. *A Contested Good? Understanding Private Higher Education in South Africa,* 2003. (Copublished with PROPHE, University at Albany.)

Damtew Teferra and Philip G. Altbach, eds. *African Higher Education: An International Reference Handbook,* 2003. (Commercial edition published by Indiana University Press, Bloomington, IN.)

Alma Maldonado-Maldonado, Yingxia Cao, Philip G. Altbach, Daniel C. Levy, and Hong Zhu. *Private Higher Education: An International Bibliography,* 2004. (Commercial edition published by Information Age Publishers, Westport, CT.)

Francesca B. Purcell, Robin Matross Helms, and Laura Rumbley. *Women's Universities and Colleges: An International Handbook,* 2004. (Commercial edition published by Sense Publishers, Rotterdam, Netherlands.)

Philip G. Altbach and Toru Umakoshi, eds. *Asian Universities: Historical Perspectives and Contemporary Challenges,* 2004. (Commercial edition published by the Johns Hopkins University Press, Baltimore, MD. Japanese-language edition published by Tamagawa University Press, Tokyo, Japan. Chinese-language edition published by China Ocean University Press, Quingdao, China.)

Philip G. Altbach and Daniel C. Levy, eds. *Private Higher Education: A Global Revolution,* 2005. (Commercial edition published by Sense Publishers, Rotterdam, Netherlands.)

James JF Forest and Philip G. Altbach, eds. *International Handbook of Higher Education,* 2006. (Commercial edition published by Springer Publishers, Dordrecht, Netherlands.)

D. Bruce Johnstone. *Financing Higher Education: Cost Sharing in International Perspective,* 2006. (Commercial edition published by Sense Publishers, Rotterdam, Netherlands.)

Philip G. Altbach, *International Higher Education: Reflections on Policy and Practice,* 2006.

Philip G. Altbach, Leslie A. Bozeman, Natia Janashia, and Laura E. Rumbley, *Higher Education: A Worldwide Inventory of Centers and Programs.* Revised Edition, 2006. (Commercial edition published by SensePublishers, Rotterdam, the Netherlands).

Pamela N. Marcucci and D. Bruce Johnstone, *International Higher Education Finance: An Annotated Bibliography,* 2007.

Tradition and Transition: The International Imperative in Higher Education

Philip G. Altbach

Center for International Higher Education
Lynch School of Education, Boston College
Chestnut Hill, Massachusetts

January 2007

©2007. Center for International Higher Education, Boston College and Sense Publishers.

Boston College Center for International Higher Education
207 Campion Hall
Chestnut Hill MA 02467
USA

Web site: http://www.bc.edu/cihe/

Sense Publishers
POB 21858
3001 AW Rotterdam
The Netherlands

Website: http://www.SensePublishers.com

This edition is not for sale. Copies may be requested from the Center for International Higher Education. A commercial edition is published by Sense Publishers, Rotterdam, the Netherlands.

Funding for this book is provided by the Ford Foundation and Boston College.

Table of Contents

Acknowledgments

This book is part of the research program of the Center for International Higher Education at Boston College. The Center receives funding from the Ford Foundation and the Lynch School of Education. Edith Hoshino and Laura E. Rumbley provided editing assistance. Salina Kopellas and Louise Nally assisted in the preparation of the text. I appreciate the colleagueship and collaboration of Damtew Teferra and Jane Knight, who have coauthored chapters in this book. I am indebted to the publishers that have permitted the use of previously published materials—all of the chapters in this book are reprinted with the permission of the publishers and journals involved. All have been revised and updated for this book.

Chapter 1. "The Logic of Mass Higher Education," *Tertiary Education and Management* 5, no. 2 (1999). © Springer Publishers.

Chapter 2. Originally published as "Globalization and the University: Myths and Realities in an Unequal World," *Current Issues in Catholic Higher Education* 23 (Winter 2003) © Association of Catholic Colleges and Universities.

Chapter 3. "Academic Freedom: International Realities and Challenges," *Higher Education* 41, no. 1–2 (2001). © Springer Publishers.

Chapter 4. "Comparative Perspectives on Private Higher Education," in *Private Prometheus: Private Higher Education and Development in the 21st Century*, ed. P. G. Altbach (Chestnut Hill, MA: Center for International Higher Education, Boston College, 1999). © Center for International Higher Education.

Chapter 5. Originally published as "Empires of Knowledge and Development," in *The Struggle to Compete: Building World-Class Universities in Asia and Latin America*, ed. P. G. Altbach and J. Balán (Baltimore: Johns Hopkins University Press, 2007). © Johns Hopkins University Press.

Chapter 6. Higher Education's Landscape of Internationalization: Motivations and Realities (with Jane Knight), in *The NEA 2006 Almanac of Higher Education* (Washington, DC: National Education Association, 2006). © National Education Association.

Chapter 7. "The Academic Profession: The Special Challenges of Developing Countries," in *The Decline of the Guru: The Academic Profession in Developing and Middle-Income Countries*, ed. P. G. Altbach (Chestnut Hill, MA: Center for International Higher Education, Boston College, 1999). © Center for International Higher Education.

Chapter 8. "The Deterioration of the Academic Estate: International Patterns of Academic Work," in *The Changing Academic Workplace: Comparative Perspectives*, ed. P. G. Altbach (Chestnut Hill, MA: Center for International Higher Education, Boston College, 2000). © Center for International Higher Education.

Chapter 9. "The Past and Future of Asian Universities: 21st Century Challenges," in *Asia's Universities: Past Lessons, Future Prospects*, ed. P. G. Altbach and T. Umakoshi (Baltimore: Johns Hopkins University Press, 2004). © Johns Hopkins University Press.

Chapter 10. "Challenges and Prospects of African Higher Education" (with Damtew Teferra), in *African Higher Education: An International Reference Handbook*, ed. D. Teferra and P. G. Altbach (Bloomington: Indiana University Press, 2003). © Indiana University Press.

Chapter 11. Originally published as "Doctoral Education in the United States: Present Realities and Future Trends," *College and University* 80 (Fall, 2004). © American Association of Colleges and Universities.

Chapter 12. "Research and Training in Higher Education: The State of the Art, in *Higher Education: A Worldwide Inventory of Centers and Programs*, Philip G. Altbach, Leslie A. Bozeman, Natia Janashia, and Laura E. Rumbley, revised edition (Chestnut Hill, MA: Center for International Higher Education, 2006). © Center for International Higher Education.

Introduction

This book examines some of the central issues affecting higher education worldwide. A comparative perspective can illuminate central themes and contribute to our understanding of trends. While it is seldom possible to transplant academic models from one country or system to another, we can learn lessons from the experiences of other countries. The title of this book highlights contemporary realities. Academe worldwide is bound by tradition—a history of more than eight centuries in the West and the impact of the European academic model on the rest of the world. Such tradition may inhibit reform, but it is a valuable reminder of the core values of the university in a period of profound change. The beginning of the 21st century is also a time of considerable transition in academe. Mass enrollments have created changes in the administration, orientation, and financing of higher education worldwide. Technology is a new force that is challenging the traditional university. The worldwide knowledge economy and the pressures of globalization create further tensions. This book shows the interplay between tradition and transition—examining the established norms and values of the university and the forces of change in the university of the 21st century.

The focus also concerns the international imperative—to understand academic change from a comparative and international perspective and the growing international forces that are influencing higher education. While universities in the Middle Ages were international institutions, using Latin for instruction and attracting students and teachers from many countries, the current period has seen a resurgence of internationalism. There is a significant international flow of both students and professors and a growing trend to offer degrees and other academic programs "off-shore" through a variety of transnational educational enterprises. While English has not become "the Latin of the 21st century," it is without question the dominant language for communicating science and scholarship; and it is increasingly used as a language of instruction, even in non-English-speaking environments.

Global Issues and Explanations

Globalization explains everything and has thus lost much of its explanatory power. The world economy is increasingly affected by international trends, and the knowledge economy of the 21st century is quintessentially global in scope and impact. Other aspects of modern society are also increasingly affected by international trends—including higher education. Yet, many analysts attribute all developments in higher education to the impact of globalization, thus forgetting that academic institutions are embedded in national systems and respond to national authorities and local market forces. Global trends are certainly a key variable, but they are by no means the only one. It is important not to exaggerate the idea of globalization in context. The complex interplay between national, regional, and local realities, on the one hand, and broader international trends on the other is central to any effective analysis of the contemporary university.

The pressure to expand enrollments and provide access to wider segments of the population can be observed everywhere, but such developments are more the result of realities within nations and societies than dictated by international agencies or the dominant economic powers. Somewhat more difficult to analyze is, for example, the trend toward the privatization of public higher education and the growth of private higher education in much of the world or the concept of higher education as a "private good" rather than a "public good." It can be argued that the World Bank and its related agencies have pressed an agenda that includes increased private funding for higher education, propelled by their overall economic perspective, but the paucity of funding at the national level is of even greater importance.

The "logic" of higher education expansion stems from local demand as well as from the needs of increasingly sophisticated economies. Academic institutions and governments have had to accommodate the imperative of mass enrollments. Not only is the United States perceived as having a successful academic system, but it was also the first country to cope with mass higher education. Such developments as differentiated academic systems, a public-private mix, charging tuition for study, accreditation systems, and the like are all necessary adjustments to increased access and mass higher education.

This book also focuses on several other elements of the new global reality. Academic freedom is central to the success of any academic institution or system, but it has been largely ignored in current debates. The focus here relates to the topic's relevance and its complexity in the new environment. Academic freedom includes the freedom to teach and learn, as well as to conduct research and communicate knowledge and analysis through publication, without restriction. Academic freedom continues to be contested terrain. In a few places, there are direct restrictions on teaching and research. Professors, and sometimes students, may suffer consequences—including being fired from their posts or occasionally being jailed or worse. In some countries or universities, certain topics, especially in the social sciences, are banned. In others, specific interpretations may be unacceptable. Subtle threats to academic freedom are more widespread. Corporate involvement in university research has sometimes determined the direction of research and restricted the dissemination of results. Ownership of databases and scholarly journals by multinational media firms has introduced commercial considerations into knowledge dissemination. Academic freedom is occasionally threatened by the academic community itself—by professors or sometimes students who wish to control the intellectual climate on campus. Thus, academic freedom remains part of the agenda for higher education worldwide and requires constant reinterpretation and vigilance.

In many countries, the expansion of the private higher education sector accompanies massification. Private higher education is now the fastest-growing sector. In many countries once dominated by public higher education systems   such as several in Latin America—more than half the students attend private institutions. Private sectors have emerged in places, including a number of African countries, where public higher education once constituted the sole institutional pattern. Public universities have been privatized to some extent and are expected to generate more of their own income, through tuition charges as well as other revenue-generating activities. These are all elements of new global reality discussed in this book.

The research university, invented by the Germans in the 19th century and expanded in concept and size in the United States, is at the pinnacle of academic systems worldwide. It is now a key part of the new knowledge economy, and most countries seek to build one or more research universities in the struggle to compete in higher education worldwide. For developing countries, the challenges of building and sustaining research universities are difficult.

The Academic Profession

The academic profession is much affected by both tradition and transition. Discussion of the future of higher education often ignores the professoriate. It is incorrectly assumed that well-qualified teachers will always offer instruction and researchers will undertake the cutting-edge basic research so necessary for 21st-century economies. While it is true that teachers can be found to fill classrooms, it is not assured that they will be of adequate quality or well trained. In many countries, most academics do not hold a doctorate and many have only a bachelor's degree. Part-time instructors are the fastest-growing segment of the academic labor force—in Latin America a large majority of the academic profession consists of part-time instructors; and the proportions are growing everywhere, even in industrialized nations. In much of the world, a full-time academic salary is inadequate to support a middle-class family, and thus many university teachers must hold more than one job.

At one time, at least in most industrialized nations, an academic career offered high status, adequate (if modest) income, and a substantial degree of employment security. This is no longer the case for a growing number of academics even in industrialized nations. Terms of employment have been changed in a number of countries. For example, tenure has been abolished in the United Kingdom, and in much of Europe the traditional civil service status of professors is being eliminated or redefined. There are fewer full-time, career-ladder positions everywhere. The attractions of an academic career are being diminished.

In developing and middle-income countries, the situation is even more dire. Never highly attractive, academic careers are becoming increasingly problematic, especially in comparison with other options in growing economies such as India and China. In Russia and other countries of the former Soviet system, which at one time provided relatively attractive academic careers, the terms and conditions of academic work have deteriorated and opportunities for highly educated people have flourished outside the universities.

The results are already evident—enrollments in doctoral programs have declined in many fields in numerous countries, and the qualifications of people seeking advanced degrees are lower. The "best and brightest" are simply no longer interested in an academic career. The implications of dramatic changes in the structure and conditions of the academic career will in a few years be experienced worldwide. Will the next generation of academics retain the ability and motivation to perform the best teaching and research? It is unclear whether the terms and conditions of the academic career will provide the opportunities for the best-quality work.

There is also an unprecedented international flow of academic talent—typically from poor to wealthy countries. Many of the most talented academics leave their home countries to work where they can earn the highest salaries and enjoy the best working conditions. This trend inevitably weakens academic systems in developing countries. What constituted in an earlier period a "brain drain" with talent being permanently lost to the country of origin is now a much more complex relationship with scholars maintaining links with their home countries, contributing expertise, and sometimes returning.

The situation of the academic profession is complex and, in general, problematic. A combination of factors contributes to deteriorating working conditions and low morale. The future of higher education depends on the academic profession, and one cannot be optimistic about the future in light of the circumstances of the professoriate.

These are among the themes analyzed in *Tradition and Transition*. The goal is to analyze in a comparative context some of the central challenges facing higher education. The relationship between societal pressures such as mass access in a context of public underinvestment in higher education is but one of these problems. This book seeks to link societal challenges and institutional responses.

Global Issues

1

The Logic of Mass Higher Education

Mass higher education had become the international norm by the end of the 20th century. Today, most countries have large academic systems that educate a growing number of young people and require substantial resources. China and India, which enroll, respectively, 21 and under 15 percent of the relevant age group in postsecondary education, have large academic systems. China now enrolls the world's largest student population, at 23 million; the United States is second with 17 million; and India follows, with about 10 million. Worldwide, there are more than 70 million students in postsecondary education. The Vancouver-based Commonwealth of Learning estimates that 150 million students will be in need of postsecondary education by 2020. Virtually all industrialized and many middle-income countries have built mass higher education systems, enrolling more than a quarter of the age cohort. Most are moving toward enrolling 40 percent or more, and a few now enroll half of that population sector.

We refer to "massification" as the process by which academic systems enroll large numbers—and higher proportions of the relevant age group—of students in a range of differentiated academic institutions. Even countries that until recently have had small and elitist academic systems are facing pressures for expansion. There is no country that is immune from the pressure for massification.

The United States, which enrolls more than half of the age group and has traditionally permitted nontraditional students (older individuals and others without standard academic credentials) into postsecondary education, is the leader in terms of access. However, both

Western Europe and a number of Pacific Rim countries in Asia are approaching American participation rates. Academic systems have expanded for several reasons. A degree from a postsecondary educational institution is increasingly seen as a prerequisite for economic success. The skills imparted through university or other postsecondary study are in demand for the increasingly complex and technology-based economies of the 21st century. The certification provided through a college or university degree is important in modern society. University degrees are also seen as essential for social mobility.

In most parts of the world, higher education was limited in size and scope until the 1960s. Sociologist Martin Trow, writing in the early 1970s, divided the world's academic systems into three categories—elite (under 15 percent of the relevant age group participating in post-secondary education), mass (between 20 and 30 percent), and universal (above 30 percent)—arguing that higher education was inevitably moving toward universal access (Trow 1973). He argued that the traditional university structure in most countries could accommodate up to 15 percent of the age group, but that a higher percentage would require structural changes. Trow proved to be both too optimistic and too pessimistic. The countries at the upper end of the scale, such as the United States and Canada, stopped expanding higher education and currently enroll slightly more than half of the age group. Countries that Trow identified as moving toward mass higher education at the end of the 1960s have dramatically expanded—most of Western Europe now enrolls more than 30 percent of the age cohort—and some have reached a 50 percent rate of inclusion. Most dramatically, a few Latin American countries; such Asian nations as South Korea, Taiwan, the Philippines; and some countries in Central and Eastern Europe are expanding rapidly and are close to universal access.

The 1990s saw the emergence of mass and universal access in many parts of the world. All the larger Western European nations—Germany, the United Kingdom, France, and Italy—have expanded significantly, and all now enroll 30 percent or more of the age cohort. Higher education expansion in Central and Eastern Europe slowed in the aftermath of the fall of communism, although growth is again beginning to take place in this region. The Asian middle-income countries that had been experiencing rapid economic growth were hit by economic problems in the late 1990s. In general, economic cycles have not significantly affected expansion either in this part of the world or elsewhere. Expansion has been growing rapidly in most of the developing world—including China and India (which now have the world's first- and third-largest student populations) and Latin America (which has seen dramatic growth). Only in sub-Saharan Africa, beset by severe long-term economic and political crises, did growth slow significantly in some places. Despite some regional variations, the 21st century continues a pattern of expanded access to higher education.

While confirming global expansion and the creation of mass systems of higher education, it is important not to overgeneralize these trends. Some academic systems have already reached a level of maturity or are subject to social or economic conditions that will stymie expansion. Japan, for example, already has a high level of participation in higher education and is experiencing a drop in the university-age population, and it suffered through a long economic downturn during the 1990s. Experts predict that total student numbers will decline modestly, and some less prestigious private colleges and universities will fail as a result of an enrollment slump. By way of comparison, the United States, which also has a high rate of participation, is currently experiencing expansion due to short-term demographic growth in the 18- to 22-year-old population. Nontraditional students—older people who may have been unable to obtain a degree when they were young or who see the need to upgrade their skills—are demanding access to higher education, and most countries have moved to accommodate them.

The mass higher education systems emerging worldwide have an inherent logic that will characterize key elements of academe in the coming decades. Traditional patterns of organization and governance will, of course, continue to exist; universities are highly conservative institutions, and change comes slowly. But the logic of mass higher education will affect all countries and academic systems.

The American higher education system serves as a kind of model for the rest of the world in an era of mass higher education, given that the United States was the first country to experience mass access to higher education—beginning in the 1920s and dramatically expanding in the 1950s. The patterns and structures that evolved in the United States have provided models for other countries to examine—and in some cases emulate—as they confronted expansion (Altbach 1998a). Most other academic systems were elitist until the middle of the 20th century or even thereafter and thus did not need to cope with large numbers of students. As they grew, these systems were forced to adapt to new realities, which often proved to be a difficult task. Italy, for example, still relies on a traditional academic organizational structure that does not function well with larger enrollments. Britain restructured its academic system in the 1980s to deal with larger student numbers. In developing countries, the elite models imposed by colonial rulers have remained basically unreformed and no longer work well. Many of the world's academic systems are groping for new models that will operate effectively in the context of mass higher education.

This chapter discusses some of the central realities of the "massification" of higher education worldwide (*Academic Reforms in the World* 1997). The following topics are central to the phenomenon of mass higher education in the 21st century:

- the challenge of funding;
- new sectors of higher education, including private higher education, for-profit higher education, and new vocational institutions;
- distance learning as a means of coping with demand;
- the differentiation and complexity of academic institutions;
- the managerialization of academic institutions and creation of the "administrative estate";
- the nature of the academic profession; and
- diversity of students and student culture.

The Challenge of Funding

Higher education is expensive. The cost of providing instruction, libraries and laboratories, and the other accoutrements of higher education has grown dramatically (Financing Higher Education 1998). Libraries and laboratories in particular now require major investments of resources. The new communications technologies, as well as keeping abreast of the dramatic growth in knowledge, are also costly.

Significant changes in attitude on the funding of higher education have evolved since the 1980s. Earlier, in most countries a consensus existed that higher education was a "public good" contributing significantly to society by imparting knowledge and skills to those who were educated at universities and other postsecondary institutions. Since higher education was considered a public good, it was agreed that society should bear a large part of the cost. In the 1980s, with the World Bank and extending to many governments, higher education began to be viewed as mainly a "private good," benefiting the individual more than society as a whole (World Bank 1994). The logic of this change in thinking places more of the burden for financing higher education on the "users"—students and their families. In many countries, policies require students to pay a growing proportion of the cost of postsecondary education.

Many countries have experienced a significant change in attitudes with regard to public spending. The 1980s witnessed a gradual breakdown of the consensus built up following World War II on the role of the state in funding not only higher education but public services in general and an accompanying policy of high taxes to pay for these state services. The administrations of Margaret Thatcher in Britain and Ronald Reagan in the United States had a major impact in this area. Even in Sweden, the Social Democrats lost their majority for a time, and the welfare state was to some extent weakened. The collapse of the Soviet Union and of state socialism in Eastern Europe further strengthened conservative thinking. Finally, the impact of world economic trends and competitiveness placed pressure on many governments to trim public spending (Kuttner 1997). In the wake of the 1992 Maastricht Treaty and the advent of euro-based economic policies in the European Union, public spending growth has been limited and in some countries cut. Australia and New Zealand have also been at the forefront of this trend. One of the countries that have moved most rapidly from state support to a market model is Chile (Brunner 1997). Although initiated by a military regime, Chile's subsequent democratic governments (both center-right and left) have retained similar economic policies. Other Latin American nations have moved in this direction as well—although market-oriented neoliberal approaches remain controversial. Many analysts have related these policies with globalization and the neoliberal policies stressed by the World Bank and other international agencies and have linked them to the continuing funding problems faced by academic systems everywhere (Stiglitz 2002).

Thus, at the same time that higher education is faced with significant expansion in the number of students, the government—the traditional source of funding in most countries—is less willing to invest in postsecondary education, placing significant pressure on systems of higher education. Expansion cannot be halted because public demand is immense, and many European countries guarantee access to those who pass secondary school examinations. Higher education institutions and systems have had to accommodate more students with fewer financial resources.

In much of Western Europe, including the United Kingdom, expansion has continued or has even accelerated because government policy has remained committed to increased access. In Germany, France, and Italy higher education remains essentially free while at the same time government funding has not increased to match enrollment growth. The result has been overcrowding at the universities and a deterioration in the conditions of study. In Germany, student discontent resulted in the largest demonstrations since the 1960s. After major political turmoil, fees were introduced in Britain for the first time as a way to provide funding to handle increased enrollments and reduced government allocations. Introduced by the Conservatives, fees were supported by the Labour government now in power. Indeed, Labour legislated "top-up" fees, giving academic institutions for the first time the power to set their own fee levels. In other parts of the world—such as in Latin America, Central and Eastern Europe, and parts of Asia—private initiative has been encouraged as a way of serving increased demand for postsecondary education, and private higher education is increasing its share of total enrollments.

New Sectors of Higher Education

As higher education expands, traditional institutions such as universities grow. In addition, new types of institutions are inevitably added in order to serve larger numbers, and also to provide more diverse education and training for a more disparate clientele. The university remains at the core of an expanded higher education system. Other forms of postsecondary education provide both expanded access and diversity. Because of the financial pressures discussed earlier as well as private institutions' ability to respond more rapidly to new demands, private higher education has quickly expanded.

Nonprofit private universities and colleges now constitute a significant part of the postsecondary systems of many countries. Such schools are beginning to emerge in countries where the private sector has not previously been active (e.g., Malaysia, Hungary) (Geiger 1986; Altbach 1999). Private sectors can be quite diverse in terms of quality, orientation, and focus, as well as sponsorship and financial aspects. Religious institutions are a significant part of the private higher education sector in many countries. In Latin America, where the Roman Catholic Church established many of the oldest and most prestigious universities, religiously sponsored higher education is especially influential.

These nonprofit institutions have been overshadowed—at least in terms of numbers—by newer, more entrepreneurial private universities and by specialized institutions, many of which are of questionable quality (Altbach 1998b). A similar phenomenon exists in Central and Eastern Europe, where there has been a proliferation of private institutions established to serve specific segments of an expanding market for higher education. Many of the newer private institutions have scarce resources, and most focus on fields of high demand—such as management studies, computer science, and information technology. Private institutions may also offer instruction in fields that are inexpensive to teach, such as some arts and social science subjects that require no laboratory facilities or other costly equipment. The newer private institutions are often entrepreneurial—they take advantage of "market niches," advertise their "products," and operate much like private businesses.

The private higher education sector enrolls a majority of students in many countries. It has traditionally enrolled 80 percent of the student population in Japan, South Korea, Taiwan, and the Philippines. More than half the students in Indonesia now attend private institutions. Similarly, the private sector now enrolls more than half the students in Mexico, Argentina, Brazil, and several other Latin American countries and is a growing sector in Central and Eastern Europe. In the United States, private enrollments have remained steady at around 20 percent of the total for a half century or more, and Western Europe has not seen dramatic growth. Clearly, private higher education is the fastest-growing segment of postsecondary education, and it has provided the capacity to serve growing demand.

While for-profit private postsecondary schools have long existed in many countries, they have seldom been considered as a legitimate part of the academic system. In the past several decades, the for-profit sector has grown rapidly in many countries—depending on whether legal and regulatory systems permit such institutions—and now constitutes a significant part of the postsecondary system. Traditionally, the for-profit sector consisted mainly of small vocationally oriented schools that provided specific job-oriented skills. In many countries, these schools were not formally recognized and could not award degrees. The quality of the for-profit sector varied tremendously, and often there was no way of assessing standards or quality. For students, it was an environment of "caveat emptor"—let the buyer beware. In the United States, this sector consisted almost exclusively of trade schools offering specialized instruction in highly applied fields. Some of these schools were able to take advantage of government-sponsored loan programs. In Japan, schools preparing students to take university entrance examinations, the *yobikos* and the *jukus*, are a central part of the for-profit sector. In the Philippines and a number of other countries, some colleges and universities operate on a for-profit basis.

In the past decade, there has been dramatic growth of the for-profit sector. In the United States, the University of Phoenix, which has the ability to offer degrees and is accredited by one of the regional accrediting agencies, has pioneered degree-granting activity in the for-profit sector (Sperling and Tucker 1997). This institution, with branches in a dozen states, is now the largest private university in the United States, and its stock is traded on the stock exchange. It offers vocationally tailored degrees in such fields as management studies by using information technology and part-time faculty. In many other countries, new for-profit schools have been established, mainly in high-demand fields. For example, schools specializing in computer science and information technology are widespread in India, which has a major software and computer industry. These for-profit schools cannot offer degrees, are largely unregulated, and are of varying quality. In India, as well as in other countries, there are significant problems of measuring the quality and effectiveness of this new sector and ensuring that students have reliable information concerning the institutions.

While the traditional university remains the central institution in postsecondary education worldwide, the university represents a small part of the total postsecondary enterprise. Higher education is becoming increasingly vocational in focus, and the institutional mix of higher education reflects this interest. In the United States, the community college sector has grown in size and importance. These two-year institutions, which are mainly vocational in focus, now enroll 25 percent of American students (Cohen and Brawer 1996). Similar accommodation to vocational interests can be seen in other countries. Examples of such vocationally oriented nondegree schools in Europe are the *Fachhochschulen* in Germany, the HBO institutions in the Netherlands, and similar institutions in other European countries. Much of the growth in higher education in Europe and in some other countries is taking place in the nonuniversity sector.

Distance Higher Education
Mass higher education has stimulated an interest in distance education. The advent of new technologies has permitted distance education to develop in new and unexpected ways. In fact, the evolution in distance education is still in its early stages. Distance education is not, of course, a new idea. Correspondence courses and other methods of delivering education without bringing students together have long been in existence. The University of South Africa, for example, has for more than a half century mainly offered academic degrees through correspondence. The pioneering contemporary distance education effort, the British Open University, also started in the 1960s, before the advent of the new technologies. It began its educational programs with a combination of written course materials, television, and direct meetings with course tutors in small group settings. While the Open University is somewhat less expensive than traditional higher education, it is not dramatically cheaper. Now, with more reliance on purely distance methods, costs have been reduced (Mason 1998). Increasingly, distance education providers rely on the Internet for all instruction and evaluation—with the concept becoming almost synonymous with the use of Internet-based technology.

This decade has seen the development in many countries of distance higher education that makes use of the new technologies. By 2000, 8

of the 10 largest distance–higher education providers were in developing or middle-income countries, with the largest, Adadolu University in
Turkey, serving 578,000 students and China's TV University following
with 530,000 (Task Force on Higher Education and Society 2000, 31).
In Japan, the University of the Air uses a range of methods for delivering instruction, including television. Everyman's University in Israel
has also built up a clientele for its services. The most dramatic expansion of distance higher education has been in several developing countries. Thailand has two large distance education institutions offering
degree programs throughout the country, enrolling more than a half
million students. The Indira Gandhi Open University in India offers
instruction to even larger numbers in most of the country's states.

Distance higher education is still in the process of development (Van
Dusen 1997). Few studies have been undertaken on the effectiveness of
the instruction provided through distance education. The financial conditions are also not clear, although the limited existing data show that
costs are lower but not dramatically so. The mix of computer-mediated
instruction, direct contact with an instructor (perhaps through video-
conferencing, Web-based communication, or e-mail), and reading material is part of a powerful combination of instructional techniques that are
in the process of being molded into an effective tool for learning.

Many questions remain concerning the true costs, the appropriate
use of technologies, and issues related to monitoring. Many have
rushed to use distance education as a "quick fix" to provide access, hop-
ing that the technologies will catch up with the demand. Too little attention has been paid to effectiveness and quality (Robins and Webster
2002).

Distance education is ideally suited to the international delivery of
educational initiatives. It is easy to send educational programs across
borders, and there are already many Internet-based educational offerings. Questions of control and cultural or other biases that may be part
of cross-border education have yet to be answered. There is much to be
learned about how the process of teaching and learning works in cross-
cultural contexts.

Already, millions of students are participating in this sector worldwide, the large majority of them in developing countries. Distance
higher education allows students to be admitted without the construction of expensive campuses and libraries or the hiring of teachers to put
in individual classrooms. While distance programs may not result in
dramatic savings in direct instructional costs, they do eliminate construction and other infrastructure expenditures.

In the industrialized nations, however, distance higher education has not always proved financially successful, nor has it consistently attracted large enrollments. The British Open University, for example, established an American branch that proved to be unsuccessful and was closed. The Western Governors University, organized by several public-university systems in the western part of the United States, did not attract many students and was also eliminated, as was a distance initiative by a consortium of prestigious American private universities.

Distance higher education is an integral part of a mass higher education system (Brown and Duguid 1996). It can serve students in remote locations, permits rapid expansion, and is flexible in implementing rapid changes in curriculum. However, it remains unclear if the best-quality education can be delivered in remote locations without providing students access to libraries or to direct contact with instructors. Theoretically, at least, distance higher education at its best could provide a quality education. Whether the kind of programs now offered in countries such as Thailand or India can truly achieve excellence remains an open question.

The Diversity and Complexity of Academic Institutions

Not only do new institutional types and ways of delivering instruction form part of mass higher education, existing universities also are changing. In most cases, institutions are growing in size and in the diversity of programs offered to students. Clark Kerr's description of the multiversity in the United States is relevant internationally (Kerr 1995). While universities retain their basic core functions and governance structure, departments, faculties, and schools grow in size and number. Whole new institutes or other academic units may be added. The very mission of the university may also expand. The traditional dedication to teaching and research may extend to direct involvement with industry and other institutions in society and service to many constituencies. In most cases, growth takes place by accretion—by adding on new functions and responsibilities and increasing the size of existing units without changing the basic structure of the institution.

This pattern of institutional growth has been both a strength and a weakness. It has permitted universities to expand to meet society's needs and to maintain their centrality in the higher education system. At the same time, it has made universities more difficult to manage and has severely damaged traditional patterns of governance. The size and complexity of the modern university has increased bureaucracy, alienated both faculty and students, and undermined the ideal of participation and shared governance. The tradition of control by the professors, enshrined in the medieval University of Paris and protected through the centuries, may be facing its most serious threat in the current period. It is worth keeping in mind that the concept of shared governance and a strong element of faculty control originated in the German Humboldtian ideal in the 19th century and was adapted later in the American university model in the early years of the 20th century (Ben-David and Zloczower 1962). As universities have grown larger, it has been very difficult to maintain traditional forms of governance. Institutions have necessarily become more bureaucratic, and direct faculty control or even significant faculty participation has declined.

In this respect, Western Europe is moving closer to the United States in terms of basic institutional control. The Netherlands is a leading example of this trend in governance reform. In the United States, the traditional power of the faculty has been eroded by administrative control due in part to the logic of expanding institutions and in part to demands for accountability, although professorial power remains stronger in the research universities than in other institutions (Hirsch and Weber 2001).

Not only has governance changed as the result of institutional expansion, the work of the university has also expanded; and new offices, departments, schools, and other structures have emerged to take on these new functions. In the United States, the proliferation of organized research units, often called centers or institutes, reflects the expanded research role of the leading universities. These research units often have a good deal of autonomy, especially when they are funded by external agencies. Links with industry are considered a central part of the contemporary mission of many universities, and administrative offices have been established to facilitate university-industry relationships. Public service has grown in importance as well, with offices being established to administer this area. As student numbers have grown, universities have often added staff to deal with students. In all cases, the increase has meant more administration and control.

As the curriculum has expanded, new departments and institutes have been created. Interdisciplinary teaching and research have also grown in importance, and academic units have been established to foster interdisciplinary work. Entire new fields have emerged in the past several decades. Computer science and informatics, for example, did not exist several decades ago. Now, these fields are among the most important in academe. The field of management studies has gained in importance, as have fields such as international trade. New discoveries in the biomedical sciences have led to new departments, institutes, and centers.

The logic of mass higher education has induced significant changes in the universities. There are some discernible worldwide patterns, although approaches differ according to national circumstance and the history of universities. The universal reality constitutes a decline in professorial power and the growth of academic bureaucracy. Administrators, increasingly career-track professionals, have increased in number and hold enhanced power in the modern mass university.

There are a number of approaches to differentiation of higher education worldwide. A few examples will illustrate patterns. In the United States, higher education does show differentiation of public higher education within the states. While California is the best known and perhaps the most effective example of a statewide system in the public higher education sector, multicampus systems exist in almost every state. The traditional American pattern of boards of trustees and a strong president accountable directly to the trustees is generally compatible with the expansion of universities.

In Western Europe, universities are experiencing governance reforms. The Dutch have pioneered the trends that will likely occur in other countries: enhancing the influence of the administration, requiring greater direct accountability to government, the diminishing of professorial power, and the elimination of meaningful student participation in governance. Changes in the British higher education system during the Thatcher regime in the 1980s also brought significant alterations in governance. Vice chancellors and other executives were given greater power. Higher education was made more directly accountable to government with the abolition of the University Grants Committee. The elimination of the "binary" structure that separated the universities and the polytechnics into two separate categories also made the system more closely linked to government and increased competitiveness (Warner and Palfreyman 2001; Williams 2003).

The Rise of the Administrative Estate

Administrative power was pioneered in US universities, which have traditionally carried out a strong executive function in higher education. College and university presidents are appointed by the board of trustees rather than elected by the faculty; and senior administrators, such as vice presidents and deans, are in turn appointed by the president, generally with the advice of relevant faculty. Senior administrators control the budget, academic planning mechanisms, and the other levers of institutional power. Institutional patterns vary, with the most prestigious universities having a greater degree of professorial power and autonomy than those lower in the academic hierarchy (Youn and Murphy 1997).

As their functions expand and diversify, universities add administrators to deal with them. In the United States, the fastest-growing sector in higher education is academic administration. While the number of faculty members has remained fairly steady, administrators have increased in number (Shattock 2003). The new functions are usually too complex for faculty members to handle on a part-time and nonexpert basis. They require full-time attention and specialized expertise in accountancy, law, management, health services, statistics, and other types of expertise required by the contemporary university. The demands for accountability have also added to the number of administrators needed to generate the statistics, reports, financial documentation, and other data for government authorities, trustees, and accrediting bodies. Pioneered in the United States, the field of "institutional research," which is focused on providing internal statistics and other data and analysis for the internal use of academic institutions, has reached Europe and will inevitably spread to other parts of the world. Legal officers manage the university's legal relationships with external groups as well as with students or professors. The legal staff may also have responsibility for patents and licenses produced by university researchers. Administrators have little direct relation to the professoriate and do not owe their jobs to the faculty. They have become a new "estate" of the university—a self-perpetuating group central to the operation of the institution.

The American model is one approach to handling the administrative functions of institutions. In Germany and some other European nations, universities have a dual administrative structure, with an elected rector presiding over the academic functions of the university and a government-appointed administrator (the chancellor), who has responsibility for the purely administrative aspects of the institution. The chancellor is a civil servant and not an academic, and he or she typically stays in the position for an extended period while the academic rector serves for a two- or three-year term. As the administrative structure and budget of the university have grown, the power of the chancellor has increased. At the same time, the German *Länder* (states) and governments in some other countries have devolved part of their budgetary and other controls to the academic institutions, giving the institutions more autonomy. Academic institutions have become more complex but in some ways more autonomous.

The Academic Profession
As noted, the academic profession has lost some of its power and autonomy within the university. Academic work, for a growing number of people within the profession, is changing. Indeed, the academic pro-

fession itself is adapting to the new realities. New types of academics are taking their places in the universities and colleges—clinical professors, research professors, part-time and adjunct academic staff, and others are all part of the mass system. The professorial ideal of autonomy to teach without much control from external authority is less often achieved. In many countries, workloads have increased and class size has grown.

Academic work is to some extent becoming more specialized. Growing numbers of teachers are hired only to teach and not to engage in research or contribute to the growth of scholarship. Elite professors, employed by research-oriented universities, produce the large proportion of published scholarship and obtain most of the research grants but are becoming more of a minority within the academic profession. In the United States, it is estimated that fewer than one-fifth of the professoriate is in this "research cadre" (Haas 1996; Schuster and Finkelstein 2006). The rest of the American professoriate engages mainly in teaching rather than in research and service. While the professoriate in most European countries, as well as Japan and South Korea, expresses a high degree of interest in research, a relatively small portion of the profession is actually producing published scholarship (Enders 2001).

Significant structural changes are taking place in the academic profession. In many countries, the proportion of full-time academics is declining as part-time teachers grow in number. This is true in the United States, where it is estimated that more than 30 percent of teaching is now carried out by part-time faculty. The number of full-time but nonpermanent faculty members has also increased. These teachers often carry a higher teaching load than permanent staff members and cannot obtain regular professorial positions. In Latin America, part-time faculty are the norm, although some countries have sought to increase the number of full-time professors because of the assumption that part-time faculty lack loyalty or commitment to the institution at which they are teaching. Other parts of the world are moving toward the Latin America case without anticipating the inevitable repercussions.

These changes in the nature of the academic labor force will have significant implications (Altbach 2003). Fewer well-qualified young people will be attracted to academe once they realize that they cannot expect a full-time career. Average salaries will drop as the profession increasingly consists of part-time and temporary junior staff. Research orientation and productivity will decline as fewer professors are focused on research. Institutional loyalty and commitment will dissipate, and the university will have fewer professors to participate in governance.

Widespread criticisms have been voiced of the permanent employment status of the professoriate in most countries. Faculty members, especially senior professors, hold "tenure" in most countries—their jobs are for all practical purposes guaranteed until the age of retirement. Permanent appointment status protects the academic freedom of the professoriate, and it is a way of attracting the highest-quality individuals to the profession. In many countries, permanent status was traditionally awarded after a few years of probationary employment. In the United States and some other countries the evaluation process for tenured appointments comes after six years of service and is generally quite rigorous in nature. In some countries, permanent appointment is anticipated but not strongly protected. While patterns of appointment and promotion vary, the standard system begins with probationary appointments and ends with a permanent position.

Critics argue that permanent appointment precludes regular evaluation and prevents accountability. It is also thought to place too great a burden on academic institutions, denying them the flexibility to reduce staffing in some fields while expanding in others or to adjust to changing financial circumstances. Tenure, it is argued, promotes "deadwood"—unproductive professors undeserving of their positions. In Britain, traditional tenure was abolished for new appointees in the 1980s, although academic staff have remained de facto permanent employees. In the United States, while no basic change has taken place, "posttenure review" that includes accountability for professors but stops short of limiting tenure is more common. In Germany and most other European countries, fewer initial appointments are being made to "tenure-track" positions, although the traditional ironclad tenure system remains.

Mass higher education has reduced both the power and the autonomy of the professoriate. The "traditional" professor is no longer the standard for academic appointments. Alternative academic career paths now exist, most of which are not as favorable to the professoriate as in the past. The terms and conditions of academic work are being changed to reflect the realities of mass higher education. These changes are perhaps inevitable, but they also create problems for the future of the university. Will the most qualified individuals be attracted to academic careers under the new circumstances? Will the universities be able to produce the research that increasingly complex societies and economies require? Will a sufficient portion of the professoriate be committed to the ethos and governance of the university? These and other questions are of considerable importance as the formal principles of mass higher education affects the professoriate.

Students

Of course, students are at the heart of the mass university. The growth in numbers of students completing secondary education, interest in social mobility, the needs of industrial and postindustrial societies, and the emphasis on obtaining diplomas and degrees has contributed to the rising demand for higher education. In many countries, including some developing countries, a university degree is a requirement for a middle-class occupation. Student numbers have risen dramatically from the 1960s to the 1980s, when some countries saw a reduction in growth. For most developing countries, expansion did not stop—it continues unabated. Even in the United States, Germany, and much of the rest of Europe, where there is little or no rise in the university-age population, a combination of increasing graduation rates from secondary education and demand from nontraditional age groups has kept up the pressure on universities to expand access. As mentioned earlier, nontraditional students refer to those who are older or who may lack standard secondary education credentials. In only a few countries, such as Japan, has demand for higher education stagnated, mainly because of the decline in the number of university age students; and even in Japan demand would experience growth if access were opened to nontraditional age groups. In a number of European countries, including Russia, population declines will mean fewer students going on to postsecondary education, assuming that access remains relatively stable.

The composition of the student population has changed with the advent of mass higher education. In the industrialized countries, higher education has been dominated by the middle classes for a century or more; and as the middle class has expanded, the universities have grown. Access for the working class is now widespread. In developing countries, higher education is increasingly available to the middle classes and even to working-class young people. In many countries, nontraditional students are gaining access to higher education. The proportion of women students has dramatically increased: in the United States and most European countries, women comprise at least half the student population, with major variations by field of study. This increasingly diverse student population means a breakdown in a common student culture.

Students also differ more in their academic abilities and interests, and this too has had an impact on the university. In differentiated academic systems, students are selected into different types of institutions according to their interests and abilities. New types of institutions have been created for students who may not be suited for traditional academic study. For example, in the United States, the two-year vocationally oriented community colleges require only graduation from secondary school for entry. They are "open door" institutions. There is considerable interest internationally in the concept of relatively open-access community colleges as a way to increase access and provide postsecondary education at a relatively low price.

Students are less carefully selected, contributing in part to the large numbers who drop out of postsecondary education or take a longer time to complete their academic degrees. This "wastage" has financial and other implications but is part of the reality of mass higher education. Academic systems that traditionally had a laissez faire approach to study and degree completion are tightening up requirements and instituting accountability measures for students. Students who do not make satisfactory academic progress are given deadlines and then terminated. Many countries are moving toward an American-style course-credit system because it provides regular assessment of students and a way of monitoring academic progress.

Students are increasingly looking at postsecondary education as a way to enhance employment opportunities, income, and social mobility. They are less interested in the intrinsic values of higher education. Students see themselves as consumers of educational products. This change has significant implications for student attitudes, the relationship between students and academic institutions, and the way the university and other postsecondary institutions relate to students.

Conclusion

Mass higher education has also brought with it significant changes in how academic institutions relate to society. When higher education served an elite, universities were small and the budget for postsecondary education was relatively modest. A general consensus existed concerning the role of the university in society, and considerable autonomy was granted to universities. Higher education is now central to all societies. Universities provide the essential training for virtually all occupations necessary for technologically based societies and for the business and government sectors as well. Universities provide new knowledge through research. Higher education is a matter of major concern for large segments of the population because sons and daughters attend postsecondary institutions. Further, higher education is now expensive, both in terms of the government budget and increasingly the direct costs to individual students and their families. For many countries, higher education comprises a significant part of the state budget, which makes governments more concerned about the performance and policies of postsecondary education (Neave and van Vught 1994). As higher education has moved from periphery to center, it has naturally received more attention from society, resulting in more accountability.

In many countries, mass higher education has been forced on the universities. In much of Europe, access is guaranteed to students who complete their secondary school examinations; growing numbers passed these examinations and chose to enter the universities. Governments in general did not, however, provide the funding needed to produce a quality education for these students, and as a result, the conditions of study have deteriorated. In many developing countries, the rise of a middle class and a growing economy increased the demand for access; and higher education was forced to accept growing numbers of students, again often without adequate funding. In the United States, where expansion first took place, a combination of increased public funding, an active private sector, and the growth of a highly differentiated academic system with institutions of varying quality and purposes led to the development of a reasonably effective mass higher education system.

The challenges are tremendous. The emergence of a for-profit sector in many countries, the continuing deterioration of standards, the problems of institutionalizing a differentiated academic system serving varied purposes, and the difficulties of funding mass higher education have all contributed to current tensions. One thing is, however, certain: mass higher education is a permanent reality of higher education throughout the world.

References

Academic reforms in the world: Situation and perspective in the massifica-tion stage of higher education. 1997. Research Institute for Higher Education seminar reports, no. 10. Hiroshima: Research Institute for Higher Education, Hiroshima University.

Altbach, P.G. 1998a. The American academic model in comparative perspective. In *Comparative higher education: Knowledge, the universi-ty and development,* 55–73. Norwood, NJ: Ablex.

————. 1998b. The anatomy of private higher education. *International Higher Education* no. 12:9–10.

————, ed. 1999. *Private Prometheus: Private higher education and devel-opment.* Westport, CT: Greenwood.

————, ed. 2003. *The decline of the guru: The academic profession in devel-oping and middle-income countries.* New York: Palgrave.

Ben-David, J., and A. Zloczower. 1962. Universities and academic sys-tems in modern societies. *European Journal of Sociology* 3 (1): 45–84.

Brown, J. S., and P. Duguid. 1996. Universities in the digital age, *Change* July–August, 11–19.

Brunner, J. J. 1997. From state to market coordination: The Chilean case. *Higher Education Policy* 10 (3): 225–37.

Cohen, A., and F. Brawer. 1996. *The American community college.* San Francisco: Jossey-Bass.

Enders, J., ed. 2001. *Academic staff in Europe: Changing contexts and con-ditions.* Westport, CT: Greenwood.

Financing higher education: Innovation and changes. 1998. *European Journal of Education* 33:5–130.

Geiger, R. L. 1986. *Private sectors in higher education: Structure, function and change in eight countries.* Ann Arbor: University of Michigan Press.

Haas, J. E. 1996. The American academic profession. In *The interna-tional academic profession: Portraits from fourteen countries,* ed. P. G. Altbach, 343–88. Princeton, NJ: Carnegie Foundation for the Advancement of Teaching.

Hirsch, W. Z., and L. E. Weber. 2001. *Governance in higher education: The university in a state of flux.* London: Economica.

Kerr, C. 1995. *The uses of the university.* Cambridge, MA: Harvard University Press.

Kuttner, R. 1997. *Everything for sale: The virtues and limits of markets.* New York: Knopf.

Mason, R. 1998. *Globalising education: Trends and applications.* London: Routledge.

Neave, G., and F. van Vught, eds. 1994. *Government and higher educa-*

tion relationships across three continents: The winds of change. Oxford: Pergamon.

Robins, K. R., and F. Webster, eds. 2002. The virtual university? Knowledge, markets, and management. Oxford: Oxford University Press.

Schuster, J. H. and M. J. Finkelstein. 2006. The American faculty: The restructuring of academic work and careers. Baltimore, MD: Johns Hopkins University Press.

Shattock, M. 2003. Managing successful universities. Buckingham, UK: Open University Press.

Sperling, J., and R. W. Tucker. 1997. For-profit higher education: Developing a world-class workforce. New Brunswick, NJ: Transaction.

Stiglitz, J. 2002. Globalization and its discontents. New York: Norton.

Task Force on Higher Education and Society. 2000. Higher education in developing countries: Peril and promise. Washington, DC: World Bank.

Trow, M. 1973. Problems in the transition from elite to mass higher education. In Policies for higher education. Paris: OECD.

Van Dusen, G. C. 1997. The Virtual university: Technology and reform in higher education. Washington, DC: Graduate School of Education, George Washington University.

Warner, D., and D. Palfreyman, eds. 2001. The state of UK higher education: Managing change and diversity. Buckingham, UK: Open University Press.

Williams, G., ed. 2003. The enterprising university: Reform, excellence, and equity. Buckingham, UK: Open University Press.

World Bank. 1994. Higher education: The lessons of experience. Washington, DC: World Bank.

Youn, T., and P. Murphy, eds. 1997. Organizational studies in higher education. New York: Garland.

2

Globalization and the University: Realities in an Unequal World

Since the 1990s, globalization has come to be seen as a central theme for both society and higher education. Some have argued that globalization, broadly defined as largely inevitable global economic and technological factors affecting every nation, will liberate higher education and foster needed change. Technological innovations such as the Internet, market forces, the expansion of the private sector in higher education, and massification will permit everyone to compete on the basis of equality. Knowledge interdependence, it is explained, will help everyone. On the other side, critics claim that globalization strengthens worldwide inequality, fosters the franchising of higher education institutions, and tends to keep academic power in the hands of the wealthy universities of developed countries. All contemporary pressures on higher education, from massification to the growth of the private sector, are characterized in general as resulting from globalization. There is a grain of truth in each of these positions—and a good deal of misinterpretation as well. This essay will seek to "unpack" the realities of globalization in higher education and to highlight some of the impact on the university.

Academe around the world is affected differently by global trends. The countries of the European Union, for example, are adjusting to new common degree structures and other kinds of harmonization that are part of the Bologna process and related initiatives. Countries that use English benefit from the increasingly widespread use of that language for science and scholarship. Of special interest here is how globalization is affecting higher education in developing countries, which will experience the bulk of higher education expansion in the first half of the 21st century (Task Force on Higher Education 2000).

From the beginning, universities have been global institutions—in that they functioned in a common language, Latin, and served an international clientele of students. Professors, too, came from many countries, and the knowledge imparted reflected scholarly learning in the Western world at the time. Since universities have always figured in the global environment, they have been affected by circumstances beyond the campus and across national borders. This reality is all too often overlooked in analyses of 21st-century globalization. A long-term perspective when considering the university reveals the deep historical roots of the ethos and governance of universities. As Clark Kerr noted, of the institutions that had been established in the Western world by 1520, 85 still exist—the Roman Catholic Church, the British Parliament, several Swiss cantons, and some 70 universities. Among these institutions, the universities may have experienced the least change (Kerr 2001, 115).

Today's globalization, at least for higher education, does not lack precedents. From the beginning, universities have incorporated tensions between national conditions and international pressures. While English now dominates as the language of research and scholarship, in the 19th century German held sway, as did Latin in an earlier era. Students have always traveled abroad to study, and scholars have always worked outside their home countries. Globalization in the 21st century is truly worldwide in reach—few places can elude contemporary trends, and innovations and practices seem to spread ever faster due to modern technology. But, again, similar trends have occurred in other periods as well.

It is also the case that all of the universities in the world today, with the exception of the Al-Azhar in Cairo, stem from the same historical roots—the medieval European university and, especially, the faculty-dominated University of Paris. This means that the essential organizational pattern of the contemporary university worldwide stems from a common tradition—this is an important element of globalization. Much of the non-Western world had European university models imposed on it by colonial masters: academic systems in India, Indonesia, Ghana, and the rest of the developing world stem from common Western roots. Even those countries not colonized by Western powers—such as Japan, Thailand, Ethiopia, and a few others—adopted the Western academic model (Altbach and Selvaratnam 1989). This is the case even in countries, such as China, with well-established indigenous academic traditions (Hayhoe 1999).

The American university itself, so influential worldwide, constitutes an amalgam of international influences. The original colonial model, imported from England, was combined with the concept of the German research university of the 19th century and the American ideal of service to society to produce the modern American university. Foreign models were adapted to domestic realities in creative ways. As the European Union moves toward the harmonization of national higher education systems in the "common European space," foreign influences again emerge—degree structures, the course-credit system, and other elements in modified form—to produce evolving academic patterns. Just as Japan adapted German academic models and some American traditions as it built its modern university system after 1868, the European Union is looking to "best practices" worldwide in the 21st century.

Given the centrality of the knowledge economy to 21st-century development, higher education has assumed a higher profile both within countries and internationally because of its roles in educating people for the new economy and in creating new knowledge (Altbach 1998a). As evidence, the World Trade Organization is now focusing on higher education. Currently, a debate is under way concerning the General Agreement on Trade in Services (GATS). Multinational corporations and some government agencies in the rich countries are seeking to integrate higher education into the legal structures of world trade through the WTO. These developments indicate how important universities and knowledge have become in the contemporary world (Larsen, Martin, and Morris 2002; Knight 2002; Altbach 2002).

Terminology
It will be useful to discuss some of the terms in the current debate about globalization. For some observers, globalization means everything—an inchoate catch-all for the external influences on societies. For others, it represents only the negative side of contemporary reality.

This essay examines the international environment of higher education and seeks to analyze how that environment affects national higher education systems and individual academic institutions. The focus is not on the specific issues of the management of academic institutions—such as changes in administrative structures or academic appointments—although these may be influenced by global trends. Rather, the discussion concerns how societies and universities have dealt with mass enrollments, privatization, and the new technologies, among other issues.

In this discussion, the term *globalization* is viewed as the broad economic, technological, and scientific trends that directly affect higher education and are largely inevitable in the contemporary world. These phenomena include information technology in its various manifestations, the use of a common language for scientific communication, the imperatives of society's mass demand for higher education (massification) and for highly educated personnel, and the "private good" rationale about the financing of higher education. Academe is affected, for example, by patterns in the ownership of multinational publishing and Internet companies, the investment by private companies and governments in research and development worldwide, and international currents of cultural diffusion. These and other trends within globalization help to determine the nature of the 21st-century economy and society. Globalization is by no means a new phenomenon, and the medieval universities were affected by the global trends of the period. The emergence of the research university from the German model in the 19th century was greatly influenced by the global industrial revolution among other factors. Globalization has increased salience in the interdependent world of the 21st century. All countries and academic institutions are affected by these trends and must contemplate them as part of higher education reality and policy.

The term *internationalization* usually refers to specific policies and programs undertaken by governments, academic systems and institutions, and even individual departments to facilitate student or faculty exchanges, engage in collaborative research overseas, offer academic programs in English (or other languages), or a myriad of other initiatives. Internationalism is not a new phenomenon and indeed has been part of the work of many universities and academic systems for centuries. With much room for initiative, institutions and governments can choose the ways in which they deal with the new environment. Internationalism constitutes the ways that contemporary academe deals with globalization. While the forces of globalization cannot be held at bay, it is not inevitable that countries or institutions will necessarily be overwhelmed by them, or that the terms of the encounter must be dictated by others. Internationalization accommodates a significant degree of autonomy and initiative (Knight 1997; Knight 2005; Scott 1998; de Wit 2002).

Another new trend in higher education can be called *multinationalization*, which refers to academic programs or institutions located in one country offering degrees, courses, certificates, or other qualifications in other countries. The programs are often sponsored jointly with local institutions, but this is not always the case (Teather 2004). A joint degree sponsored by institutions in two or more countries, often called "twinning," is an example of a multinational academic enterprise.

Offshore institutions constitute another form, which may be carried out through franchising—selling the right to offer academic programs or degrees (sometimes referred to as "McDonaldization")—or simply by opening a branch institution (Hayes and Wynyard 2002). The American University of Bulgaria, offering US-style academic programs in English in Bulgaria and accredited in the United States, is an example. Increasingly, the Internet is used in the delivery of multinational academic programs. Multinationalization is, in some ways, a subset of internationalization—that is, the result of institutions in two or more countries entering into agreements to deliver academic programs.

History shows that when universities shut themselves off from economic and social trends they become moribund and irrelevant. European universities, for example, largely ignored the Industrial Revolution and ceased to be relevant to the needs of society or the intellectual and scientific ideas of the day. Indeed, the French Revolution abolished the universities entirely. Napoleon established the *grandes écoles* to provide relevant training for the leaders of society and to advance science and technology. Wilhelm von Humboldt had to reinvent the German university model in 1809 to connect it to the development of science and industry in Prussia (Ben-David and Zloczower 1962). In the 21st century, many of the most important trends are tied to global economic and social forces. Institutions and systems possess great latitude in how they deal with globalization and other social influences, at times effectively coping with such changes. At other times, the innate conservatism of academe prevented this. Thus, those who identify a single model for higher education in the 21st century are clearly wrong.

Centers and Peripheries
Concentrating on developing countries and on smaller academic systems immediately reveals the specter of inequality. While the Internet and other manifestations of globalization are heralded as disseminating knowledge equally throughout the world, the evidence shows mixed outcomes. In some ways, globalization does open access, making it easier for students and scholars to study and work. But in many respects, existing inequalities are only reinforced while new barriers are erected. The debate within higher education mirrors analyses of globalization generally. Economists Joseph Stiglitz and Dani Rodrik, among others, have argued that in some respects globalization works against the interests of developing countries, reinforcing international inequalities (Stiglitz 2002; Rodrik 1997; Rodrik 1999). Neither Stiglitz or Rodrik oppose globalization—both see it as inevitable—but they

reveal often overlooked, critical problems.

Powerful universities and academic systems—the centers—have always dominated the production and distribution of knowledge. In the late 20th century the research universities in the major English-speaking countries and a few others in the major industrialized countries have constituted those centers. Smaller and weaker institutions and systems with fewer resources and often lower academic standards—the peripheries—have tended to be dependent on the centers. Academic centers provide leadership in science and scholarship and in research and teaching. They are in the vanguard with regard to organizational structure and mission of universities and in knowledge dissemination. The centers tend to be located in larger and wealthier countries, where the most prestigious institutions benefit from the full array of resources, including funding and infrastructures—such as libraries and laboratories to support research, academic staff with appropriate qualifications, strong traditions, and legislation that supports academic freedom. The academic culture fosters high achievement levels by individual professors and students and by the institutions themselves. These top institutions often use one of the major international languages for teaching and research and in general enjoy adequate support from the state.

The world of centers and peripheries is growing ever more complex (Altbach 1998c). The international academic centers—namely the leading research-oriented universities in the North, especially those that use one of the key world languages (particularly English)—occupy the top tier. High-quality universities do exist elsewhere—for example, in Germany, France, Japan and several smaller European countries. A number of universities in China, Singapore, Taiwan, and South Korea aspire to reaching the status of top research institutions. Even within countries at the center of the world academic system in the early 21st century—the United States, Britain, Germany, France, and to some extent Australia and Canada—there are many peripheral institutions. For example, perhaps 100 of America's 3,200 postsecondary institutions can be considered research universities. These institutions receive more than 80 percent of government research funds and dominate most aspects of American higher education. The rest of the American higher education system lies on the periphery of the research centers. These segments, including the comprehensive universities, community colleges, and other institutions play important roles in both the academic system and in society; but they are not considered leaders in the academic system. While hardly a new development, this stratification has probably become more pronounced in recent years.

Countries that established relative equality among universities are fostering diversification—the United Kingdom has created a ranked system, and in 2006 Germany identified several universities to receive funding so that they can achieve world-class status.

Other countries possess similarly stratified academic systems. Some universities play complex roles as regional centers, providing a conduit of knowledge and links to the top institutions. For example, the major universities in Egypt provide academic leadership for the Arabic-speaking world and are links to the major centers, while contributing relatively little top-class research themselves. China's key universities are significant producers of research, mainly for internal consumption, while at the same time serving as links to the wider world of higher education.

It has now become more difficult to earn the status of a major player in international higher education—that is, to achieve "center" status (Altbach 1998b). The price of entry has risen. Top-tier research universities require ever greater resources, and in many fields scientific research involves a large investment in laboratory facilities and equipment (Altbach forthcoming). Enabling institutions to remain fully networked for the Internet and information technology is also costly, as are library acquisitions—including access to relevant databases. Universities in countries without deep financial resources will find it virtually impossible to join the ranks of the top academic institutions. Indeed, any new institution, regardless of location, will face similar challenges.

Academic institutions at the periphery and the academic systems of developing and some small industrialized countries depend on the centers for research, the communication of knowledge, and advanced training. The major journals and databases are headquartered at the major universities—especially in the United States and the United Kingdom—since international scholarly and research journals are largely published in English. Most of the world's universities are mainly teaching institutions—in developing countries virtually all are in this category—that must look elsewhere to obtain new knowledge and analysis. Many smaller developing countries, for example, lack the facilities for research, do not provide degrees beyond the bachelor's, and are unable to keep up with current journals and databases due to the expense. Structural dependency is endemic in much of the world's academic institutions.

A New Neocolonialism?
The era of the Cold War was characterized by the efforts of the major powers to dominate the "hearts and minds" of the peoples of the world.

The Soviet Union, the United States, and others spent lavishly on student exchanges, textbook subsidies, book translations, institution building, and other activities to influence the world's academic leaders, intellectuals, and policymakers. The goals were political and economic, and higher education was a key battlefield. The rationale was sometimes couched in the ideological jargon of the Cold War but was often obscured by rhetoric about cooperation (Altbach 1971). Some critics labeled such policies and initiatives as neocolonialism—an effort to dominate foreign countries by means other than naked military or economic force.

Many programs offered benefits to the recipients in the form of scholarships to study abroad, high-quality textbooks, scientific equipment, and other resources. Participation in programs took place on an entirely voluntary basis, but the level of assistance became difficult to cut back in the context of scarcity. Acceptance meant increased ties to the donor countries and institutions and long-term dependence on the countries providing the aid. Installation of laboratory equipment or computers, for example, meant continuing reliance on the supplier for spare parts, training, and the like.

We are now in a new era concerning power and influence. Politics and ideology have taken a subordinate role to profits and market-driven policies. Now, multinational corporations, media conglomerates, and even a few leading universities can be seen as the new neocolonialists—seeking to dominate not for ideological or political reasons but rather for commercial gain. Governments are not entirely out of the picture; they seek to assist companies in their countries and have a residual interest in maintaining influence as well. An example of governmental support for commercial interests and income generation in higher education is the American and Australian advocacy of open-markets in the World Trade Organization's General Agreement on Trade in Services (GATS) negotiations—supporting easy entry of universities and for-profit providers into developing countries. As in the Cold War era, countries and universities are not compelled to yield to the terms of those providing aid, fostering exchanges, or offering Internet products, but the pressures in favor of participation tend to prevail. Involvement in the larger world of science and scholarship, and obtaining perceived benefits not otherwise available, present considerable inducements. The result is the same—the loss of intellectual and cultural autonomy by those who are less powerful.

The Role of English
English is the Latin of the 21st century. In the current period, the use

of English is central for communicating knowledge worldwide, for instruction even in countries where English is not the language of higher education, and for cross-border degree arrangements and other programs. The dominance of English is a factor in globalization that deserves analysis if only because higher education worldwide must grapple with the role of English (Crystal 1997).

English is the most widely studied foreign language in the world. In many countries, English is the required second language in schools and the second language of choice in most places. English is the medium of most internationally circulated scientific journals. Universities in many countries stress the value that their professors publish in internationally circulated scientific journals, almost by definition in English, placing a further premium on the language. Internet Web sites devoted to science and scholarship function predominantly in English. Indeed, English serves as the language of online academic and scientific transactions. The largest number of international students go to universities in English-speaking countries.

English is the medium of instruction in many of the most prominent academic systems—including those of the United States, the United Kingdom, Australia, Canada, and New Zealand—all of which enroll large numbers of overseas students. Singapore, Ethiopia, and much of anglophone Africa use English as the primary language of instruction as well. English often functions as a medium of instruction in India, Pakistan, Bangladesh, and Sri Lanka. Other countries are increasingly offering academic programs in English—to attract international students unwilling to learn the local language and to improve the English-language skills of domestic students and thus enable them to work in an international arena. English-medium universities exist in many countries—from Azerbaijan and Bulgaria to Kyrgyzstan and Malaysia. In many countries—such as Japan, the Netherlands, Germany, and Mexico—universities offer English-medium degree programs and courses at local universities. Many European Union nations offer study in English as a way of attracting students from elsewhere in the EU. English is clearly a ubiquitous language in higher education worldwide.

The role of English affects higher education policy and the work of individual students and scholars. Obviously, the place of English at the pinnacle of scientific communication gives a significant advantage to the United States and the United Kingdom and to other wealthy English-speaking countries. Not surprisingly, many scientific journals are edited in the United States, which gives an advantage to American authors; for not only are they writing in their mother tongue, but the peer review system is dominated by people accustomed to both the language and methodology of US scholars. Others must communicate in a foreign language and conform to unfamiliar academic norms. As mentioned earlier, in many places academics are pressured to publish in internationally circulated journals—the sense being that publication in the most prestigious scientific journals is a necessary validation of academic work. Increasingly, international and regional scientific meetings are conducted exclusively in English, again placing a premium on fluency in the language.

English-language products of all kinds dominate the international academic marketplace, especially journals and books. For example, textbooks written from a US or UK perspective are sold worldwide, influencing students and academics in many countries and providing profits for publishers who function in English. The English-language databases in the various disciplines are the most widely used internationally. Universities must pay for these resources, which are priced to sell to American or European buyers and are thus extraordinarily expensive to users in developing or middle-income countries. Nevertheless, English-language programs, testing materials, and all the other products find a ready market in these countries.

Countries that use "small languages" may be tempted to change the medium of instruction at their universities entirely to English. A debate took place in the Netherlands on this topic, and it was decided to keep Dutch as the main language of instruction—largely out of concern for the long-term survival of the Dutch language and culture—although degree programs in English are flourishing in the country. Where collaborative degree programs are offered, such as in Malaysia, the language of instruction is almost always English and not the language of the country offering the joint degree.

English is supplanting such languages as French, German, and Spanish as the international medium of scholarship. These other languages are in no danger of disappearing in higher education, but their world role has shrunk. The use of English tends to orient those using it to the main English-speaking academic systems, and this further increases the influence of these systems' countries. Regardless of the consequences, however, English will continue as the predominant academic language.

The Global Marketplace for Students and Scholars

Not since the medieval period has such a large proportion of the world's students been studying outside their home countries—more than 1.5 million students at any one time—and some estimate that the number of overseas students is predicted to grow to 8 million by 2020. Large numbers of professors and other academics travel abroad temporarily for research or teaching, and substantial numbers of academics migrate abroad as well to pursue their careers. Aspects of globalization such as the use of English encourage these flows and will ensure that growth continues. The global marketplace will expand as academic systems become more uniform and academic degrees more accepted internationally, immigration rules favor people with high skill levels, and universities look to hiring the best talent worldwide.

The flow of academic talent at all levels is directed largely from South to North—from the developing countries to the large metropolitan academic systems. Perhaps 80 percent of the world's international students come from developing countries, and virtually all of them study in the North. Most of these students pursue master's, doctoral, and professional degrees. Many do not return to their countries of origin. Close to 80 percent of students from China and India, two of the largest sending countries (to the United States), do not return home immediately after obtaining their degrees—taking jobs or postdoctoral appointments in the United States. The years since the collapse of the Soviet system have also seen a flow of scientists from Russia to Western Europe and North America. Students from industrialized countries who study abroad typically do not earn a degree but rather spend a year or two in the country to learn a language or gain knowledge that they could not acquire at home.

Most international students pay for their own studies, producing significant income for the host countries—and a drain on the economy of the developing world. According to estimates, the money spent abroad by students from some developing countries more than equals incoming foreign aid. These students not only acquire training in their fields but also absorb the norms and values of the academic systems in which they studied. They return home desiring to transform their universities in ways that often prove to be both unrealistic and ineffective. Foreign students serve as carriers of an international academic culture—a culture that reflects the major metropolitan universities and may not be relevant for the developing world.

In 2002, universities in the United States hosted almost 85,000 visiting scholars. Although statistics are not available, it is estimated that visiting scholars number 250,000 worldwide. The predominant South-North flow notwithstanding, a significant movement of academics occurs among the industrialized countries and to some extent within other regions, such as Latin America. As part of the Bologna initiatives of the European Union, there is more movement within Europe. Most visiting scholars return home after their sojourns abroad, although a certain number use their assignments as springboards to permanent emigration.

The flow of highly educated talent from the developing countries to the West is large—and problematic for Third World development. For example, more Ethiopian holders of doctoral degrees work outside of Ethiopia than at home, and 30 percent of all highly educated Ghanaians and Sierra Leoneans live and work abroad (Outward Bound 2002, 24). Many African countries experience this pattern. South Africa is losing many of its most talented academics to the North, while at the same time it is recruiting professors from other countries in Africa. This migration has seriously weakened academic institutions in many developing countries.

Migration does not affect only developing countries. Academics from developed countries will also go abroad to take jobs that offer more attractive opportunities, salaries, and working conditions, as illustrated by the ongoing small but significant exodus from the United Kingdom to North America. To combat this trend, UK authorities have provided funds to entice their best professors to remain at home. Being at the center of research activity and having access to the latest scientific equipment sometimes lures scholars from small but well-endowed academic systems, such as those in Denmark or Finland, to the metropoles. In some fields, such as engineering specialties and computer science, the percentage of professors from other countries working at US universities is very high—reflecting the fact that almost half the doctoral students in these fields are foreigners. Academic migration takes place throughout the academic system, especially in the sciences, engineering, information technology, and some management areas. Such migration occurs both at the top of the system, with some world-famous scholars attracted abroad by high salaries, and at the bottom, where modest salaries are able to draw foreigners to jobs that are unappealing to local applicants.

Academic migration follows complex routes. Many Egyptian, Jordanian, and Palestinian academics work at Arabian Gulf universities, attracted by better salaries and working conditions than are available at home. Indians and Pakistanis are similarly drawn to the Gulf as well as to Southeast Asia. Singapore and Hong Kong attract a broad range of expatriate academics. Mexico and Brazil employ scholars from elsewhere in Latin America. South Africa, Namibia, and Botswana currently recruit Africans from elsewhere on the continent. Some of the best scholars and scientists from Russia and a number of Central European countries have taken positions in Western Europe and North

America. The existing traffic among member states will likely grow once the EU implements policies to harmonize academic systems, a process now under way.

The most significant "pull" factors include better salaries and working conditions and the opportunity to be at the centers of world science and scholarship (Altbach 2003). The discrepancies in salaries and conditions between North and South mean that in most developing countries academics cannot aspire to a middle-class lifestyle or have access to the necessary tools of research and scholarship.

One of the many "push" factors involves the limited extent of academic freedom in many developing countries. Academics can be subject to restrictions and even arrested if they stray from officially approved topics. Favoritism and corruption in academic appointments, promotions, and other areas further erode the environment of the university. In many higher education systems, job security or stability is unattainable. Conditions at Third World universities stem largely from the scarcity of resources and the pressure of increased student numbers on overburdened academic institutions. While the "pull" factors at the centers will retain their influence, the "push" factors can be moderated. Overall, however, the migration of academic talent will continue in the current globalized environment.

People have long equated the migration of talent with brain drain; however, the life stories of emigrants have changed (Choi 1995). Many academics now keep in close contact with their countries of origin, maintaining scientific and academic relationships with colleagues and institutions at home. Growing numbers of academics have even gone back after establishing careers abroad as economic and political conditions at home have changed. Some academics from South Korea and Taiwan, for example, left the United States to accept senior academic appointments in their home countries once academic working conditions, salaries, and respect for academic freedom had improved. More commonly, expatriate academics return home for lecture tours or consulting, collaborate on research with colleagues in their countries of origin, or accept visiting professorships. Facilitated by the Internet, these links are increasingly accepted as appropriate and useful. Such trends are especially strong in countries with well-developed academic systems, such as China, India, and South Africa, among others.

The migration of academic talent is in many ways promoted by the industrialized countries, which have much to gain. Immigration policies are in some cases designed to encourage talented personnel to migrate and establish residency—although, at least in the United States, security concerns in the aftermath of 9/11 have changed the equation to some extent. In many countries, academic institutions make it easy for foreigners to fit into the career structure. Countries that place barriers to foreign participation in academe, such as Japan and now perhaps the United States, may find it more difficult to compete in the global knowledge sweepstakes. Industrialized countries benefit from a large pool of well-educated scientists and scholars—people educated by developing countries—who choose to take their talents and skills to the highest bidders. In this way, the developing world has supported the North's already overwhelming lead in science and scholarship. The renewal of links between academics who migrate and their countries of origin mitigate this situation somewhat, although developing countries and some smaller industrialized nations still find themselves at a disadvantage in the global academic labor market.

The Curriculum
The field of business administration exemplifies the global dominance of ideas by the major English-speaking academic systems. In most countries, business administration is a new field, established over the past several decades to prepare professionals for work in multinational corporations or in firms engaged in international commerce as well as in local business. The dominant pattern of professional studies is the MBA degree—the American-style master's of business administration. This degree originated as the way to prepare American students for work in US business, based on American curriculum ideas and business practices. A key part of many MBA programs is the case study, again developed in the US context. The MBA model has been widely copied in other countries, in most cases by local institutions but also by American academic institutions working with local partners or setting up their own campuses overseas. While the programs sometimes are modified in keeping with the local context, the basic degree structure and curriculum remain American.

Another example of the export of the curriculum is the proposed incorporation of some general education in the first degree. Part of the US undergraduate curriculum for two centuries, general education provides a broad background in the disciplines along with critical thinking skills. *Higher Education in Developing Countries: Peril and Promise*, an influential report sponsored by the World Bank and UNESCO, advocates general education as an alternative to the existing largely specialized undergraduate curriculum common in higher education worldwide (Task Force on Higher Education 2000). The future of general education as a curriculum reform is not clear.

There is an increasing use of common textbooks, course materials, and syllabi worldwide, stimulated by the influence of multinational publishers, the Internet, and databases, as well as the growing number of professors who return home after their study abroad with ideas concerning curriculum and instructional materials. These materials originate mainly in the large academic systems of the North—especially the United States, the United Kingdom, and France.

Disciplines and fields vary in terms of how globally homogenous they have become. Such fields as business administration, information technology, and biotechnology are almost entirely dominated by the major academic centers. Other fields—such as history, language studies, and the humanities—are largely nationally based, although foreign influences are felt in methodology and approaches to research and interpretation. Curricular influences, like scientific research and the knowledge distribution system, proceeds largely from North to South.

The Multinationalization of Higher Education
The emergence of a global education marketplace exhibits itself in the form of a variety of multinational higher education initiatives—ranging from "twinning" programs linking academic institutions or programs in one country with counterparts in another, to universities in one country setting up branch campuses in another. Cross-border higher education ventures include many that use the Internet and other distance education means to deliver their programs. Many for-profit companies and institutions have invested in multinational educational initiatives, as have a range of traditional higher education institutions (Observatory on Borderless Higher Education 2004; OECD 2004). Multinationalization is a subset of internationalization since it results from specific policy initiatives of those involved.

History shows that the export of educational institutions and the linking of institutions from different countries generally represented a union of unequals. Earlier "export models" involved colonialism—the colonial power simply imposed its institutional model and curriculum, often diluted and designed for intellectual subservience, on the colonized (Ashby 1966). In almost all cases, the institution from the outside dominated the local institution, or the new institution was based on foreign ideas and nonindigenous values. Examples include the British in Africa and Asia, the Dutch in what is now Indonesia, and the French in Africa and Asia. The Spanish monarchy asked the Roman Catholic Church to set up universities in Latin America and the Philippines; religious orders such as the Jesuits undertook what might now be referred to as multinational higher education. In the 19th century, American Protestant missionaries established universities based on the US model in Lebanon, Egypt, Korea and Turkey, among other places—for example, the American University of Beirut. During the Cold War, both the United States and the Soviet Union exported their academic institutions and ideas mainly to the developing world, generally tied to foreign aid, and in some cases set up universities reflecting their views—such as the University of Nigeria-Nsukka (Hanson 1968).

The same inequality is characteristic of the 21st century, although neither colonialism nor Cold War politics impels policy. Now, market forces, access demand, and monetary gain motivate multinational higher education initiatives. When institutions or programs are exported from one country to another, academic models, curricula, and programs from the more powerful academic system prevail. Thus, programs between Australian and Malaysian institutions aimed at setting up new academic institutions in Malaysia are always designed by Australian institutions. Rarely, if ever, do academic innovations emanate from the periphery to the center.

Both traditional colonialism and the government-sponsored foreign assistance programs of the Cold War era exported institutional models, practices, and curriculum from the metropole to developing countries. In the past decade, the number of institutional exports based on nongovernmental programs have risen, usually on the initiative of the exporting country. In the 1980s, for example, American colleges and universities directed their attention to Japan as a higher education market. Several hundred US institutions explored the Japanese market, and more than a dozen established campuses—usually in cooperation with a Japanese institution or company (Chambers and Cummings 1990). A small number of Japanese institutions looked into the feasibility of a US connection, with a few even setting up branch campuses. However, most Japanese programs involved bringing Japanese students to the United States for study, while US programs focused on educating Japanese students in Japan. Generally, the institutions engaging in export activities were not the most prestigious schools. By 2000, very few of the branches were still operating. In Japan, the difficulty of obtaining Ministry of Education certification for US programs proved overwhelming, and the initiatives on both sides were affected by the protracted economic slowdown in Japan. The US-Japan initiatives were unusual in that both sides were industrialized countries.

Some of the export initiatives taking place today are indicative of global trends. A small number of prestigious American universities are establishing campuses worldwide, usually in popular professional fields such as business administration. The University of Chicago's business school established a campus in Spain that has been moved to

London. Chicago degrees are offered to European students, using the standard Chicago curriculum—taught in English mostly by Chicago faculty members—with an international focus. It includes a period of study at the home campus as well. Some other US universities have developed similar programs.

An unusual but interesting model of multinationalization is being undertaken by Singapore, which has invited a number of prestigious foreign universities—including the University of Pennsylvania's Wharton School and INSEAD (the Paris-based European business school)—to start programs in Singapore. The government carefully selects the institutions and provides incentives to encourage them to come to Singapore. The establishment of a branch of Cornell University's medical school in the Arabian Gulf is another example. A further trend has been the establishment of US-style universities in such countries as Kyrgyzstan, Qatar, and Bulgaria, among other places. These schools typically originate through local initiative, and many have strong links to American universities. Some are supervised by the US partners and accredited in the United States. The language of instruction is English and the curriculum US based. The quality of these American clones varies considerably, with some simply capitalizing on the cachet of an American-style education.

In keeping with the standard export model, a university in an industrialized country will set up a program abroad, often but not always in a developing country, at the invitation of a host institution. The host may be an educational institution or a corporation without any link to education or some combination of the two. Examples of these arrangements can be found in Malaysia to satisfy unmet demand by local students. Universities from Australia and the United Kingdom are most active in Malaysia, but some new programs have generated complaints of low quality, poor supervision, or inadequate communication between the providers and the hosts. In Israel, a number of small and generally low-prestige American colleges began to offer academic degrees when the market was opened up in the 1990s by the Israeli government. After considerable criticism, restrictions were later placed on the programs—many of which have ceased to exist.

In another export model, foreign academic degree programs are "franchised" by local institutions. The foreign university lends its name and provides the curriculum, some (often quite limited) supervision, and quality control to a local academic institution or perhaps business firm. The new institution is granted the right to award a degree or certificate from the foreign institution to local students. Unfortunately, these franchising arrangements have led to many abuses and much criticism. Many articles have appeared in the British press charging that some UK institutions, mostly the less prestigious ones, involved in overseas programs are damaging the "good name" of British higher education. Meanwhile, "buyers" (fee-paying students) overseas think that they are getting a standard British degree, when in reality they are receiving the degree but not the level of education provided in the United Kingdom.

There are a large number of "twinning" programs worldwide. This arrangement links an academic institution in one country with a partner school in another. Typically, the university in the North provides the basic curriculum and orientation for an institution in the South. In such arrangements, academic degrees are often jointly awarded. Twinning has the advantage of aiding institutions in the South in developing new curricular offerings, with the stamp of approval of an established foreign university. Again, the higher education "products" come from the North, often with little adaptation to local needs.

As can be seen in this brief discussion, there are many facets to the 21st century multinational higher education enterprise—programs and initiatives usually involving academic or other institutions from more than one country. However, some common perspectives and motivations can be identified. With few exceptions, a central goal for all of the stakeholders, especially those in the North, is to earn a profit. Institutions in the South that are attracted to multinational initiatives may also be interested in making money, but they also want to meet the growing demand for higher education and for new degree programs that may not be available in local schools. As with other aspects of globalization in higher education, multinational arrangements between institutions are marked by inequality.

Information Technology

The information age carries the potential of introducing significant change in higher education, although it is unlikely that the basic functions of traditional academic institutions will be transformed. The elements of the revolution in information technology (IT) that are transforming higher education include the communication, storage, and retrieval of knowledge (Castells 2000). Libraries, once the repositories of books and journals, are now equally involved in providing access to databases, Web sites, and a range of IT-based products (Hawkins and Battin 1998). Scholars increasingly use the Internet to undertake research and analysis and to disseminate their own work. Academic institutions are beginning to use IT to deliver degree programs and other curricula to students outside the campus. Distance education is

rapidly growing both within countries and internationally. IT is beginning to shape teaching and learning and is affecting the management
of academic institutions.

Information technology is integral to our analysis—this new technology is central to the global academic environment of the 21st century. At the same time, universities and other institutions use IT to create
or enhance their international initiatives. IT also permits multinational programs to more easily be set up—rapid and reliable IT-based communications permits links among institutions worldwide.

As with the other aspects of globalization, significant inequalities
exist. Inevitably, the information and knowledge base available through
the Internet reflects the realities of the knowledge system worldwide.
The databases and retrieval mechanisms probably make it easier to
access the well-archived and electronically sophisticated scientific systems of the advanced industrialized countries than the less networked
academic communities of the developing countries. Further, commercial interests increasingly dominate the Internet, selling knowledge
products for the benefit of corporations.

For scholars and scientists at universities and other institutions that
lack good libraries, the Internet simplifies the obtaining of information. This change has had a democratizing effect on scientific communication and access to information. At the same time, however, many
people in developing countries have only limited access to the Internet
(Teferra 2003). Africa, for example, has only recently achieved full connectivity to the Internet.

The Internet and the databases on it are dominated by the major
universities in the North. The dominance of English on the Internet
also affects access and usage of information. Multinational publishers
and other corporations have become key players, owning many of the
databases, journals, and other sources of information. Academic institutions and countries unable to pay for access to these information
sources find it difficult to participate fully in the networks. Tightening
copyright and other ownership restrictions through international
treaties and regulations will further consolidate ownership and limit
access (Correa 2000).

Distance education, while not a new phenomenon, comprises
another element of higher education profoundly affected by IT. The
University of South Africa, for example, has been offering academic
degrees through correspondence for many decades. The Open
University in the United Kingdom has effectively used a combination
of distance methods to deliver its highly regarded programs. Both of
these institutions serve students outside their home countries. IT has

greatly expanded the reach and methodological sophistication of distance education, contributing to the growth of distance education institutions. Of the 10-largest distance education institutions in the world, 7 are located in developing countries, and all use IT for at least part of their programs. Universities and other providers in the industrialized nations are beginning to employ IT to offer academic programs around the world, a significant portion of which are aimed at developing countries. Entire degree programs in fields such as business administration are offered through distance education on the Internet, and many providers view the international market as critical for the success of their programs. These providers include corporations, such as some of the major multinational publishers, for-profit educational providers like Laureate Education, Inc. and others. Some universities now offer degree and certificate programs through the Internet to international audiences. Firms such as Microsoft, Motorola, and others are offering competency certificates and other training programs in fields relating to their areas of expertise.

As with the other aspects of globalization discussed in this analysis—the leading providers of IT consist of multinational corporations, academic institutions, and other organizations in the industrialized nations. The Internet combines a public service—e-mail and the range of Web sites to which access is free—with a commercial enterprise. Many databases, electronic journals, e-books, and related knowledge products are owned by profit-making companies that market them, often at prices that make access difficult to users in developing countries.

Nevertheless, developing countries have been able to take advantage of IT. For example, most of the largest universities using distance education are located in developing countries. The African Virtual University is an effort by a number of African nations to harness the Internet and other distance techniques to meet their needs. AVU's success so far has been limited, and many of the courses and programs are based on curriculum from the North. E-mail is widely used to improve communication among scientists and scholars and to create networks in the developing world. The information revolution will neither transform higher education, nor is it a panacea for the higher education needs of developing countries. However, IT is one of the central elements of globalization in higher education.

International Agreements and Frameworks
In the new era of globalization in higher education, new international agreements and arrangements have been drawn up to manage global

interactions. The links between countries range from bilateral treaties on student and faculty exchanges to the mutual recognition of degrees—for example, the many binational commissions governing the American Fulbright scholarship and exchange programs. Of the current international agreements in higher education, perhaps the most comprehensive are the European Union's: the comprehensive Bologna framework, designed to introduce changes to harmonize the higher education systems of all EU member states, and specific exchange and scholarship programs such as ERASMUS and SOCRATES (de Wit 2002). In contrast, NAFTA (the North American Free Trade Agreement) and ASEAN (the Association of Southeast Asian Nations) have few implications for higher education.

The debate over the inclusion of higher education in the framework of the WTO through the General Agreement on Trade in Services (GATS) proposal has significant implications for the themes of globalization, internationalization, and multinationalization discussed in this essay. While GATS is still being debated in the WTO, it is not yet implemented into the WTO framework. GATS seeks to establish "open markets" for knowledge products of all kinds—including higher education. GATS treats knowledge as a commodity that should be freely traded around the world. The proponents commend free trade as a universal benefit permitting competition in the marketplace of ideas and knowledge products.

GATS and related WTO arrangements also seek to provide a legally binding framework for the circulation of educational services and for the protection of intellectual property (Knight 2004; OECD 2004). Thus, GATS and the WTO are very much related to TRIPS (Trade Related Intellectual Property) arrangements and copyright regulations (Altbach 1995). The motivating force behind all of these regulatory frameworks is to rationalize the global trade in knowledge and to ensure open markets and protections for the owners of knowledge products. The WTO and its related agreements, as well as international copyright, have the force of law—they are international treaties supported by a legal enforcement regime. These arrangements were created to protect the sellers and the providers, not the buyers and users, and as a result they have negative implications for developing countries (Raikhy 2002). For example, copyright laws have been further strengthened to protect the owners of knowledge, while failing to open access through "fair use" provisions or meaningful special arrangements for developing countries (WTO and Higher Education 2003).

Groups favoring GATS and the regulatory framework in general are the sellers and owners—multinational knowledge companies, governments focusing on exports, and other stakeholders (OECD 2002). Testing companies such as the US-based Educational Testing Service, multinational publishers, information technology and computer firms, for-profit educational providers such as Laureate Education, Inc. are examples of businesses devoted to global education that see GATS as benefiting their interests. In many countries, the government agencies most focused on GATS constitute not the ministries of education but rather departments concerned with trade and export promotion. In the United States, the Department of Commerce has taken the lead, not the Department of Education. In the United Kingdom, the Department of Trade and Industry has been in the forefront. Education groups in the United States, Canada, and a number of other countries have been skeptical or opposed to the GATS proposal. The American Council on Education, which represents most university presidents in the United States, for example, has spoken out against GATS. Some developing countries, such as South Africa, are quite critical of GATS, while India and a few others that may have the potential to export educational products are ambivalent. Most developing countries have not yet taken a position on the concept of free trade in education and knowledge products.

While the complicated details of a GATS treaty have not been worked out, the basic issues are straightforward. Should education in all of its manifestations be considered as a commodity to be traded in the marketplace, regulated in the same fashion as are automobiles or bananas? In a 2002 interview, Lawrence Summers, a former US treasury secretary and former president of Harvard University, stated "I'm skeptical as to whether bringing educational issues under the auspices of trade negotiations would be helpful.... To start with, many educational institutions are nonprofit, their motivations are different from the motivations of commercial firms that we think of in a trade context. There may be some egregious practices that should be addressed, but I would be skeptical about treating education in a way that had any parallels with financial services, with insurance, or with foreign investments" ("The World According to Larry" 2002, 38).

While GATS would bring developing countries into a global framework of commerce and exchange in higher education, it would remove aspects of autonomy from educational decision making. Extending the principle of free trade to education would open national markets in GATS signatory countries to testing companies, providers of distance education, and many other organizations. Regulation or control of these entities would prove difficult if not impossible to achieve. Institutions or companies could, in principle, count on having access to foreign education markets. Since developing countries typically import rather than export their educational products or institutions, it is unlikely that GATS would promote their exports—although countries such as Egypt or India may have a limited regional market. Developing countries represent the markets that sellers from the industrialized world are eager to target. Most developing countries, having few educational "products" to export, would be at the mercy of the multinational providers.

Current arrangements—in which all countries retain authority over educational imports and exports, subject to some regulatory arrangement such as international copyright, patent treaties, local accreditation and licensing arrangements, and the like—nonetheless permit a great deal of international higher education exchange, as this essay illustrates. It can be argued that international education markets are already appropriately open and additional legal requirements to open them further are not needed. Cross-border educational transactions of all kinds are being actively pursued worldwide. As the main importers of products and services from abroad, developing countries would be most directly affected by GATS.

Conclusion

Globalization in higher education and science is an inevitable development. Historically, academe has always been international in scope and has always been characterized by inequalities. Modern technology, the Internet, the increasing ease of communications, and the flow of students and highly educated personnel across borders enhance globalization. No academic system can exist by itself in the world of the 21st century.

The challenge is to recognize the complexities and nuances of the global higher education context—an academic world fraught with inequalities in which market and commercial forces increasingly dominate. The traditional domination of the North over the South remains largely intact. Ameliorating inequalities in the context of mass higher education is not an easy task.

References

Altbach, Philip G. 1971. Education and neocolonialism. *Teachers College Record* 72 (1): 543–58.

———. 1995. *Copyright and development: Inequality in the information age.* Chestnut Hill, MA: Bellagio Publishing Network and the African Books Collective.

———. 1998a. *Comparative higher education: Knowledge, the university, and development.* Greenwich, CT: Ablex.

———. 1998b. Gigantic peripheries: India and China in the world knowledge system. In *Comparative higher education: Knowledge, the university, and development,* ed. Philip G. Altbach, 133–46. Greenwich, CT: Ablex.

———. 1998c. The university as center and periphery. In *Comparative higher education: Knowledge, the university, and development,* ed. Philip G. Altbach, 19–36. Greenwich, CT: Ablex.

———. 2002. Knowledge and education as international commodities: The collapse of the common good. *International Higher Education,* no. 28:2–5.

———. 2003. Centers and peripheries in the academic profession: The special challenges of developing countries. In *The decline of the guru: The academic profession in developing and middle-income countries,* ed. Philip G. Altbach, 1–22. New York: Palgrave.

———. Forthcoming. Empires of knowledge and development. In *World class worldwide: Transforming research universities in Asia and Latin America,* ed. Philip G. Altbach and Jorge Balán. Baltimore, MD: Johns Hopkins University Press.

Altbach, Philip G., and Viswanathan Selvaratnam, eds. 1989. *From dependence to autonomy: The development of Asian universities.* Dordrecht, Netherlands: Kluwer.

Ashby, Eric. 1966. *Universities: British, Indian, African—A study in the ecology of higher education.* Cambridge, MA: Harvard University Press.

Ben-David, Joseph, and Awraham Zloczower. 1962. Universities and academic systems in modern societies. *European Journal of Sociology* 3 (1):45–84.

Castells, Manuel. 2000. *The rise of the network society.* Oxford: Blackwell.

Chambers, Gail S., and William K. Cummings. 1990. *Profiting from education: Japan-United States international ventures in the 1980s.* New York: Institute of International Education.

Choi, Hyaeweol. 1995. *An international scientific community: Asian scholars in the United States.* Westport, CT: Praeger.

Correa, Carlos M. 2000. *Intellectual property rights, the WTO and devel-*

oping countries. London: Zed Books.

Crystal, David. 1997. *English as a global language*. Cambridge: Cambridge University Press.

de Wit, Hans. 2002. *Internationalization of higher education in the United States and Europe*. Westport, CT: Greenwood.

Hanson, John W. 1968. *Education, Nsukka: A study in institution building among the modern Ibo*. East Lansing: Michigan State University.

Hawkins, Brian L., and Patricia Battin, eds. 1998. *The mirage of continuity: Reconfiguring academic information resources for the 21st century*. Washington, DC: Council on Information and Library Resources.

Hayes, Dennis, and Robin Wynyard, eds. 2002. *The McDonaldization of higher education*. Westport, CT: Praeger.

Hayhoe, Ruth. 1999. *China's universities, 1895-1995: A century of cultural conflict*. Hong Kong: Comparative Education Research Centre, University of Hong Kong.

Kerr, Clark. 2001. *The uses of the university*. Cambridge, MA: Harvard University Press.

Knight, Jane. 1997. Internationalisation of higher education: A conceptual framework. In *Internationalisation of higher education in Asia Pacific countries*, ed. Jane Knight and Hans de Wit, 5–19. Amsterdam: European Association for International Education.

———. 2002. *Trade in higher education services: The implications of GATS*. London: Observatory on Borderless Higher Education. http://www.obhe .ac.uk.

———. 2004. GATS, trade and higher education: Perspective 2003— where are we? In *Mapping borderless higher education: Policy, markets and competition*, ed. Observatory on Borderless Higher Education, 39–88. London: Association of Commonwealth Universities.

———. 2005. Internationalization: Concepts, complexities, and challenges. In *International handbook of higher education*, ed. James J.F. Forest and Philip G. Altbach, 207–42. Dordrecht, Netherlands: Springer.

Larsen, Karl, John P. Martin, and Rosemary Morris. 2002. *Trade in educational services: Trends and emerging issues*. Paris: Organization for Economic Cooperation and Development.

Observatory on Borderless Higher Education. 2004. *Mapping borderless higher education: Policy, markets and competition*. London: Association of Commonwealth Universities.

OECD. *See* Organization for Economic Cooperation and Development.

Organization for Economic Cooperation and Development. 2002. *GATS: The case for open services markets*. Paris: OECD.

———. 2004. *Internationalization and trade in higher education*. Paris:

OECD.

Outward Bound. 2002. *Economist*, September 28, 24–26.

Raikhy, P. S. 2002. Trade in education under the WTO policy regime: Implications for India. In *Internationalization of higher education*, ed. K. B. Powar, 127–33. New Delhi: Association of Indian Universities.

Rodrik, Dani. 1997. *Has globalization gone too far?* Washington, DC: Institute for International Economics.

———. 1999. *The new global economy and the developing countries: Making openness work*. Washington, DC: Overseas Development Council.

Scott, Peter, ed. 1998. *The globalization of higher education*. Buckingham, UK: Open University Press.

Stiglitz, Joseph. 2002. *Globalization and its discontents*. New York: Norton.

Task Force on Higher Education and Society. 2000. *Higher education in developing countries: Peril and promise*. Washington, DC: World Bank.

Teather, David, ed. 2004. *Consortia: International networking alliances of universities*. Melbourne: Melbourne University Press.

Teferra, Damtew. 2003. *Scientific communication in African universities: External agencies and national needs*. New York: RoutledgeFalmer.

The world according to Larry. 2002. *Foreign Policy*, July–August: 30–39.

WTO and higher education. 2003. *Chinese Education and Society*, 36 (5): 3–104.

3

Academic Freedom:
International Realities and Challenges

I n many parts of the world, academic freedom is far from secure, and in some places it is under attack. A prominent Iranian social scientist was sentenced to death for calling for democracy (the sentence was lifted in 2004 after an international outcry), a Hong Kong academic pollster was warned by his university's vice chancellor not to publish polls critical of the region's chief executive, and academics in Serbia were routinely arrested for opposing the Milosevic regime. Indonesian academics who took part in the democracy movement that succeeded in toppling the Suharto regime were occasionally jailed or fired by the Suharto government, which had never been much committed to freedom of expression in any case (Human Rights Watch 1998). In Malaysia and Singapore, some topics are simply taboo for research and publication due to government pressure. Academic freedom is by no means secure worldwide.

Academic freedom is situated at the very core of the mission of the university. It is essential to teaching and research. Many would argue that a fully developed higher education system cannot exist without academic freedom. At the beginning of the 21st century, there is considerable cause for optimism about academic freedom. After all, most of the countries that were formerly part of the Soviet Union, as well as the countries of Central and Eastern Europe, have achieved reasonable levels of academic freedom, although as yet not always the full range. Most countries and academic systems at least recognize something called academic freedom and express a commitment to it. Yet, academic freedom is far from secure, and those concerned about the core values of the university need to be ever vigilant. A global reassessment is needed.

While there are now few countries in which professors are completely under the thumb of repressive authorities, a more common pattern is one of occasional government crackdowns in an atmosphere of constraint. Indeed, the threats, current and potential, are sufficient to warrant heightened awareness and positive steps to ensure that academic freedom can flourish. Yet, surprisingly, academic freedom does not rank high on the international agenda. The topic is seldom discussed at academic conferences, nor does it appear in the declarations and working papers of agencies such as UNESCO or the World Bank (Burgan 1999). Those who are responsible for leading and funding higher education are far too concerned with finance and management issues. More attention needs to be given to the mission and values of the university, for without academic freedom, universities cannot achieve their potential nor fully contribute to the emerging knowledge-based society.

Elusive Definitions

While it seems a simple concept and in essence is, academic freedom is also difficult to define. From medieval times, the term has meant the freedom of the professor to teach without external control in his or her area of expertise, and it has implied the freedom of the student to learn. The concept was further defined with the rise of the research-oriented Humboldtian university in early 19th-century Germany. The Humboldtian concept enshrined the ideas of *Lehrfreiheit* and *Lernfreiheit*—freedom to teach and to learn.

These concepts of academic freedom gave special protection to the professor in the classroom and within the parameters of the professor's field of expert knowledge. From the beginning, the university was considered a special place, devoted to the pursuit and transmission of knowledge. Academe claimed special rights precisely because of its calling to pursue truth. The authorities, whether secular or ecclesiastical, were expected to grant universities a special degree of autonomy. Academic freedom was never absolute, however. In the medieval university, both church and state exercised some control over what could be taught in universities. Professors whose teachings conflicted with the doctrines of the Roman Catholic Church were sometimes sanctioned, and loyalty to the civil authorities was also expected. Nonetheless, greater freedom of expression existed in the universities than elsewhere in society.

In the German university of the early 19th century, the concept of academic freedom was expanded as research became part of the academic mission. The professor was given almost absolute freedom regarding research and expression in the classroom and laboratory. But that freedom did not necessarily extend to protection of expression on broader political or social issues. Nor was it considered a violation of academic freedom that socialists and other dissenters were not eligible for academic appointments.

As the research university idea crossed the Atlantic at the end of the 19th century, the concept of academic freedom was expanded. By the early years of the 20th century, the American Association of University Professors had defined academic freedom within the classroom and laboratory as encompassing all aspects, not just those within the field of scholarly expertise. The AAUP also extended the concept to provide high levels of protection for professorial expression outside of the university. Professors were considered valuable social critics and were accorded special protections of speech and writing on all topics. At about the same time in Latin America, as a result of the university Cordoba reform movement of 1918, a very broad definition of academic freedom came to be applied to the entire university community. Civil authorities were forbidden to enter the university buildings without the permission of the academic community. The concept of the "autonomous" Latin American university was born at this time (Walter 1968).

At the beginning of the 21st century, some confusion exists over the proper definition of academic freedom. Generally, the broader New World definition has gained acceptance within the academic community. But nowhere has academic freedom been fully delineated, and nowhere does it have the force of law. In some countries, both university and civil authorities assume the narrow Humboldtian definition. Elsewhere, within academe and outside, the broader New World ideal prevails. There is no universally accepted understanding of academic freedom.

Controversy has arisen concerning whether the claims of academic institutions and individual professors for special rights and freedoms bring obligations as well. For example, some have argued that universities should not take overtly political stands or become enmeshed, as institutions, in political debates or movements. It is argued that institutions, and to some extent individual academics, have a responsibility to remain disengaged from partisan controversies to provide the best objective analysis (Trow 1985). This perspective is especially salient in developing countries, where the academic community's involvement in struggles for independence created a tradition of political engagement. In Latin America, for example, professors and students actively participated in the struggles against military dictatorships and sometimes supported leftist movements in the 1960s and 1970s, often bringing the wrath of the regime down upon the university. In such countries as Argentina, Brazil, and Chile, large numbers of professors and students were jailed, forced into exile, or even killed by repressive regimes. While no one would condone repression, some have argued that academic institutions should keep aloof from partisan politics, making a distinction between the right of individual professors to speak out on political or social issues and the concept of institutional neutrality (Ashby 1974). In the United States, there were debates during the 1960s concerning whether universities as institutions should take stands on such issues as opposing the war in Vietnam. No one opposed the right of individual faculty or students to participate in antiwar movements, but many felt that the institution itself should remain neutral. The issue of the appropriate role for universities in social and political spheres remains an unresolved part of the debate about the role of academic freedom.

There has also been considerable debate over the influence of political or ideological ideas on universities. In the United States, critics of "political correctness" have charged factions within academe of imposing their views on academic departments or disciplinary associations, violating as a result the norms of academic freedom (Kors and Silverglate 1998). The intrusion of partisan politics or sometimes ethnic issues into academic appointments, university elections, and publication and research is evident in many countries in Latin America and South Asia and is by no means unknown in other parts of the world. These pressures, usually emanating from within the universities themselves, threaten academic freedom. The intrusions introduce extraneous conflicts and nonmeritocratic factors into the process of academic governance, teaching, and research and affect relations among academics. Such conflicts are often not seen as related to academic freedom. If academic freedom means the free pursuit of teaching and research, as well as decision making on grounds of solely academic criteria, the intrusion of political or other factors into decision making regarding personnel or other matters violates the norms of both governance and academic freedom (Metzger 1988).

Many have argued that the liberty conferred by academic freedom creates a reciprocal responsibility (Shils 1991; Poch 1993; Russell 1993). Those entrusted with teaching and research in higher education, it is claimed, have a special obligation to dedicate themselves to truth and objectivity in all their scholarly work. These critics argue that academe and politics should not be intertwined. Universities are not political institutions, and those involved in the academic enterprise need to recognize that academe's survival depends on its ability to keep an appropriate distance from partisan politics. Others have a more absolutist view of academic freedom—namely that faculty members should have the right to participate in any activities they deem appropriate and that representative bodies of the faculty may similarly be engaged. There is as yet no consensus in the academic community, and thus there is considerable debate about the appropriate limits to academic freedom.

Academic freedom also needs to be reconsidered in the era of the Internet and distance education. Are professors entitled to academic freedom in the cyberclassroom? Does the cyberprofessor have the freedom to design and deliver a course without external restrictions from sponsors (often profit-making companies), especially when development costs may be high? Who owns knowledge products developed for Internet use? These questions impinge on the tradition of academic freedom and need to be answered as higher education moves to new modes of knowledge provision.

Historical Precedents

Academic freedom has a long and controversial history. For centuries, church and civil authorities placed restrictions on the academic community in terms of teaching, research, and public expression. The Catholic Church forbade the teaching of theological and scientific doctrines at universities that were contrary to accepted doctrine. Martin Luther, a professor of theology, found himself in conflict with church officials because of his theological views and was removed from his professorship. It was only later, when some German universities in areas that had turned Protestant became sympathetic to his views, that he was able to resume his academic duties. As the result of many struggles, and especially following the rise of the research university in the early 19th century, freedom of expression gradually expanded, and professors were given more latitude in their teaching and research.

But academic freedom has always been contested terrain—even in academic systems with strong historical traditions. Academic freedom was effectively obliterated in Nazi Germany despite the fact that this modern ideal was a German invention. Not only were direct restrictions placed on what could be taught at German universities during the Third Reich, but tenured professors who did not conform to the new ideology, as well as professors who were Jewish or known to be politically dissident, were fired. Few voices were raised in protest in Germany against these developments, and both the German professors' organizations and the student unions supported the Nazi suppression of academic freedom. In many cases, the universities themselves implemented the changes. During the 1950s Cold War era, the anti-communist hysteria in the United States led to academic freedom being challenged by governmental authorities seeking to rid the universities of alleged communists. In some cases, such as at public universities in California and New York, a number of professors were forced from their positions by state regulations, especially by the refusal of some to sign loyalty oaths (Schrecker 1986). At other institutions, investigations "exposed" leftist professors, leading to firings or forced resignations. Some universities protected faculty members in the name of academic freedom, while others gave in to outside pressure and fired professors. Loyalty oaths imposed by several state governments placed added stress on the academic profession and resulted in a small number of additional losses when universities were forced to fire faculty members who refused to sign the oaths. While only a few academics were actually fired during this period, academic freedom was imperiled in an atmosphere of repression, and many academics feared dismissal. These examples show that even in countries with strong academic traditions and commitments to academic freedom universities can suffer serious consequences.

The Latin American academic tradition also contributed an important concept to the debate about academic freedom. The idea of university autonomy, enshrined in the Cordoba Reforms of 1918, has long been a powerful force in Latin America (Walter 1968). What originated as a student protest resulted in a significant reform of universities in Argentina and most of Latin America. Many of the continent's public universities are by law and tradition autonomous, which has implications for relations with the state as well as for academic freedom. The concept of autonomy provided significant protection for professors and students during periods of political unrest in Latin America. That protection has not been comprehensive—especially during the era of military dictatorships during the 1960s and 1970s—but has nonetheless played a central role in determining the continent's thinking about higher education.

In countries that experienced colonial rule, academic freedom is less firmly rooted historically and less well protected. The colonial powers—whether British, French, Japanese, Dutch, or others—feared unrest from subject peoples (Ashby 1966). Modeled on the metropolitan home university, universities established in the colonies were generally not permitted freedoms that were allowed in the metropole. As it turned out, the colonizers' fears of unrest were justified, since intellectuals and students often stood in the forefront of struggles for independence. As a result of these colonial academic traditions, the circumstances of revolutionary independence struggles, or postindependence instability and crisis, academic freedom did not take root in many developing countries. Governments have often been quick to interfere in academic affairs in order to maintain stability. The academic community, both professors and students, has been involved in protest movements. In short, the conditions for building traditions of academic freedom in many developing countries were not auspicious, and academic freedom remains tenuous.

Contemporary Realities

With more data, it would be possible to create a "world academic freedom barometer" as has been developed for human rights, corruption, and other issues. Such a mechanism, while useful, would be quite difficult to put together due to the problems discussed earlier of defining academic freedom. The following survey may serve as the first step in such a comprehensive survey (From Beijing to Belgrade 1999).

SEVERE RESTRICTIONS

In a few countries, academic freedom is nonexistent. Perhaps the most egregious example is Burma, where universities are periodically closed for extended periods of time when unrest occurs. The regime does not trust the academic community. In countries with unstable governments, universities are closed from time to time—usually to combat student unrest, but also to repress criticism by the faculty and others. Regimes that are willing to shut down universities are also likely to place severe restrictions on the academic freedom of faculty—especially concerning their freedom to speak out on social or political issues but also including views expressed in the classroom and in the course of research.

In countries such as Burma, North Korea and to a lesser extent Syria, where universities represent an integral part of a repressive governmental apparatus, restrictions are built into the academic and political system—rather than being caused by social unrest or political crises. The absence of academic freedom is endemic and complete. In some scientific disciplines, it is possible to teach and do research with only minimal restriction. In the social sciences and other sensitive fields, there are severe restrictions on what can be taught or written. Violations can result in loss of jobs, jail sentences, or worse. Political or intellectual dissent on campuses is not permitted.

Iran is an interesting case in point. Oppositional ideas and movements have emerged from the universities, especially the University of

Tehran, for decades. Students and faculty provided leadership opposing the shah and were a key force in the overthrow of the monarchy and the establishment of a theocratic regime. Students also provided the leadership for the takeover of the US embassy in the 1970s, a landmark event solidifying the new regime. Starting in the 1990s, the academic community has been calling for a liberalization of Iran's theocratic regime, and conservatives in the government and among Islamic religious authorities see the universities as a threat. The professors are caught in the middle of a power struggle in society. The fundamentalist regime has repressed academic freedom on campus, threatened professors, and in at least one case sentenced a critical professor to death— a sentence overturned as the result of internal pressure and international outcry. In 2006, renewed campus student activism called for a liberalization of Iranian society. The Iranian example shows how campus opinion can change and how regimes may alter their perspectives on the role of the universities.

CRISES AND SOME RESTRICTIONS

In a much larger group of countries, while a measure of academic freedom is present in many scientific fields, significant restrictions do exist. The involvement of professors in activities viewed as antiregime is not tolerated. Penalties for transgressions can be severe and include not only loss of academic jobs, but sometimes prosecution and imprisonment. Certainly China, Vietnam, and Cuba are examples of countries in which restrictions on academic freedom are an integral part of university life, especially in the social sciences and other fields that are considered politically or ideologically sensitive. Yet even in these countries, the universities generally enjoy an academic environment similar to that in countries with greater degrees of academic freedom in most fields. Participation in international scientific and scholarly networks is permitted, and in most disciplines, teaching and research are only minimally inhibited by government control. At times of political tension, such as during the 1989 Tienanmen Square crisis in China, governmental repression increases dramatically. Indeed, Chinese universities were kept on a tight leash by the government for years after Tienanmen, reflecting the historical importance of the Chinese universities as centers of political dissent (Hayhoe 1999). Afterall, the Chinese imperial government was toppled in considerable part by university-based demonstrations a century earlier.

Some Islamic countries fall into this category. The absence of democratic traditions in society, potential political instability, intellectual struggles between fundamentalist and secular forces in the universities, and weak academic traditions combine to create tensions between academe and government. With some exceptions, there are few universities with strong traditions of academic freedom and autonomy. This makes the professoriate more vulnerable to external pressure. In Egypt, Algeria, and some of the Arabian Gulf states, academics who support fundamentalist groups may face arrest or other restrictions. In Sudan, dissident views from the opposition engender repression. In most countries, there are de facto restrictions on some research topics and interpretations. The range of academic freedom extends from severe restrictions in Syria to modest problems in Egypt (the arrest of a respected Egyptian sociologist was seen by many in the academic community as punishment for his oppositional views—he was later released after an international pressure), to relative openness in Kuwait and several of the Gulf countries.

LIMITED ACADEMIC FREEDOM

A still larger group of countries might be characterized as relatively free, especially within the classroom and with regard to research in fields that are not considered politically or ideologically sensitive by the state. In general, these countries claim a commitment to academic freedom, but serious difficulties still arise from time to time. The limits are seldom clearly articulated, and the penalties imposed for violations of the restrictions are often unstated and not fully understood in the academic community. Testing the limits of academic freedom in these countries may be dangerous, and the perception that limits exist creates a significant chilling effect among academics.

Government authorities may impose fairly harsh penalties, often without warning. In the mid-1990s, the Ethiopian government, for example, fired more than 40 professors, and jailed some professors at the University of Addis Ababa for undisclosed reasons that had overtones of political repression. This heralded continuing violations of academic freedom in the country. In many nations, it is clear that antiregime sentiments, expressed in the classroom or in public discourse, may cause problems. In Serbia, student opposition to the Milosevic regime created repression in the universities as the government sought to maintain its control—since the downfall of Milosevic conditions have improved.

In many countries scholars do experience a considerable degree of academic freedom. However, political or other crises may create severe difficulties for the universities with respect to academic freedom, creating an atmosphere of general unease for many academics. Much of Africa and a number of Asian countries find themselves in this situation (Diouf and Mamdani 1994). Countries in this category include those whose governments are weak and lack legitimacy. Their academic traditions are not well established, often as a result of colonialism, and the universities tend to be dependent on the state for support. Nigeria, which has a large academic system and sporadically enjoys a considerable degree of academic freedom, often faces restrictions, especially during military regimes. Smaller African countries with weaker academic traditions generally have less academic freedom. In Asia, Cambodia, emerging from decades of repression, is slowly rebuilding its universities. Academic freedom will be difficult to establish because of governmental instability, dependence on a few sources of funding, and the almost total destruction of higher education during the Khmer Rouge years (Chamnan 2000).

The challenge of instituting academic freedom under conditions of political instability is considerable. Universities often function as centers of political and intellectual dissent, and regimes are thus reluctant to allow institutions the freedom and autonomy that may contribute to instability. An academic community that is unused to academic freedom and perhaps engaged in political struggle may not be in a position to create academic freedom or to exercise the self-discipline involved.

LESS THAN COMPLETE ACADEMIC FREEDOM

In some nations, restrictions are imposed on faculty research topics as well as on the freedom of public expression by academics. Although many professors resist them, these restrictions are widely accepted in the academic community. Sanctions for violating the often unstated norms can range from mild rebukes by administrators to loss of jobs or, in rare cases, prosecution in the courts. Singapore and Malaysia are countries that have long had informal bans on certain research topics and the expression of oppositional views. Ethnic conflict, certain religious issues, and local corruption are among the topics deemed inappropriate for academic research, especially if research findings might raise questions about government policies. Academics must also watch what they say in the classroom on sensitive issues since the penalties for violating these norms can be serious. In Singapore, the former prime minister, Lee Kwan Yew, would occasionally come to National University of Singapore faculty meetings to criticize individual academics for their writings and to encourage the faculty to work in support of what he defined as the national interest. The situation in both countries has become more open in recent years as more tolerant political leaders have assumed power. In the Arab world, in countries that have a modicum of academic freedom, there are taboo subjects for research as well—for example, some aspects of Islam or the Arab-Israeli conflict.

Many countries have such restrictions on academic freedom (Altbach 1988). Government authorities make it clear to university officials that continued good relations, budgetary allocations, and research funds depend on the appropriate academic and political behavior on the part of the faculty.

THE REEMERGENCE OF ACADEMIC FREEDOM

In two quite different parts of the world academic freedom is gaining in strength. First, Latin America has a strong tradition of academic freedom and autonomy, going back at least to the 1918 Cordoba Reforms (Walter 1968). Political turmoil throughout much of Latin America in the 1960s and 1970s led to military coups, social instability, and guerrilla struggles. Many groups in the universities, especially the large public autonomous institutions located in capital cities, were deeply involved in the struggles, always on the side of the leftist dissidents. In Peru, for example, several of the key leaders of the violent Sendero Luminoso movement that created severe civil unrest were former professors, and the movement had some support in the universities. Throughout Latin America, some activist students left the campuses to join, or even lead, guerrilla movements against the government. It is not surprising that the military authorities, which had little use for academic freedom in any case, violently confronted the academic community. Academic freedom and the idea of university autonomy suffered serious setbacks during this period. Professors known for their dissenting views were forced into exile, jailed, and even killed. Student movements were violently repressed. Peru, Brazil, Argentina, Uruguay, El Salvador, Chile, and other countries all experienced severe restrictions on academic freedom during this period. As violent dissent decreased and military rulers were gradually replaced with democratic governments, the situation in Latin America changed, and academic life returned to normal.

While Latin American universities have been involved in national politics at least since the Cordoba movement, and partisan politics continues to infuse campus elections and, in some universities, academic life generally, it was possible to rebuild and even strengthen academic freedom when democracy was restored. The Latin American experience shows that strong traditions of academic freedom can survive periods of severe repression.

The second region that has seen a resurgence of academic freedom is Central and Eastern Europe and the former Soviet Union. These countries have a venerable academic history; some of oldest universities in the world include those in the Czech Republic and Poland. However, academic freedom was basically abolished, first during the years of Nazi occupation and later during the over four decades or more of communist rule. Universities were considered arms of the state, ideological loyalty was expected, and severe sanctions were often imposed for violating political or academic orthodoxy, including removal from academic posts and prosecution. Academic freedom was seen as a "bourgeois" concept, inappropriate in a socialist society, because all elements of society, including the universities, were subject to the needs of the state for economic development and social reconstruction.

With the collapse of communism in the region, universities found themselves in a very different environment. Academic freedom was restored as a central value of higher education, and the ideological accoutrements of the communist era were dismantled. Some, however, have argued that the practice in many of these countries of summarily removing professors who were identified as having been overly loyal to the communist regimes violated due process and was in some ways a violation of academic freedom. Teaching and research are no longer considered to be subject to ideological and political goals, and in most of these countries academic freedom and the ideal of academic autonomy have been restored. The financial and other pressures of the post-communist era, however, have created a set of new problems that affect academe in the region.

Without question, there is now a considerable degree of academic freedom in much of the region. Promotions are now more likely to be decided on the basis of merit. Most academics need not fear direct sanctions for pursuing any research or teaching. Countries with long academic traditions, stable democratic governments, fairly robust economies, and closer ties to the major Western nations—such as the Czech Republic, Hungary, and Poland—quickly reestablished academic norms that valued academic freedom and autonomy for the universities. As of 2004, academic freedom is largely absent in Belarus and is in a precarious state in Ukraine and in several of the Central Asian republics. With the restoration of a tenuous peace and the end of the Milosevic regime in Serbia, academic freedom has been generally restored in Serbia, Bosnia-Herzegovina, and Kosovo. Conditions are much better in Russia and in most of Central Europe. Weak traditions of academic freedom, the fact that universities have been largely dependent on governments that have only limited legitimacy, and decades of severe repression have made it difficult to build strong norms of academic freedom in parts of the region.

INDUSTRIALIZED COUNTRIES

At the beginning of the 21st century, academic freedom as an ideal and in most cases in practice is strong in the industrialized nations. Countries such as Japan and Germany, in which academic freedom was abolished, have reestablished strong traditions after World War II. The American anticommunist restrictions lasted just a few years in the 1950s. All industrialized nations value academic freedom in teaching and research and have accepted freedom of expression for professors within the university and in society. It is widely recognized that academic freedom is necessary for universities to fulfill their missions of teaching and research. Few if any external restrictions are placed on university activities or on professors or students. Despite this generally healthy situation, there are some issues that deserve attention.

In the United States, some have argued that the greatest threat to academic freedom lies within the academy. Critics claim that the dominant forces in the professoriate, mainly in the social sciences and humanities, seek to enforce "political correctness"—imposing academic orthodoxy, usually from a liberal or radical perspective, on some disciplines and seeking to silence those with opposing viewpoints (Kors and Silverglate 1998). Several scholarly associations, such as the Modern Language Association, have experienced fierce ideological battles. Few if any academics with divergent views have been restricted or have lost their jobs, but the debate about the politicization of some academic disciplines has raised questions about the tolerance of diverse perspectives within universities. Politicization or the influence of ideology on academic institutions or disciplines is not limited to the United States. During the 1960s, ideology played a role in academic politics and in the disciplines in Western Europe, in many cases intruding into elections and appointments to academic posts.

Some argue that the increased involvement in academe of corporations and the growth of privately sponsored research have transformed research funding and that this has implications for academic freedom (Slaughter and Leslie 1997; Slaughter and Rhoads 2004). Academe, it is argued, has become "corporatized," and the interests of firms have become predominant on campus. Basic research is being de-emphasized in favor of applied work that will yield quick results for corporate sponsors. Government support for basic research has either declined or failed to keep pace with scientific needs. A growing portion of research funding, especially in the biomedical sciences, is directly provided by corporations, and the results are considered proprietary—leading to patents and other rewards for the sponsor. Research findings are sometimes actually suppressed because of corporate funding agreements.

This is considered by many as a violation of the freedom of academics to disseminate the results of their research. The prospects of basic research have been seen as jeopardized by these transformed funding patterns.

A related issue, not usually encompassed in the context of academic freedom, is the growth of what some have called "managerialism" in higher education—the notable increase in the power of administrators and other officials as distinct from the authority of the professoriate in the governance and management of academic institutions. Academic freedom and autonomy are related, and these governance trends reduce the autonomy and power of the professoriate. The authority of the professors to determine the direction of the university, develop the curriculum, and maintain full control in the classroom and in the selection and implementation of research topics is compromised by this trend. There seems little doubt that the shift in power and authority from the professoriate to professional managers and external governing bodies will dramatically affect the traditional role of the academic profession—with repercussions on academic freedom as well.

Another relevant aspect of contemporary realities is how the academic profession itself views academic freedom. A survey of academics in 14 countries (all middle-income and mostly industrialized nations, on all continents except Africa) found a range of views as to whether the academic profession is strongly protected. More than 75 percent of the respondents reacted positively to this question in all of the countries but two—Brazil and Russia, where majorities answered negatively. Yet, in all of the countries included except Israel, about 20 percent of the faculty responded negatively. Similar numbers reported that they felt no restrictions on their research and teaching. However, when asked to respond to the statement "In this country, there are no political or ideological restrictions on what a scholar may publish," significant numbers expressed disagreement—34 percent in the United States, 25 percent in the United Kingdom, and 27 percent in Mexico (Boyer, Altbach, and Whitelaw 1994, 101). These findings indicate that while academics are reasonably sanguine about the state of academic freedom in these countries, there remains some sense of unease.

Indeed, the challenges to academic freedom in the industrialized countries are more subtle, and perhaps in some ways more harmful than the more overt violations that have been described here and that can be readily grasped and opposed.

What Can Be Done?
History shows that academic freedom is not only a fundamental pre-

requisite for an effective university but is a core value for academia. Just as human rights are receiving more attention internationally, academic freedom must be placed at the forefront of concern for the higher education community. Higher education is international in scope—in the sense that issues affecting one country have implications in others. A sophisticated understanding of the complex issues relating to academic freedom is also required. The following items may be part of an action agenda for academic freedom.

- Academic freedom should be at the top of the agenda for everyone concerned with higher education. However, at present it is hardly discussed. Rarely are panels devoted to the topic at international conferences. The major actors in the academic enterprise seem to be concentrating on financial issues, accountability, and institutional survival.
- Academic freedom needs a universal definition. Should the scope be limited to the Humboldtian ideal of the protection of teaching and research within the confines of the university and in the area of expertise of the scholar? Or should the definition encompass expression, and perhaps action as well, on a wider range of issues both within and outside the university? At present, the lack of agreement on the nature of academic freedom makes common understanding and unified action difficult.
- Violations of academic freedom must be monitored and subjected to publicity worldwide. In the age of the Internet, keeping track of academic freedom issues and promptly disseminating information about crises and trends would be easy to accomplish. An Internet-based "early warning system" would provide information and heighten consciousness.
- A more rigorous mechanism for investigating academic freedom violations would promote international attention to severe violations. For many years—as mentioned earlier—the American Association of University Professors has monitored academic freedom in the United States. Universities found to have violated academic freedom can be censured, which serves as a warning for the academic community. When the violation is remedied, censure can be lifted. Other than being placed on a list of censured institutions, there are no sanctions, and in fact censure by the AAUP has little impact. A similar international arrangement would be more problematic and more expensive to organize but would be a valuable tool for consciousness raising.
- A solidarity network for academic freedom, such as "Scholars at Risk," is now headquartered at New York University. The network

seeks to identify individuals in trouble and to place them at universities committed to assisting them and has the broader goal of highlighting academic freedom conditions worldwide.

Conclusion

Academic freedom is a core issue for higher education. Although largely overlooked, it should be essential to every debate about the university. Academic freedom is as important as managerial accountability, distance education, and the other buzzwords of the new millennium. Indeed, without academic freedom, the mission of teaching and research cannot be truly effective. Moreover, academic freedom at the beginning of the 21st century is facing challenges, as much from the impact of new technologies and the restructuring of traditional universities as from forces that would violate academic freedom by persecuting professors. The future of the university depends on establishing a healthy environment for academic freedom.

References

Altbach, Philip G. 1988. Academic freedom in Asia. *Far Eastern Economic Review*, June 16, 24–25.

Ashby, Eric. 1966. *Universities: British, Indian, African: A study in the ecology of higher education*. Cambridge, MA: Harvard University Press.

———. 1974. The academic profession. In *Adapting universities to a technological society*, 73–87. San Francisco: Jossey-Bass.

Boyer, Ernest L., Philip G. Altbach, and Mary Jean Whitelaw. 1994. *The academic profession: An international perspective*. Princeton, NJ: Carnegie Foundation for the Advancement of Teaching.

Burgan, Mary A. 1999. A report from Paris. *Academe* 85 (July/August): 45–48.

Chamnan, Pit. 2000. Cambodia: Rebuilding the Royal University. *International Higher Education*, no. 19:16–17.

Diouf, Mamadou, and Mahmood Mamdani, eds. 1994. *Academic freedom in Africa*. Dakar, Senegal: CODESRIA.

From Beijing to Belgrade: Academic freedom around the world. 1999. *Academe* 85 (July–August): 16–39.

Hayhoe, Ruth. 1999. *China's universities: 1895–1995: A century of cultural conflict*. Hong Kong: Comparative Education Research Center, University of Hong Kong.

Human Rights Watch. 1998. *Academic freedom in Indonesia: Dismantling Soeharto-era barriers*. New York: Human Rights Watch.

Kors, Alan Charles, and Harvey A. Silverglate. 1998. *The shadow university: The betrayal of liberty on America's campuses*. New York: Free Press.

Metzger, Walter. 1988. Profession and constitution: Two definitions and academic freedom in America. *Texas Law Review* 66:1265–1321.

Poch, Robert K. 1993. *Academic freedom in American higher education: Rights, responsibilities, and limitations*. Washington, DC: George Washington University, School of Education.

Russell, Conrad. 1993. *Academic freedom*. London: Routledge.

Schrecker, Ellen. 1986. *No ivory tower: McCarthyism and the universities*. New York: Oxford University Press.

Shils, Edward. 1991. Academic freedom. In *International Higher Education: An Encyclopedia*, ed. P. G. Altbach, 1–22. New York: Garland.

Slaughter, Sheila, and Gary Rhoades. 2004. *Academic capitalism and the new economy*. Baltimore: Johns Hopkins University Press.

Slaughter, Sheila, and Larry L. Leslie. 1997. *Academic capitalism: Politics, policies, and the entrepreneurial university*. Baltimore: Johns

Hopkins University Press.

Trow, Martin. 1985. The threat from within: Academic freedom and negative evidence. *Change* (September–October): 8–9, 61–63.

Walter, Richard J. 1968. *Student politics in Argentina: The university reform and its effects*, 1918–1964. New York: Basic Books.

4

Comparative Perspectives on Private Higher Education

P rivate higher education is one of the most dynamic and rapidly growing segments of postsecondary education in the 21st century. Unprecedented demand for access to higher education combined with the inability or unwillingness of governments to provide the necessary support has brought private higher education to the forefront. Private institutions, with a long history in many countries, are expanding in scope and number and becoming increasingly important in parts of the world that have relied on the public higher education sector (Altbach 1999). It is now difficult to generalize about the private sector in higher education because of its diversity. Many of the new private institutions are at the bottom of the prestige hierarchy and cater to a mass demand, while some are small prestigious business schools. There are a few older respected private universities, often affiliated with the Roman Catholic Church, in Latin America and elsewhere, along with many diverse newer institutions. A related phenomenon is the "privatization" of public institutions in some countries (Jones 1992). With tuition and other charges rising in the public sector, the boundaries between public and private institutions look more and more porous.

Private higher education has long dominated higher education systems in Japan, South Korea, Taiwan, and the Philippines. In the 1980s, there was a dramatic shift from public to private postsecondary education in Latin America. Brazil, Mexico, Colombia, Chile, Peru, and Venezuela now enroll at least half of their students in private universities (Maldonado 2004). Private higher education is the fastest-growing sector in many countries in Central and Eastern Europe and in the countries of the former Soviet Union. For the most part, this unprecedented growth in the private sector stems from the government's inability in many countries to fund expansion.

Not only has demand overwhelmed the ability of governments to pay, but a significant change has occurred in the way that higher education is perceived. The concept of an academic degree as a "private good" that benefits the individual rather than a "public good" for society is now widely accepted. The logic of today's market economies and an ideology of privatization have contributed to the resurgence of private higher education and the emergence of private institutions where none existed before.

At a time when private higher education is undergoing a long-term worldwide expansion, it is essential to consider the role of private higher education and the specific problems facing private institutions (Geiger 1991). While private and public universities share some common roots and some similar functions, private institutions do have special characteristics. Most important among these is the financial base of private institutions. Private institutions are responsible for their own funding, along with internal governance and management, the relationship to government and public authorities, and institutional planning.

This chapter is concerned with understanding the parameters of private higher education worldwide. Will the private sector be able to manage the pressure of increased numbers, new forms of accountability, innovative technologically driven educational programs, and other developments? Or, alternatively, will the private institutions cluster at the bottom of the postsecondary system, offering low-quality programs providing a credential but little value? Will the prestigious private universities at the top of the academic hierarchy in some countries be able to provide inspiration or serve as models to the newer institutions? Will appropriate agencies be set up to protect quality and represent the interests of students and of society in this new private-enterprise educational environment?

Themes and Variations

There is tremendous differentiation in private higher education internationally. Harvard University, with an endowment measured in billions of dollars, could hardly be more different from a newly established "garage university" in El Salvador offering specialized training in only a few fields. Some private institutions are highly focused on specific fields, such as the world-renowned INSEAD international management school in Paris. Others are large multipurpose universities, like the Far East University in Manila, with more than 100,000 students; many enroll just a few hundred students. Some are among the most prestigious institutions in the country, like Waseda or Keio in Japan, Harvard and Yale in the United States, the Ateneo de Manila in the Philippines, or Javieriana University in Colombia. Most private postsecondary institutions are responsible for their own funding, although some receive government funds for specific purposes. In India, for example, more than 2,000 privately managed colleges are financed largely by public funds. In the Netherlands, all private universities receive most of their support from the government. Some nations allow private institutions virtually complete freedom, while others, such as Korea and to a lesser extent Japan, impose rigid controls. There is immense variation among private postsecondary institutions worldwide—and, in some countries, even internally.

While private higher education is growing worldwide, there are major national variations. Most of Western Europe continues to be dominated by public universities. While their number and role within academic systems are growing, private institutions still constitute a tiny minority. Some are religious, mainly Catholic, universities and seminaries, while a growing number are specialized institutions, especially business schools. A few, such as the University of Buckingham in England, are multipurpose private universities. But more than 95 percent of students in Western Europe attend public institutions. Significantly, it is in Eastern Europe and the former Soviet Union that private higher education is having its greatest European success. In this region, governments are unable to devote sufficient funds to expanding public universities; the idea of state domination was discredited after the fall of communism; and there is little regulation of the new private institutions.

While many of the most famous American universities are private, more than 80 percent of students in the United States attend public institutions of higher learning. The proportion of enrollments at public colleges and universities has steadily increased for the past half century, and the 80:20 ratio seems stable. In the United States, private institutions fall into several categories. At the top of the academic hierarchy are such prestigious private universities as Harvard, Yale, Princeton, Stanford, the University of Chicago, the Massachusetts Institute of Technology, and others. Top-ranked private colleges such as Amherst, Smith, Williams, and Swarthmore can be included in this category. These private universities and colleges are highly selective and all have large endowment funds. Religiously affiliated universities and colleges—ranging from top-ranking institutions such as Georgetown, Notre Dame, and Boston College to many small "bible colleges" and struggling liberal arts colleges affiliated with both Catholic and Protestant groups—are another key category in the private sector. There are also many secular private colleges and universities. Finally, a group of little-known "proprietary" (profit-making) specialized institutions, most of which are small, are included, although few are accredited. These schools are not central to the academic enterprise in the United States. The over 2,000 American private colleges and universities are quite diverse; a large majority of them depend on student tuition fees for survival. They constitute a unique and vibrant segment of American higher education.

In comparative terms, private higher education is most powerful in Asia. In a number of Asian nations—including Japan, South Korea, the Philippines, and Indonesia—private postsecondary institutions dominate the higher education systems in terms of numbers. In all of these countries almost 80 percent of students attend private institutions. While public universities are the most prestigious in each of these countries, several private schools also rank at the top of the hierarchy. Substantial private sectors exist in Thailand and Taiwan, among other countries. In Asian nations traditionally dominated by the public sector, such as Malaysia, the fastest-growing segment of higher education is private. Even in China and Vietnam, with communist systems, private higher education is growing rapidly. There are 2,000 private postsecondary institutions in China, although only a handful are officially recognized by the government. Most undergraduate education in India is provided by private colleges affiliated with public universities. In India, unlike all other Asian nations, there is substantial, although declining, public funding for the private colleges.

Latin America has traditionally had a private higher education sector—one dominated by the Catholic Church (Levy 1986). The oldest institutions are church-related and typically among the most prestigious. In the past several decades, an entirely new group of institutions has been established, and in most countries these now outnumber church-related universities. These new institutions are diverse secular postsecondary institutions—some are multipurpose universities offering degrees in fields with strong market demand and some are specialized schools offering instruction in single fields from management to tourism studies. A few have achieved high standing and respect, but most are clustered at the lower levels of the academic hierarchy. This explosive growth has created a private sector that now educates a majority of students in Brazil, Mexico, Colombia, and other countries.

Aside from Western Europe, the region relying most on public higher education is sub-Saharan Africa, and even in this area private higher education is the fastest-growing segment of postsecondary education. The public-oriented traditions of the main colonial powers, the British and the French, and the limited financial resources available in the private sector in most African countries have meant that, traditionally, little private higher education has existed. In the past decade, however, the private sector has grown dramatically, as it became clear that government could not finance access. Catholic religious organizations have been active throughout the region, as have Protestant groups, in Zimbabwe, Kenya, Ghana, and several other countries. Other private initiatives are emerging as well. Shortages of capital and student inability to pay for the cost of tuition will make the expansion of private higher education in Africa a more difficult and probably slower process than it has been in most other regions, although there is evidence of a growing middle class able to pay for private higher education (Kruss and Kraak 2003).

This global summary of private higher education development shows national and regional variations and indicates explosive expansion. Private postsecondary education is a significant force almost everywhere, and it is a growing phenomenon even where it has not previously been in the mainstream. There is considerable diversity among private institutions, but most of the expansion is taking place at the low end of the higher education system. The role played by private higher education—which is able to adapt quickly to changing market conditions, student interests, and the needs of the economy—is bound to grow.

Issues and Trends
As private higher education moves to the center of higher education systems worldwide, certain central issues and trends require discussion and analysis. We are concerned with raising questions in a comparative framework.

FINANCING PRIVATE HIGHER EDUCATION
There are many models of funding private higher education. In the large majority of cases, institutions are financed by tuition payments from students. The central reality of most private institutions is that tuition payments are the financial basis of the institution. Tuition levels must be high enough to provide sufficient funds for institutional survival, which requires careful planning relating to student numbers, the cost per student, and expenditure levels. Errors in these calcula-

tions, the failure to meet enrollment goals, or unanticipated expenses can wreak havoc on institutional budgets and even threaten an institution's survival. Most new private postsecondary institutions do not have much of a financial cushion. Tuition dependency also means students must be able to afford to pay the fees charged. This, in turn, has an impact on the social class of students and the kinds of programs that are offered. In this way, private institutions may exacerbate class or other divisions in society.

A relatively small proportion of private institutions have other financial resources available to them. Universities sponsored by religious organizations sometimes receive funds from these groups or at least rely on help with staffing. In a few countries, a small number of universities can depend on endowment or other funds contributed by alumni or other supporters. This is especially the case in the United States, where a sizable minority of private schools have substantial endowment incomes that provide continuing operating funds. All but the most prestigious of these colleges and universities, however, remain dependent on tuition revenues. In a few countries, government support is available to private postsecondary institutions. In the United States, while direct funding is not provided, students in private institutions are eligible for government loans and grants, and private universities can compete for government research funding. In India, the large majority of students studying at private colleges are financed in part with government money. The Philippines has a fund for private universities that provides some resources. Japan and a few other countries provide limited financial support to private schools. With the possible exceptions of India and the Netherlands, the bulk of funding for private postsecondary institutions is generated by the institutions themselves. As the private sector grows, there will be debate over how it should be paid for and whether private institutions should have access to government funding programs for research, student aid, construction, and the like.

OWNERSHIP AND PROFITS

Traditionally, colleges and universities everywhere have functioned as nonprofit institutions operating under legal authority from the state to provide education and engage in research and other education-related activities. These universities have been owned by nonprofit agencies, such as religious organizations, scientific societies, and other groups that have legal authority for ownership and management. For the most part, these arrangements do not permit institutions to earn a profit, although the institutions are guaranteed a high level of autonomy. In some cases, the university is "owned" by a sponsoring organization, in others by the academic staff and administrators, and in still others by boards of trustees or governors composed in part of academics or dominated by outsiders. Legal arrangements vary from country to country.

Religious organizations have long been involved in establishing and supporting academic institutions. Many of the earliest academic institutions were established by the Roman Catholic Church, not only in Europe, but later in Latin America and Asia. The only existing university older than the European medieval universities, the Al-Azhar University in Cairo, is an Islamic institution. Protestant religious organizations have also been active in higher education, including establishing the first academic institutions in the United States. Christian organizations were also involved in establishing many of the early universities in Asia—in the Philippines, Korea, China, Japan, and elsewhere (Lutz 1971). A major motivation was to inculcate Christianity in local elites and ultimately to convert people to Christianity. In some cases, such as in the Philippines, a goal was also to educate Church personnel. Hindu organizations in India, Shinto and Buddhist groups in Japan, Buddhists in Thailand, and Muslims in Malaysia, Indonesia, and elsewhere have all been active in establishing academic institutions. Today, while the goals of religiously affiliated institutions are different to some degree from secular institutions, religious organizations of all kinds remain active in private higher education worldwide.

In some countries, Japan and South Korea among them, universities can be established and owned by individuals or by limited, often family-dominated, groups through boards of trustees. In such cases, academic institutions remain legally nonprofit, but the border between nonprofit and profit making is sometimes difficult to discern. Ownership groups, such as trustees or governors, often have the ability to appoint their own successors and are thus able to maintain control over an extended period of time.

There is a growing trend toward for-profit private higher education institutions. These schools may specialize in such fields as business management, computer studies, or related areas that might be in high demand, although they are sometimes multipurpose institutions. Profit-making higher education institutions are dependent for their existence on the legal provisions of countries. However, even where the founding of such institutions is discouraged, it is possible for existing regulations to be shaded toward profitability. In the United States, a largely ignored proprietary profit-making postsecondary education sector has long existed, mainly focusing on vocationally oriented fields at the lower end of the prestige hierarchy. These proprietary schools are seldom authorized to offer degrees and instead give certificates for specialized skills. The University of Phoenix, part of the Apollo Group that is listed on the New York Stock Exchange, has joined the ranks of for-profit higher education (Ruch 2001). This institution offers academic programs in high-demand areas that do not require much investment in facilities, such as business studies and educational administration. Phoenix has no campus and works from offices in most major metropolitan areas in the United States. It has established branches in several other countries. The University of Phoenix offers its programs through traditional classroom-based methods as well as by distance education methods. It is now the largest private university in the United States and is accredited by a regional accreditation agency.

The Philippines has long had for-profit universities, with several institutions listed for many years on the stock exchange. In Latin America, where most countries do not permit for-profit higher education institutions, at least some of the new institutions seem to be interested in producing revenue for those who established and control them. It is possible to see similar trends in other countries, including South Korea and Malaysia.

For-profit higher education is without question a major phenomenon worldwide. In a small number of countries, for-profit higher educational enterprises are permitted by law. In many others, earning profits from educational institutions is not yet accepted culturally or legally, and as a result some new schools resort to skirting existing regulations. However, for-profit higher education will continue to expand, and higher education systems will need to accommodate this trend. Where both are permitted, for-profit and nonprofit institutions are able to coexist. Few, if any, for-profit institutions are high prestige. The largest number of these institutions are small vocationally oriented schools, many of which do not have authorization to offer degrees. Nonetheless, they offer services that are in considerable demand, and it is possible to earn profits by delivering educational products. The for-profit sector creates special problems for accreditation and control, since these institutions often operate in largely unregulated segments of the higher education market.

It is difficult to generalize about international patterns of ownership and funding for private higher education since there is, and will continue to be, considerable diversity. Top universities or those that aspire to achieve elite status in the prestige hierarchy will be nonprofit institutions. They share the norms and values of top universities worldwide in terms of academic freedom and the involvement of the faculty in institutional governance. In contrast, both general-purpose universities and specialized postsecondary schools at the lower end of the academic pecking order are more likely to be for-profit. Regardless of the nature of ownership, these institutions will have less academic autonomy and more control by management. The exact configuration of ownership will depend on the legal framework and, to some extent, on the academic traditions of the nation. Countries in which regulations permit different approaches to funding and ownership will have a variety of educational models.

PRIVATE HIGHER EDUCATION AND THE ACADEMIC SYSTEM

As higher education expands and student enrollments grow, academic institutions proliferate and become more differentiated by type, role, and function. Traditional universities can no longer absorb all the demand for higher education. Moreover, the student body itself is becoming more differentiated, with a greater array of interests and goals for education and more heterogeneous in terms of ability. A higher education establishment that served 2 or 3 percent of the university-age population in traditional universities is transformed when it is called on to educate a quarter or more of the age cohort and to provide education to nontraditional students as well. This expansion and differentiation gives rise to academic systems aimed at providing some rationality and direction to higher education. Private higher education is inevitably part of this postsecondary education system.

In almost all countries, academic institutions have expanded, in number and diversity. Universities have also grown in size, and many public schools are integrated within multi-institutional systems. Ministries of education and other government authorities have sought to understand —and control—the mass phenomenon of higher education. In some countries, coordinating agencies have been set up to ensure that postsecondary institutions serve societal needs with a minimum of duplication. In others, academic institutions have been brought into centralized systems that allocate responsibilities and resources. Coordination and control have proved to be difficult; and the cost, legal and financial, of providing the activities has been high.

Private higher education has become an essential part of most national systems (Umakoshi 2004). As governments have sought to coordinate and in some cases to control the academic system, they have found the private sector even more difficult to deal with than the public sector. Because resources do not generally come from public sources, ownership is not in government hands; and because accountability is extended to many institutions and groups, the private sector poses special challenges. Tight control over the private sector has been part of the South Korean higher education system. Government agencies impose limits on enrollments, tuition, numbers of teaching staff, and salaries. These regulations have recently been modified, but Korea and, to a lesser extent, Japan represent countries with strong government authority over the private sector. The United States, in contrast, has relied on the nongovernmental accreditation system to ensure an acceptable level of quality of private institutions.

Most private institutions seek to fit into the academic system of a nation because their survival depends on attracting students and offering degrees and other qualifications that directly appeal to public demand—generally this means applied fields, such as management training, and a variety of vocational subjects. As noted, in most countries, especially in the developing world, most of the newer private schools rank near the bottom of the academic hierarchy. Their low ranking is due not only to the length of time it takes to build up an academic reputation and status but also because these institutions offer applied programs and have very limited resources.

Significant exceptions to this generalization do exist, even among newer institutions. In Pakistan, the Aga Khan University, with generous funding from the Aga Khan Foundation, has rapidly achieved top ranking. In Argentina, several private universities, notably San Andres and DiTella, have built impressive reputations. The INSEAD management school in Paris was able to establish itself as a top school almost from the beginning. In American higher education, private institutions such as Stanford and the University of Chicago, both established at the end of the 19th century, quickly became top-ranking institutions. In all of these cases, impressive financial resources and skilled leadership permitted rapid development in an academic and social environment requiring these innovative institutions.

AUTONOMY AND ITS LIMITS
Private higher education operates with considerable autonomy in most countries. Because private institutions typically receive little if any public funding and because legal structures do not regulate most academic activities or programs, private postsecondary institutions usually enjoy a great deal of autonomy. Autonomy is, of course, not comprehensive. Laws relating to nonprofit organizations or corporations govern certain aspects of private higher education. In many countries, government regulations concerning higher education do apply, at least to some extent, to private institutions. Some other countries have initiated special legislation covering private higher education.

How much autonomy does private higher education deserve to

have? Should institutions operate with total freedom to determine their goals, standards, tuition charges, curricula, personnel policies, academic standards, and other aspects? Or should private schools be subject to controls to ensure that national norms of quality and academic practices are observed? Should private universities be regarded as an integral part of an academic system and subject to governmental direction? Should private institutions be measured for quality or for relevance? How much responsibility does private higher education have to the public good? How accountable should private higher education be to regulations and standards? Should the extent of accountability be based on social conditions? Should private higher education in developing countries attain the same autonomy as in wealthier nations?

These questions go to the heart of private higher education. Countries give differing answers. A few countries impose fairly strict controls on private institutions, but most permit them a significant degree of autonomy. The international trend provides more leeway to private higher education while subjecting the private sector to accountability—to offer accurate information to potential students, ensure minimum standards of quality, and manage fiscal affairs.

THE MULTINATIONALIZATION OF PRIVATE HIGHER EDUCATION

Academic institutions in one country are beginning to establish links, branches, and collaborative arrangements with universities in other countries. This "multinationalization" trend flows mainly from institutions in the North linking with universities in the South. Collaboration takes many forms, including offering specific degree programs abroad, franchising curricula and degrees, establishing academic centers abroad, and other arrangements. A significant element is establishing branch campuses or programs in other countries. For example, several prominent management schools of American private universities are opening a management institute in India in collaboration with local business firms. Much of multinationalization involves private postsecondary institutions, in part because external controls are less extensive and especially because more entrepreneurialism exists in the private sector.

Multinationalization permits private institutions to quickly establish new academic programs by importing them from abroad. In general, however, the importing institutions rely on foreign providers for academic programs and expertise—without active collaboration over designing new structures and curricula. Concerns have also been raised about measuring quality and accountability of cross-border academic programs. Despite these and other issues, multinational educational initiatives do permit private universities to establish programs quickly in response to local market demands.

The Responsibilities of Private Higher Education

Few have thought about the responsibilities of the private sector to society. Higher education delivers a unique product—knowledge and the credentials to apply knowledge in modern society. Higher education has traditionally been considered both a public and a private good—providing skills to enable individuals to raise incomes and achieve more prestigious careers, as well as improving the human resources needed for societal growth and the operation of a modern economy. There has been much debate about the primary contribution of higher education—whether students and families should pay because the benefits are largely private or society should pay because the benefits serve the public good.

Data from virtually every country show that postsecondary education ensures a higher income and greater opportunities for graduates. Comparisons between persons who have attended college or university and those who have not show consistent benefits to degree holders. Even those who have attended a college or university without earning a degree have higher earnings. There are variations among countries, but the pattern holds globally.

Universities contribute significantly to society in aspects beyond teaching and offering degrees. University libraries provide major repositories of knowledge. Universities serve as centers of research and development and in most countries form the primary sources of basic research. Universities often constitute important cultural centers—sponsoring publishing enterprises, dance companies, and orchestras and serving as venues for cultural performances and institutions. In many countries, universities provide one of the few arenas where independent and critical thought takes place. These aspects comprise central responsibilities of universities that are difficult to measure and do not produce income.

How do private institutions relate to the core functions of higher education? The majority of private universities and postsecondary institutions worldwide provide training and credentials in their areas of expertise, but little else. With the exception of universities operated by religious organizations, social responsibility ranks low on the agenda of private academic institutions. Moreover, few private schools function as research centers or support major libraries.

Private institutions provide access to individuals who can afford to pay for instruction and in some countries permit wider access to postsecondary education because public universities cannot absorb the demand. Thus, despite the fact that few private universities offer scholarship programs for students from poor economic backgrounds or provide academic support programs for underprepared students, they do create opportunities for access to students who would otherwise be unable to attend. Private universities can contribute to social mobility simply by expanding the number of places available in higher education institutions. However, letting market forces fully determine who studies at private universities ensures that only those who can afford the tuition will be able to attend.

Private higher education should have a responsibility to provide information to the public concerning program quality, the usefulness of degrees and certificates, and other details of their offerings. All too often, the prevailing practice is based on caveat emptor—buyer (student) beware. Where they do exist, accrediting systems provide certain controls over the quality of educational programs. The educational marketplace lacks transparency, since the measurement of the educational product is a difficult task and there are few established traditions of quality assurance. Public universities have put budgetary and program accountability measures in place in many countries—but private institutions generally lack accountability and transparency. Indeed, in an era of private-sector expansion, accountability and accreditation are major challenges for higher education with regard to ensuring that students learn about the "educational product" they are buying and linking private higher education to national priorities and plans for postsecondary education.

The professoriate forms the core of any university, and thus the relationship of private institutions and the academic profession must be contemplated. While they constitute traditional elements of the modern university, academic freedom and autonomy are sometimes seen to be in conflict with the market orientation of private higher education. The professoriate has traditionally worked on curriculum development, and there is a commitment to freedom to pursue knowledge in the classroom. However, these norms are often missing in the private higher education sector. Much of the private sector is new, and so it is mandatory that the traditional values of academe be instilled into the practices of the institutions and in their faculties at the beginning if this sector is to effectively work as part of the higher education system.

The Future

Private higher education, given its rapid expansion and significance in the world's higher education systems, faces special challenges and responsibilities. The following issues need to be explored.

- What elements compose private higher education? What kinds of institutions exist? Only limited knowledge is available on the patterns of private higher education development worldwide and how the private sector fits into the higher education system.
- Private higher education is largely market driven. To what extent should the market control developments? Should restraints be imposed? How do controls work in countries, such as Korea, where they exist?
- How should the older, established, and often high-status private universities relate to newer, less-well-endowed institutions? Do the former have a special responsibility to assist or monitor emerging universities?
- What is the appropriate balance of accountability and autonomy in the private sector of higher education?
- How should private higher education be accredited?
- How should the for-profit private sector be regulated? What is the appropriate role of this sector?
- How can distance education be successfully integrated into private higher education? Because it is cost-efficient, distance education will inevitably become part of private higher education.
- What is the appropriate role for government in private higher education? How should public and private institutions interact? Should private higher education be funded by public sources? How should funding mechanisms work?
- How should coordinating agencies responsible for ensuring that the higher education needs of a nation are met deal with private higher education—as an integral part of the postsecondary education system?
- What should the role of the new vocational postsecondary institutions be in the higher education system?
- In Latin America especially, but in other parts of the world as well, what should the role of the Roman Catholic Church, and other religious organizations, be in higher education? What responsibilities do religious universities have for the broader higher education system?
- Fundamentally, what are the public responsibilities of the private higher education sector? How can the public good be served by private institutions?

AN AGENDA FOR THE 21ST CENTURY

In the early 21st century, private higher education is the most dynamic segment of postsecondary education in much of the world. In developing countries, the private sector is without question essential for meeting enrollment needs in the coming decades. Private higher education's prominence is linked with the ideology of privatization that is so influential at present and with the trend worldwide to cut public spending. The inability of governments to meet the demand for access to postsecondary education worldwide contributes to the rise of the private sector. For these reasons, the ongoing expansion of private higher education is inevitable.

The character and quality of private higher education are difficult to portray. The majority of private institutions are positioned at the lower end of the hierarchy in most countries, yet some prestigious and esteemed private universities exist. Private postsecondary institutions tend to be small and specialized, but there are some large multipurpose private universities. While few private institutions have a research focus, examples of research-oriented private universities can be found not only in the United States but in Chile, the Philippines, Japan, and elsewhere.

A growing trend toward the multinationalization of the private sector in higher education is further blurring educational distinctions as well as national boundaries. Private interests such as corporations, publishers or IT companies in one country, usually developing or middle-income countries, are linking up with public or private universities in industrialized nations, to offer educational programs and degrees. This multinationalization complicates the control and monitoring process. The private sector is more aggressive about establishing international links than are public academic institutions.

The private sector needs an effective mix of autonomy and accountability. It needs to be encouraged to introduce new models and approaches for the delivery of higher education and to ensure cost-effectiveness and an orientation toward innovation. At the same time, accountability is needed to ensure that these new ideas deliver a quality educational product. Accreditation and quality control are integral to the growth of private higher education.

In some countries, the trend toward for-profit private postsecondary institutions creates special challenges. For-profit institutions may be able to provide specific kinds of postsecondary training but, given their nature, cannot create universities with the traditional academic values of autonomy and academic freedom. An orientation to the "bottom line" will simply not permit this. For-profit higher education is a part of the postsecondary education system that requires special monitoring precisely because the values of the corporation and the marketplace are to some extent at odds with the traditional values of the university.

Despite the need for private higher education in a period of enrollment expansion, potential problems exist. Will private higher education be so dominated by market demand and short-term requirements that it will not be able to retain commitment to the pursuit of knowledge and truth and to the values of academic freedom and free inquiry? While not every academic institution needs to foster research or to model itself after Oxford or Harvard, the traditional norms of academe are important for everyone. Even schools that focus exclusively on vocational training and specialized degrees should encourage professionalism, academic freedom, and high standards in their educational programs.

The societal role and responsibilities of private higher education is seldom discussed. Higher education has a responsibility to maintain meritocratic values while promoting social mobility. Public universities have provided opportunities for advancement to many graduates, and they provide access to culture and undertake social analysis. Public universities bring the benefits of science and technology to the society through continuing education, book publishing, and by other means. However, these objectives are seldom on the agendas of private higher education institutions.

The 21st century will see private higher education grow in size, scope, and significance in many nations, especially in the developing and middle-income countries. Even in the wealthy countries of Western Europe and North America, private higher education will become more central to the academic enterprise. This sector is diverse, complex, and requires careful analysis. So far, the multiple roles of the new private sector remain unexamined, allowing the market to determine the nature and direction of private higher education.

References

Altbach, Philip G., ed. 1999. *Private Prometheus: Private higher education and development in the 21st century.* Westport, CT: Greenwood Press.

Geiger, Roger L. 1991. Private higher education. In *International higher education: An encyclopedia*, ed. P. G. Altbach, 233–46. New York: Garland.

Jones, David R. 1992. Privatization. In *The encyclopedia of higher education*, ed. B. Clark and G. Neave, 956–69. Oxford: Pergamon.

Kruss, Glenda, and Andre Kraak, eds. 2003. *A contested good? Understanding private higher education in South Africa.* Chestnut Hill, MA: Center for International Higher Education, Boston College.

Levy, Daniel C. 1986. *Higher education and the state in Latin America: Private challenges to public dominance.* Chicago: University of Chicago Press.

Lutz, Jessie Gregory. 1971. *China and the Christian colleges, 1850–1950.* Ithaca, NY: Cornell University Press.

Maldonado-Maldonado, Alma, et al. 2004. *Private higher education: An international bibliography.* Chestnut Hill, MA: Center for International Higher Education, Boston College.

Ruch, Richard S. 2001. *Higher ed, Inc.: The rise of the for-profit university.* Baltimore: Johns Hopkins University Press.

Umakoshi, Toru. 2004. Private higher education in Asia: Transitions and development. In *Asian universities: Historical perspectives and contemporary challenges*, ed. P. G. Altbach and T. Umakoshi, 33–51. Baltimore: Johns Hopkins University Press.

5

Peripheries and Centers: Research Universities in Developing Countries

The research university is a central institution of the 21st century—essential to the creation and dissemination of knowledge. As one of the key elements in the globalization of science, the research university is at the center of science, scholarship, and the new knowledge economics. The research university educates the new generation of personnel needed for technological and intellectual leadership, develops new knowledge so necessary for modern science and scholarship, and, just as importantly, serves as an element of worldwide communication and collaboration.

All but a few research universities are located in the developed economies of the industrialized world. Any of the recent world rankings of top universities show that the main research-oriented universities are found in a few countries. This essay, however, looks at the realities and prospects for research universities in developing and middle-income countries—a small but growing subset of research universities worldwide. If knowledge production and dissemination are not to remain a monopoly of the rich countries, research universities must become successful outside the main cosmopolitan centers. In establishing and fostering research universities, developing countries face problems that are to some extent unique.

Research universities are defined here as academic institutions committed to the creation and dissemination of knowledge in a range of disciplines and fields and featuring the appropriate laboratories, libraries, and other infrastructures to permit teaching and research at the highest possible level. While typically large and multifaceted, some research universities may be smaller institutions concentrating on a narrower range of subjects. Research universities educate students, usually at all degree levels—an indication the focus extends beyond research. Indeed, this synergy of research and teaching is a hallmark of these institutions, which employ mainly full-time academics who hold doctoral degrees (Kerr 2001).

Motivating this discussion is a conviction that knowledge production and dissemination must spread internationally and that all regions of the world need a role in the knowledge network (Altbach 1987). While there will always be centers and peripheries—the centers mainly concentrated in the major industrialized countries for the foreseeable future—there is room, indeed a necessity, for a wider dissemination of research capacity throughout the world. It may not be possible for each country to have a research university, but many developing and middle-income countries can develop universities with research capacity and the ability to participate in the world knowledge system. Smaller countries can form regional academic alliances to build enough strength in selected fields so as to promote participating in global science.

The argument can be made that all countries need academic institutions linked to the global academic system of science and scholarship so that they can understand advanced scientific developments and participate selectively in them. Academic institutions in small or poor countries cannot compete with the Oxfords or Harvards of the industrialized nations. But most countries can support at least one university of sufficient quality to at least participate in international discussions of science and scholarship and undertake research in one or more fields relevant to national development.

Research universities generate a growing enthusiasm worldwide. Countries conclude that such institutions are the key to gain entry into the knowledge economy of the 21st century. Not only do these institutions train key personnel, but they form windows to scientific information worldwide by providing opportunities for top-level scientific communication. Faculty members and students at these institutions connect with colleagues everywhere and participate in global science and scholarship. Even in countries such as the United States and the United Kingdom, concern is rising about maintaining the standards of existing research universities (Rosenzweig 1998). Germany worries about the international competitiveness of its top universities and has allocated resources to some key institutions, while the Japanese government has funded competitive grants to create "centers of excellence." China has placed emphasis on creating "world-class" research universities, and India is finally beginning to think about the quality of its mainstream institutions. Similar programs to enhance standards exist in South Korea, Chile, Taiwan, and elsewhere. Several of Africa's traditionally strong universities are seeking to improve their quality in an effort to achieve research university status, with assistance from external funders, although it is, in general, behind levels of academic development on the other continents.

All of these trends show a considerable shift from the 1980s, when developing countries concentrated on providing basic schooling rather than higher education. In much of the world, especially in developing countries, policymakers engaged almost exclusively with meeting mass higher education demand—largely ignoring the research role of universities. Circumstances in several of the world's regions also created crises for higher education and slowed the development of research universities. In Latin America, the military dictatorships of the 1960s and later were unfriendly toward higher education, and many of the prominent scholars went into exile. China suffered under the Cultural Revolution, which closed all of the universities for a period of time and severely damaged the system. The advent of mass higher education and the demands for access that ensued, combined with the inability of the state to financially support both quantity and quality, retarded the development of research universities. India is a good case regarding this phenomenon. Political and economic instability, combined with policies that favored basic schooling, largely destroyed the quality of sub-Saharan Africa's few academic institutions. In short, in the late 20th century few research-oriented universities existed in developing countries—even in countries that had made some earlier progress in this area.

In keeping with the rising profile of research universities in developing countries, many national policymakers, analysts of higher education, and even the international aid agencies and the World Bank, previously convinced that only basic education was worth supporting, now understand that research universities are important for national development. Research universities have emerged on the policy agenda in many developing countries, especially larger nations that seek to compete in the global knowledge economy. In Africa, the region of the world with the most severe structural, economic, and political challenges, an initiative by a partnership of donor foundations and African universities aims to build the research capacity of key African academic institutions in Kenya, Mozambique, Ghana, and several other countries. China has been particularly active in transforming a number of its major universities into research universities; the government has invested significant funding in this effort and has merged many universities to provide better economies of scale. India has created a Knowledge Commission to develop strategies for promoting academic excellence. Taiwan and South Korea have been engaged for a decade or more in building up their key institutions.

History and Perspectives

Universities, since their origins in medieval Europe, have always been concerned with the transmission, preservation, and interpretation of knowledge, although not primarily with the creation of new knowledge (Perkin 2006). While they have served as cultural and intellectual institutions in their societies, universities have not traditionally been research oriented. Science was conducted elsewhere for the most part. Wilhelm von Humboldt largely invented the modern research university when the University of Berlin was established in 1818. Von Humboldt's idea was that the university should directly enhance German national and scientific development. This revolutionary idea harnessed science and scholarship—produced, with state support, in universities—to national development. The Humboldtian concept proved to be highly successful, and the new German universities (and others that were reformed to conform to the new model) contributed to the emergence of Germany as a modern nation by producing research and educating scientists. A significant additional contribution of the Humboldtian model that impacted both science and the organization of higher education was the idea of the "chair" system—the appointment of discipline-based professors. This innovation helped to define the emerging scientific fields and also shaped the organization of the university.

Two countries focused on modernization and development—after 1862 the United States and, several decades later, Japan quickly adopted the German model. The American "land grant" model proved to be particularly successful. It combined the Humboldtian emphasis on research and science and the key role of the state in supporting higher education based on the idea of public service and applied technology (Altbach 2001b). The great American public university, as exemplified by the University of Wisconsin and the University of California in the latter 19th century, opened the door to direct public service and applied technology, and it also "democratized" science by replacing the hierarchical German chair system with the more participative departmental structure. Variations of the German, American, and Japanese research university concepts largely characterize today's research universities.

Almost all contemporary universities, regardless of location, are European in structure, organization, and concept. Academic institutions from Tokyo to Tashkent and from Cairo (although the Islamic Al-Azhar University survives with a different structure) and Cape Town are based on the Western model. This trend means, for most developing countries, that higher education institutions are not integrally linked to indigenous cultures and in many cases were imposed by colonial rulers. Even in such countries as China, Thailand, and Ethiopia, which were never colonized, Western academic models were chosen (Altbach and Umakoshi 2004). For developing countries subjected to colonialism, higher education growth was generally slow paced. Colonizers cared little about the research function of the universities, being more interested in providing midlevel training for civil servants. In much of Africa and some other parts of the developing world, universities were not established until the 20th century.

Research Universities and Academic Systems
Research universities generally constitute part of a differentiated academic system—an arrangement of postsecondary institutions with varied roles in society and different funding patterns. Countries without such differentiated systems find it difficult to support research universities, which are always expensive to maintain and require recognition of their specialized and complex academic role. Germany, for example, considers all of its universities as research institutions and, as a result, is unable to provide adequate funding to any of them. There are plans under way to recognize a few German universities as "world class" and provide enhanced resources to them, although implementing the changes is proving to be difficult. Research universities are inevitably expensive to operate and require more funds than other academic institutions. They are also generally more selective in terms of student admissions and faculty hiring and typically stand at the pinnacle of an academic system.

The creation of a differentiated academic system is, thus, a prerequisite for research universities and is a necessity for developing countries (Task Force on Higher Education and Society 2000). A differentiated system has academic institutions with diverse missions, structures, and patterns of funding. In the United States—the first country to design academic systems as a way to organize its expanding and multidimensional postsecondary institutions in the early 20th century—the "California model" is generally seen as the most successful approach. California's public system has three kinds of academic institutions, with quite different purposes (Douglass 2000). This tiered model—with vocationally oriented "open door" community colleges, multipurpose state universities, and selective research-oriented universities—has specific patterns of funding and support for each of the tiers as well as quite different missions (Geiger 2004). Britain has recently moved in a similar direction. One of the purposes of Prime Minister Margaret Thatcher's higher education policy in the 1970s was to create a tiered system in which institutions that emerged at the top of the system as a result of quality assessment—Oxford, Cambridge, and a modest number of others—could be funded more generously than other universities.

Academic systems often evolve during the massification of higher education. As Martin Trow has pointed out, most countries have inevitably moved from an elite higher education system toward mass access—with half or more of the age cohort attending postsecondary institutions (Trow 2006). Ever-larger numbers of students, with varying levels of academic ability and different studying goals, require a range of institutions to serve multiple needs. Just as important, no country can afford to educate large numbers of students in expensive research universities.

Research universities are a small part of most academic systems. In the United States, perhaps 150 out of a total of more than 3,000 academic institutions are research universities. Yet, these universities are the most prestigious and are awarded 80 percent of competitive government research funds. Academic salaries tend to be higher, teaching responsibilities for the faculty members lower, and library and laboratory facilities better than the national average. In many countries, there may be just one or two research universities because of their cost and the limited resources available. Even in fairly large countries, the number of research universities is often small—in the United Kingdom, perhaps 20 institutions and a similar number in Japan. China is aiming to establish somewhat more than 20, and Brazil has fewer than 6. Some countries may have more research universities than they can afford—Sweden and the Netherlands may be examples.

To allow research universities to flourish requires a way to differentiate them from other types of postsecondary institutions, provide funding at a higher level, and legitimize the idea that these institutions are indeed special and serve a crucial role in society.

A Confusion of Definitions
A fairly simple definition of the research university was provided earlier: an academic institution focusing intensely on the production of

research as part of its mission; offering instruction up to the doctoral level; possessing the necessary infrastructures for research—including libraries, information technology, and laboratories; employing high-quality and carefully selected academic staff (usually with doctoral degrees); maintaining working conditions that permit research activity; and selecting the best-quality students available. One can quibble with this definition, as well as whether particular universities fulfill the minimal requirements. The important task is to clearly define research universities and to differentiate them from the rest of the higher education system.

Although this essay is not primarily concerned with world-class universities, since there has been a mania to identify world-class institutions—universities at the very top of a prestige and quality hierarchy. Two new international rankings, both started after 2000, have contributed to this effort—one introduced by the *Times Higher Education Supplement* in the United Kingdom and the other by Shanghai Jiao Tong University in China (Liu forthcoming). Other national and international rankings are also available—the influential *US News and World Report* annual ranking of American colleges and universities and similar efforts by *McLean's* magazine in Canada, *Der Spiegel* in Germany, and other publications, as well as more academic analyses such as the one prepared by the University of Florida in the United States. In general, world class is a shorthand way of indicating that a university is among the most prestigious in the world—renowned among academic institutions internationally (Altbach 2003a). Almost all of today's world-class universities are in the major English-speaking countries or a few large industrialized nations. All world-class universities are research universities—without exception. But not all research universities are world class, nor should they be.

There are very few recognized world-class universities in developing or middle-income countries, and it is unlikely that many will emerge in the future. Relatively few new institutions settle into the ranks of world-class universities anywhere—high costs and competition from other postsecondary sectors are among the reasons. There will be some exceptions to this generalization. China today has several universities that are, or are close to, becoming ranked as world class—and the government is investing in them. South Korea and Taiwan have the same goal and the resources to join the world-class club. India would have the capacity to build such universities, although it has not as yet moved in that direction. Several of Latin America's great public universities—in Brazil, Mexico, and Argentina—also have world-class potential.

"Flagship" is also a frequently used term in discussions of research universities, generally referring to a leading university in a country or an academic system. These universities are the institutions looked to for influence and emulation. The flagship is typically the most prestigious university, almost always public, and often among the largest in the system or country. Systems and countries look to these institutions for leadership in higher education.

In developing countries, the leading universities have often played a central role in political and social development. These institutions have been called "state-building" universities. The National Autonomous University of Mexico (UNAM) has been used as an example (Odorika and Pusser forthcoming). UNAM has educated Mexico's political and intellectual leaders, has served as a center of political activism, houses the national library, and is the largest and most research-oriented institution in the country. Many other countries, especially in Latin America, have similar universities, which typically remain the leading academic institutions and to some extent continue to play a central role, educationally, intellectually, and often politically, for the nations. They are always among the leading research universities in the countries.

Worldwide, there is considerable confusion concerning these definitions and concepts. Policymakers may refer to world-class universities when they really mean research institutions. Academic leaders may try to "sell" their universities as world class even when the achievement of this status is impossible. A national flagship institution may seek to portray itself in a regional or international context as world class. It is useful to carefully define terms in order to aim at realistic goals.

Research Universities and Research Systems

Research universities are not the only institutions in which research is conducted. Specialized research institutes, government laboratories, corporate research centers, and other agencies carry out research, and many participate in the international scientific community. In large countries, research universities form part of a more complex research system that includes other kinds of institutions. Universities, however, serve as some of the most effective institutions for carrying out research. In addition, they provide formal training and credentials for the future generation of researchers, scholars, and teachers. Using advanced students, typically at the doctoral level, to assist with research reduces the cost of research, provides valuable training for students, and employs the insights of the new generation of talented researchers.

Research institutes, usually publicly funded, remain common establishments in many countries. The Academy of Science system of the former Soviet Union is one of the most influential patterns (Vucinich

1984). Top researchers are appointed at discipline-based (or occasionally interdisciplinary) academies that are usually attached to a research institute. These key scientists in some cases have affiliations with universities, but their main appointments and work are based in the research institutes. The hard sciences and engineering dominate the academy system—the humanities and social sciences are underrepresented. In the case of Russia and some other countries, in Eastern Europe and China, these academies are among the main providers of research. In these countries, universities have a lower research profile and little direct funding for research. Taiwan, through its Academia Sinica, operates in much the same way. The French CNRS (Centre national de recherche scientifique) and the German Max Planck Institutes have similar functions. In the United States, the National Institutes of Health resemble the European examples although in general the NIH are more focused on applied research. Many countries are moving away from the research institute model and toward embedding research laboratories in universities.

There is a growing trend, especially in the United States, of university-based research facilities that are sponsored by corporations and engaged in advanced research involving products or research themes of interest to the sponsoring company. Most focus on applied research that results in marketable products for the sponsoring corporation. American and Japanese companies have been especially active in sponsoring university-related research centers. Companies have set up research facilities near universities to take advantage of academic expertise—the relationship between biotechnology corporations and the Massachusetts Institute of Technology is well known. In other examples, corporate laboratories have been set up at universities or agreements have been made with academic units to provide funds for research in return for access to knowledge products (Slaughter and Leslie 1997). China has been very active in university-industry linkages, and there has been mixed success. Some observers have noted that not all efforts have been successful and have argued that traditional academic values are being weakened, while others have praised innovative programs (Ma forthcoming; Liu forthcoming).

Universities assemble in one place researchers, teachers, and students who create an effective community for knowledge, discovery, and innovation. Advanced doctoral-level students can provide highly motivated scientific personnel who at the same time can benefit from direct involvement in sophisticated research. Universities have a wide range of disciplines and scientific specializations, and research can benefit from interdisciplinary insight—especially significant in frontier areas such as biotechnology and environmental science. Universities can also combine basic research with applied applications in ways that other institutions cannot.

The academic environment is enriched by the unique combination of the academic norm of scientific discovery and interpretation, the link between teaching and research, and the presence of scientists and scholars from a range of disciplines. Universities also exemplify the "public good"—the idea that scientific discovery may have wider social benefits—-and their focus on basic research is unique. While science can take place in other venues, universities are a particularly effective environment for discovery.

Common Characteristics of the Research University

Despite variations among research universities worldwide, common characteristics exist that are worth noting precisely because they are so nearly universal.

Research universities, with few exceptions, are government-funded public institutions. Only in the United States and to some extent in Japan do private research universities exist—although with the current worldwide growth of private higher education it is possible that a small number of such institutions in other countries will aspire to the top ranks. This is the case for a number of reasons. Tuition-dependent private institutions can seldom fund expensive research universities. Research universities are typically large in terms of student enrollments and numbers of departments and faculties. The research function, the most expensive part of the university, requires public support because it typically does not produce direct income, especially basic research. The facilities necessary to produce top-quality research, especially in the sciences, are beyond the capacity of private universities to provide. Even in the United States, the research mission of some private universities is supported by the government through research grants given to individual scientists. In most of the world, there is no academic tradition of private research universities. Tax laws generally do not reward philanthropic assistance to private universities. As a result, few institutions except in the United States and to some extent Japan have endowment funds that permit the support of research. The growing trend internationally toward for-profit private institutions will further weaken private interest in research universities, although it is possible that a few private institutions trying to reach a competitive place at the top of the academic system may seek to become research universities.

Research universities are generally complex institutions with a range of departments and faculties. Often, but not always, they are among the largest academic institutions in their countries. Research universities frequently have professional schools and faculties (e.g., medicine, management, and arts and sciences specializations). The large size and range of disciplines permit research universities to take advantage of "economies of scale" regarding laboratories, libraries, and other infrastructures. There are some exceptions to this rule—for example, the California Institute of Technology is a small and specialized institution, as well as the campuses of the Indian Institutes of Technology. These institutions are considered research intensive.

Most research universities are, as Clark Kerr pointed out, "multiversities" (Kerr 2001)—institutions with a multiplicity of missions among which research is only one—but where research and graduate study tend to dominate. Kerr was writing about the University of California, Berkeley, but this generalization could apply to most of the world's research universities. The mission of these universities encompasses undergraduate education on a large scale and reaching out to and serving local and national communities, along with offering a range of vocational and professional credentials to students. Some universities, such as UNAM in Mexico and the University of Buenos Aires in Argentina, sponsor secondary schools as well. But in all cases, the research mission is at the top of the prestige hierarchy of the institution. This emphasis on research tends to have a negative impact on the quality of undergraduate instruction and typically has the major influence on the direction of the university (Lewis 2006; Hutchins 1995, orig. 1936). Many, however, argue that research-active faculty members bring a vitality to their teaching that benefits students, even at the undergraduate level.

Research universities are always resource intensive—they are institutions considerably more expensive to build and maintain than other academic institutions. Because of the increasingly expensive scientific equipment, rapidly expanding and costly information technology and access to worldwide scientific knowledge, and the need to pay their professors more than the norm for the rest of the academic system, research universities are considerably more expensive to operate than other academic institutions. The cost per student is always higher than for the rest of the system. Funding must be available on a sustained basis—fluctuating budgets can damage the institutions.

Finally, research universities attract the "best and the brightest" students in the nation and, in some instances, from around the world. Because of their prestige and facilities, these universities generally attract the most able students, and the admissions process is highly competitive. Similarly, research universities generally employ the most talented professors—scientists and scholars who are attracted by the research orientation, facilities, and often by the more favorable working conditions at these institutions. Research university faculty generally hold doctoral degrees—even in many countries where the doctorate is not required for postsecondary teaching.

Challenges

Research universities face severe challenges at a time when they are recognized as the pinnacle of the academic system and as central to the new globalized economy. The following factors are among the problems faced by research universities in all countries. While the scope and depth of the issues discussed here may vary, they are universally applicable.

FUNDING

As noted earlier, the basic cost of operating a research university has increased—placing more stress on traditional funding sources, mainly governmental, and forcing institutions and systems to seek new revenues. At the same time, the basic concepts underpinning public funding for higher education are being questioned. The traditional idea views higher education as a public good—serving society by means of improved human capital as well as research and service. Thus society has the responsibility to pay for much of the cost of higher education. Since the 1980s, spurred by thinking from the World Bank and international policy organizations that have shaped the "neoliberal economic consensus," higher education is increasingly seen as a private good—mainly benefiting individual graduates. From this perspective, the individual and his or her family should pay the main costs of higher education through tuition and other fees. This change in thinking occurred at the same time that massification became a key factor in many countries—dramatically increased enrollments were impossible for traditional government funding levels. Leaving aside the broader economic arguments, this combination of financial factors has been particularly difficult for the research universities, which are quintessential "public good" institutions. Their costs are high and their products—educating the top echelons of society, providing research, and serving as a repository of knowledge and a source of social analysis—may not yield practical results in the short run. Student tuition alone cannot support research universities. Further, basic research cannot be expected to fund itself. For these and other reasons, research universities face severe financial strain.

Research universities are subject to the pressures of privatization (Lyall and Sell 2006). The privatization of public universities has become a common phenomenon since public funding is inadequate to support these institutions. In the United States, for example, many of the "flagship" public research universities receive as little as 15 percent of their basic funding from their primary sponsors—the state governments. The rest of the budget comes from student tuition, research grants, income from intellectual property and ancillary services, and donations from individuals and foundations—as well as endowments. To produce sufficient income, Chinese universities have increased tuition, earned income from consulting and other work by faculty members, and established profit-making companies. In some countries—such as Russia and Uganda, among others—to earn extra funds, research universities have admitted "private" students who are charged high tuitions, in contrast to the publicly supported enrollments. Many of these activities significantly undermine the core role of the university.

RESEARCH

A culture of research, inquiry, and quality is an essential part of a research university. Because of the financial pressures described here, there is a trend toward applied and often profit-oriented research—research that can be more easily funded than basic research and may yield profits for the university. The commercialization of research has significant implications for research universities. It changes the orientation of the research community to some extent by emphasizing commercial values rather than basic research. Universities have entered into agreements with corporations to produce specific research products or provide access to university facilities. The controversial links between the University of California, Berkeley and the multinational pharmaceutical company Novartis exemplify the possible conflicts between traditional academic norms and commercial interests. The ownership of knowledge, the use of academic facilities, and the ultimate openness of scientific research are all issues raised by these new commercial linkages.

With the rising costs of university research due to expensive laboratories and equipment, large interdisciplinary scientific research teams, and other factors—raising funds to support research in the sciences grows more difficult. Even large and well-funded universities in the industrialized countries struggle to support cutting-edge research. In some fields, only the richest institutions can support frontier scientific research.

Research universities in developing countries will need to select fields of research that are affordable and linked to national needs and priorities. Appropriate links with private-sector companies, including multinational corporations, may be necessary—and a balance between applied and basic research will need to be worked out. Work in the sciences is only one part of the research agenda of a university. The social sciences and humanities are often neglected because the hard sciences are seen to be more profitable and prestigious. Yet the social sciences and humanities are quite important for the understanding of society and culture. They are also considerably less expensive than the "hard" sciences but are sometimes ignored.

The details of allocating funding for research are also central policy issues. While basic resources, from the university budget, for laboratories, libraries, and other research infrastructures are necessary, funding for specific research projects can come from a variety of sources and be allocated in different ways. A system of competitive awards encourages innovative ideas and encourages granting funds for the best projects. Such funds can come from government ministries and granting agencies, private and foreign foundations, or in some cases from business firms. An appropriate mix of funding sources and allocation mechanisms encourages competition for research funds and the best quality and most innovative research ideas.

COMMERCIALISM AND THE MARKET

The intrusion of market forces and commercial interests into higher education is one of the greatest challenges to universities everywhere. The threat to research universities is particularly great because they are quintessentially "public good" institutions. Market forces have the potential for intruding into almost every aspect of academe (Kirp 2003). Roger Geiger has written about "the paradox of the marketplace for American universities":

> Hence the marketplace has, on balance, brought universities greater resources, better students, a far larger capacity for advancing knowledge, and a more productive role in the U.S. economy. At the same time, it has diminished the sovereignty of universities over their own activities, weakened their mission of serving the public, and created through growing commercial entanglements at least the potential for undermining their privileged role as disinterested arbiters of knowledge. (Geiger 2004, 265)

For developing countries, the challenge of the market is particularly serious because there is less basic financial stability and a weaker tradition of academic autonomy. External market pressures can quickly affect the entire institution. For research universities, market forces may significantly shift the direction of research, the focus of the academic profession, and the financial balance of the institution. It is clear, however, that if research universities are forced to rely increasingly on their own resources for survival, market forces will determine institutional directions and priorities.

AUTONOMY AND ACCOUNTABILITY

The tension between autonomy and accountability is a perennial concern for academic institutions. Universities' tradition of academic autonomy constitutes the ability to make their own decisions about essential academic matters and to shape their own destiny. At the same time, external authorities—including funders, governmental sponsors, or religious organizations—held some control over higher education. Since the origins of universities in medieval Europe, these tensions were evident. In the era of mass higher education, demands for accountability have increased given higher education's rising impact on both the economy and society. Higher education is both a significant state expenditure and of growing relevance to large numbers of people. The demand for contemporary accountability almost always comes from the state, the source of much of the funding for higher education.

Research universities have a special need for autonomy, and current demands for accountability are especially problematical for them. While academe in general needs a degree of autonomy to function effectively, research universities must be able to shape their own programs, to carry out a long-term perspective, and manage their budgets and the academic community. Not only do research universities require steady funding commitments, they also need autonomy to develop and maintain their strengths. The academic community itself is the best judge of the success of programs. Basic research, especially, must have autonomy to develop, since it typically emerges from the interests and concerns of the faculty.

Accountability is, of course, an essential part of contemporary higher education—funders of academic institutions deserve to learn about spending policies and to have the power to steer public higher education institutions and systems. Students, too, have the right to know about the quality, orientation, and focus of universities. Accountability, however, is a multifaceted concept and must operate differently for research universities than for other academic institutions. The balance between accountability and autonomy must swing more toward autonomy for these institutions than for colleges and universities that focus more on teaching and service.

GLOBALIZATION OF SCIENCE AND SCHOLARSHIP

Science in the 21st century is truly global in scope. Research results are immediately available worldwide through the Internet. Scientific journals are circulated internationally, and academics contribute to the same publications. Methodologies and scientific norms are used worldwide more than ever before. Scientific equipment, ever more sophisticated and expensive, is available everywhere, and there is pressure for research universities to have the most modern laboratories if they wish to participate in global scientific research. Further, research is increasingly competitive, with researchers and universities rushing to present results and patent or license potentially useful discoveries or inventions. Science, in short, has become a "high-stakes" and intensely competitive international endeavor. Entry into advanced scientific research is expensive, as is maintaining a competitive edge.

The challenge consists not only of laboratories and infrastructures but also the definitions and methodologies of science and scholarship. Scientific globalization means that participants are linked to the norms of the disciplines and of scholarship established by the leaders of research, located in the major universities in the United States and other Western nations. The methods used in funded research and presented in the main scientific journals tend to dominate world science. Further, the themes and subject areas of interest to leading scientists and institutions may not be relevant to universities at the periphery. Involvement in world science means, in general, adherence to established research paradigms and themes.

The high cost of science creates serious problems for academic institutions without a long tradition of research and the required infrastructures and equipment. It is no longer sufficient to build an infrastructure that permits research on local or regional themes if a university wishes to join the "big leagues." Universities that wish to be considered research oriented need to participate in the international scientific network and compete with institutions and scientists worldwide. The costs of joining the league of research universities is an especially serious problem for developing countries, with funding problems and no experience of building such institutions. The world of global science is expensive to join, as is sustaining participation.

The paradox of global science is similar to globalization in general. Globalization—through information technology, better communications, the worldwide circulation of highly trained personnel, and other factors—permits everyone to participate in the global marketplace of science, scholarship, and ideas. At the same time, globalization subjects all participants to the pressures of an unequal global knowledge system dominated by the wealthy universities and imposes the norms and values of those institutions on all (Altbach 1987, 2004).

PUBLIC AND PRIVATE

As discussed earlier, almost all research universities outside the United States and Japan are public and state supported. It is very likely that this trend will continue, although with some changes. The fastest-growing sector of higher education worldwide is private, and thus the expansion of the private sector will have an impact on research universities—but only indirectly, since private higher education is not focused on research (Altbach 1999). With only a few minor exceptions, new private institutions focus on teaching and providing credentials to students in professional and other fields, often in specialized niche areas. New private universities are not full-fledged academic institutions with a comprehensive range of disciplines in most fields of science and scholarship. Specialization characterizes the rapidly expanding for-profit sector of private higher education. The sector is never concerned with building research capacity, since research does not rapidly produce profits.

Yet, a small number of nonprofit private universities may succeed in building research capacity to raise their status and contribute broadly to education and research. The Catholic University in Santiago, Chile and the American University in Cairo, Egypt are two examples of high-status private institutions that are focusing on developing significant research profiles to build national and international reputations. Institutions such as these generally have a tradition of academic excellence and access to philanthropic funds to develop research programs.

The growing role of private higher education worldwide means that a smaller proportion of universities will focus on research. This might, in some ways, benefit public research universities since the state may have some of the burden of mass higher education access lifted and be able to focus on promoting the research sector. It is, however, more likely that as the private sector takes on more responsibility for higher education, the state will continue to decrease its support for the sector, as has been the trend in many countries. The rise of the private sector, with its lack of focus on research, may threaten the research role of universities in most of the world, especially in developing countries.

RESEARCH UNIVERSITIES AS MERITOCRACIES

In some parts of the world, universities do not adhere to strict meritocratic values. Corruption is a problem, and grants and promotions may be awarded for reasons unrelated to quality and merit. For research universities, adherence to meritocratic norms and academic honesty is of special importance. Universities are, of course, part of a broader social and political system; and if the polity is rife with corruption and favoritism, academe will not be immune. The problem of academic corruption in its many facets is present in some developing countries. Systemic corruption is also evident in some of the countries of the former Soviet Union as well as elsewhere. Bribery in student admissions and the awarding of degrees, flagrant plagiarism by students and academics, widespread cheating on examinations, and other forms of clearly unacceptable behavior have become endemic. In India, for example, students have demonstrated for the right to cheat on university examinations. Furthermore, in China there has been a growing public concern about plagiarism at all levels of the academic system and violation of intellectual property at some research universities (Pocha 2006). In a healthy academic system, when such behavior takes place, it receives the condemnation of the academic community and is rooted out.

The situation is even more dangerous when it directly involves the academic profession. Poor academic salaries also contribute to unprofessional professorial practices. Widespread illegal selling of lecture notes and other course materials in Egypt by professors is linked to the need of academic staff to earn enough money to survive (Arishie 2006). Selling academic posts is a common practice in some countries, and awarding professorships on the basis of ethnic, religious, or political factors is widespread as well.

While corrupt practices are damaging in any academic environment, they are toxic to the culture and ethos of the research university. The ideal and practice of meritocratic values are central to the research university. Excellence and intellectual quality are key criteria for student admissions, academic hiring, promotion, and reward in research universities. The underpinnings of these academic institutions depend on meritocratic values. Widespread violations will inevitably make it impossible for a research university to flourish.

ACADEMIC FREEDOM

Academic freedom is a core requirement for research universities (Altbach 2001a). However, a few definitions are necessary. Of primary importance is the freedom to undertake research and publication and to teach in one's research areas and to teach without any restriction. These rights are parts of the more limited German definition of academic freedom. The right of academics to express their views in any public forum or in writing on any topic, even on subjects far from the individual's academic expertise—the broader American definition—is increasingly accepted around the world. Academic freedom is in some countries protected by specific academic legislation as well as traditional norms and values. Tenure systems in many countries and civil service status in others provide guarantees of employment security so that it is difficult, if not impossible, for governmental authorities or others to terminate a professor who is protected by these guarantees.

Research universities are particularly dependent on a strong regime of academic freedom because their faculty members are directly engaged in the discovery of new knowledge. Research university professors are also more likely than other academics to be "public intellectuals"—to be engaged in civic discourse on topics of societal importance. History shows that academic freedom—freedom in the classroom, laboratory, and scholarly publishing—is central to building a research culture.

In some countries, the norms of academic freedom are not fully entrenched, and as a result it may be more difficult to sustain top-quality research universities. Where academic freedom is entirely missing or severely restricted, as is the case in a small number of countries, research universities with reasonable standards cannot be successful regardless of financial support or resources. More common worldwide are universities with some restrictions on academic freedom. In many countries, especially developing nations, in areas of knowledge that are considered politically or socially sensitive, research, publication, or commentary are restricted. Such fields include ethnic or religious studies, environmental research, and studies of social class or social conflict, among others. The sanctions for critical analysis in these fields may be as severe as firing from academic posts, jail, or exile. More common are less serious penalties or informal warnings.

There seems to be a delicate balance concerning academic freedom and a viable research university. Singapore, for example, has long placed informal restrictions on research in a few areas considered to be politically sensitive, such as ethnic relations. Social scientists face some constraints on their freedom of research and publication and have occasionally faced criticism for straying over an unstated demarcation of what is officially sanctioned research. At the same time, Singapore has been successful in building research universities and establishing collaboration with respected universities abroad. The situation in China is similar, although restrictions are reportedly greater and sanctions for violations can be more severe. In the Middle East, there are taboos on research and publication concerning politically sensitive Arab-Israeli relations or certain religious or ethnic topics. In some African countries, criticism of the ruling regime in power can result in jail terms or job loss, although in general academic freedom is respected. It seems that reasonably successful research universities can be built under conditions of incomplete academic freedom so long as the restrictions are not too severe, although broad comparisons show universities with the greatest amount of academic freedom do best as effective research institutions.

In the United States and other industrialized countries, the main threat to traditional norms of academic freedom comes from the commercialization of research and the increasing links between universities or individual researchers and corporations interested in university-based research. Under the banner of university-industry collaboration, agreements are made that sometimes restrict access to research findings, focus the attention of research groups on commercially focused products, and support applied research at the expense of basic work (Slaughter and Rhoades 2004; Kirp 2003). This commercialization may be financially advantageous to the university and to individual researchers but often places restrictions on the free communication of knowledge, thus violating one of the principles of academic freedom.

Academic freedom is a complex and nuanced topic, central to the success of a research university. It is a core value of higher education everywhere and for all types of academic institutions—of special importance for research universities. The challenges to academic freedom in the 21st century come not only from repressive external authorities but also from the new commercialism in higher education. Problems may also originate from within the academy due to the politicization of the academic community or tensions caused by religious or ethnic relations in some countries.

THE ACADEMIC PROFESSION

The professoriate is central to higher education. Research universities rely especially on the quality and focus of the academic profession, and current developments relating to the professoriate worldwide are not favorable for either the profession or for research universities (Altbach 2003b). Research universities require academic staff with the highest possible qualifications—doctoral degrees from reputable universities. This seemingly obvious statement is necessary because the majority of academic staff in developing countries do not hold a doctorate.

Research universities require full-time professors—scholars and scientists who devote their full professional attention to teaching and research at the universities. Without a large majority of full-time academic staff, it is simply impossible to build a cadre to form a committed and effective professoriate. Not only required to fulfill the core functions of the university, full-time faculty also need to participate in governance and management because research universities need a high degree of autonomy and faculty governance. The lack of full-time faculty is one central reason why Latin American countries, for example, have failed to build research universities.

Along with full-time commitment, salaries must be sufficient to support a middle-class lifestyle. While they need not be paid salaries similar to colleagues in the most highly remunerated universities internationally, professors must be solid members of the middle class in their country. Frequently, full-time professors generate a significant part of their incomes through consulting, moonlighting at other institutions, or at some universities adding extra teaching loads in fee-producing programs. These arrangements detract from the core functions of the professoriate and make full academic productivity difficult to maintain. In some disciplines, consulting work, applied research for industry, and other links with external agencies may provide useful synergies for academic work, but in many countries outside work and dependence on outside income is deleterious to the research university. Just as problematic, academic salaries, overall, have stagnated worldwide at the same time that remuneration for similarly educated professionals outside universities has increased in some countries quite dramatically. In order to attract the "best and brightest" to academe, salaries must be competitive.

Teaching responsibilities must be sufficiently limited to allow time and energy for research. In the United States, the standard teaching load in most research universities is two courses per semester or four per academic year. In some scientific fields, even less teaching is expected. Similar teaching loads are common in Europe. In many developing countries, a much higher teaching load leaves little time for research. The most active research-focused professors in the United States undertake a significant part of their teaching in graduate (post-baccalaureate) programs, which helps to link teaching with research and increases productivity. In European countries, with doctoral programs that are mainly focused on research, professors are given sufficient time for doctoral supervision and mentoring. Few developing countries have instituted these practices.

The academic profession must have a career ladder that promotes talented professors up the ranks of the profession on the basis of performance and the quality of work; a salary structure is also determined by performance. In many countries, an initial full-time appointment is tantamount to a permanent job. In some, such as Germany, it is difficult for a junior academic to obtain a post with the prospect of promotion because of the organization of the career structure. In much of the world, promotion up the academic ranks is largely a matter of seniority rather than of demonstrated performance in teaching and research. In the majority of countries, academic salaries are determined by seniority, rank, and in some places, discipline, rather than by job performance. This is especially true for countries where academics are considered civil servants—mainly in Western Europe (Enders 2001). Civil service status provides strong guarantees of permanent employment but seldom measures productivity as an element of promotion.

The challenge is to combine reasonable guarantees of long-term employment, as both a means of ensuring academic freedom and of providing employment security and institutional loyalty. The American tenure-track system, although much criticized within the United States, may be closest to this goal (Chait 2002). The system provides initial probationary appointments with a series of rigorous evaluations that, if passed, lead to a permanent (tenured) appointment after six years. Further promotion, from the rank of associate to full professor, is also merit based and depends on a rigorous evaluation. Most American colleges and universities follow this pattern although the research universities have the most stringent evaluations. Increasingly, US universities have also instituted "posttenure review" so that productivity is measured following the award of tenure. Typically, performance and comparative salaries at peer universities as well as seniority determine salary raises.

Even in the United States the academic profession is under threat—even in the research universities. The most serious problems involve the growth of a part-time academic workforce and the relatively new category of non-tenure-track, full-time appointments (term appointments)—similar in some ways to the German pattern of appointments that do not lead to permanent careers. Now, half of the new positions at US colleges and universities are either part-time or full-time term appointments—although at research universities the proportion of tenure-track positions is higher (Schuster and Finkelstein 2006).

The academic profession is central to the success of the university everywhere. A research university requires a special type of professor—highly trained, committed to research and scholarship, and motivated by intellectual curiosity. Full-time commitment and adequate remuneration constitute other necessities. A career path that stresses excellence and at the same time offers both academic freedom and job security are required. Academics at research universities need both the time to engage in creative research and the facilities and infrastructures to make scholarly research possible.

Developing Countries: Goals, Aspirations, and Realities

Many developing and middle-income countries need research universities to participate in the expanding knowledge and service-oriented economy of the 21st century. Aspirations, however, must be tempered by realities. The goals of research universities in developing countries necessarily differ somewhat from those in large industrialized nations. For developing countries, the goals include a number of core elements.

THE CREATION AND RETENTION OF A SCIENTIFIC COMMUNITY

Research universities employ scientists and scholars in a range of disciplines. Without these institutions, highly trained academics would leave the country—as happens in many developing countries today that lack these institutions—or would fail to be trained in the first place. Research universities provide the institutional base for top professors—scholars and scientists who comprehend what is happening at the frontiers of science in all fields and can participate in the global scientific community. The institutions retain local talent at the same time as they produce additional talent. The academic community in the local research university can communicate with scholars abroad and can participate in the global scientific community.

THE RELEVANCE OF RESEARCH AND TEACHING TO INDUSTRY AND SOCIETY

Local research universities are the only institutions able to focus attention on the specific problems of the country in which they are located. External institutions have neither the interest nor the knowledge to do so. Research universities can bring international scientific trends to bear on local problems and contribute to the development of domestic industry, agriculture, and society.

CULTURE, CRITIQUE, AND CIVIL SOCIETY

Research universities constitute centers of culture and critique. In developing countries, these universities are of special importance in this regard because few other societal institutions provide relevant expertise. In many countries, not many museums, orchestras, or other cultural institutions carry out the building and interpreting of indigenous culture. Research universities are often the only places with a "critical mass" of expertise and resources in a range of cultural areas. These institutions also provide social commentary, analysis, and debate. Again, they are uniquely positioned for these roles; they have academic freedom and a community of faculty and students interested in a range of disciplines. While political authorities may find criticism unwelcome, it is of central importance for the development of a civil society.

RESEARCH AND ANALYSIS IN THE NATIONAL LANGUAGE(S)

Research universities must, of course, use the international languages of science and scholarship. Simultaneously, they need to disseminate research and analysis in local languages. Indeed, they may provide a key source for national-language development by producing scientific and literary work and building up the vocabulary of the language. In developing countries, however, the role of indigenous languages in research universities remains complex and sometimes controversial. In many countries, including almost all of Africa, India, and other regions, higher education takes place in nonindigenous languages (English, French, etc). There is also a trend toward offering instruction in English worldwide, and many universities prefer that professors write in English rather than the local language. National languages are in some cases being pushed to the side, in some ways to the detriment of building an indigenous scientific community.

EDUCATING A NEW GENERATION

The research university's mission is education—the training of the next generation of educated personnel for the society. Society's leaders—in politics, intellectual life, industry, and of course in education—are trained mostly in the local research university. The National Autonomous University of Mexico, which has educated generations of the Mexican elite, is just one example of a common trend (Odorika and Pusser forthcoming).

The goals of research universities in developing countries must be realistic. With the exception of a few of the largest and most successful developing nations, including China and India, attempting to compete with Harvard or Oxford or to build a top-ranking world-class university is not a reasonable goal. Rather, developing countries can seek to compete with second-rank but quite distinguished research universities in the industrialized world—institutions such as Indiana University or the University of Nebraska in the United States, York University in the United Kingdom, or the University of Amsterdam in the Netherlands.

Institutions need to select specific areas of science and scholarship to emphasize. Most research universities provide instruction in the main academic disciplines, and many have associated professional schools in fields such as medicine and law. A few research universities are smaller specialized institutions, such as the California Institute of Technology or the Tata Institute of Fundamental Research in India. Research universities are seldom outstanding in all fields, and the selection of disciplines is made so as to build and maintain the highest standards of quality. Other fields may be of good quality but not necessarily at the highest international levels. These decisions may be made on the basis of available resources, an examination of national or regional needs, or simply by assessing an institution's existing strengths and building on them.

Smaller developing countries may lack the funds to build and sustain a research university. Such countries may succeed in building a regional research university—information technology makes this more practicable. Some regions make such initiatives easier to implement than others. For example, because of the small countries, common languages, and similar economic and social needs, Central America might also have a similar regional potential. The same situation may exist in East Africa, francophone West Africa, and the central Asian states of the former Soviet Union. However, efforts to establish regional universities have not been very successful over the last half century. Many policy discussions have yielded few results, and at least one case, the University of East Africa—an institution designed to serve Kenya, Tanzania, and Uganda—did not succeed. However, the University of the West Indies and the University of the South Pacific have succeeded in serving distinct regions. Countries often believe that they need their own national university, and thus sharing resources with neighbors may go against national policy. It may also be possible for research universities in some of the larger developing countries to partner with institutions in small nations—such as Mexico working with Central American universities.

Conclusion

Research universities stand at the apex of a higher education system, providing access to international scholarship and producing the research that may contribute to the growth of knowledge worldwide or in local economies. These universities are also the means of communication with the international world of science and scholarship. For developing countries, research universities play a special role because they are often the sole link to the international knowledge network. Industrialized nations possess many points of access—multinational corporations, scientific laboratories, and government agencies, among others. The best local academics are employed at research universities—providing them with a home and the possibility of contributing to science and scholarship without leaving the country. Thus, research universities are centrally important for the success of any higher education system.

Maintaining research universities requires sustained funding to keep them abreast of emerging fields and advances in knowledge. These institutions have special characteristics that may not be commonplace in academic systems in many developing countries. These aspects include a cadre of full-time faculty, academic freedom, a salary structure permitting a local middle-class life style, promotion and salary enhancement based on performance rather than just seniority, reasonable guarantees of long-term appointment, absence of corruption in all sectors of academic work, and an academic culture of competition and research productivity. These elements may not be present in existing universities, which require resources as well as a cosmopolitan academic environment. Research universities constitute a kind of "flagship" for the rest of the academic system, providing examples of the best academic values and orientations.

For developing countries to join the ranks of modern economies, research universities are a requirement. These institutions link the nation to the broader world of science, technology, and scholarship. Research universities provide the skills needed by 21st century economies and societies and reflect the best academic values. Research universities are central institutions for the global economy.

References

Altbach, P. G. 1987. *The knowledge context: Comparative perspectives on the distribution of knowledge.* Albany: State University of New York Press.

————, ed. 1999. *Private Prometheus: Private higher education and development in the 21st century.* Westport, CT: Greenwood.

————. 2001a. Academic freedom: International realities and challenges. *Higher Education* 41 (1–2): 205–19.

————. 2001b. The American academic model in comparative perspective. In *In defense of American higher education,* ed. P. G. Altbach, P. J. Gumport, and D. B. Johnstone, 11–37. Baltimore: Johns Hopkins University Press.

————. 2003a. The costs and benefits of world-class universities. *International Higher Education,* no. 33:5–9.

————, ed. 2003b. *The decline of the guru: The academic profession in developing and middle-income countries.* New York: Palgrave.

————. 2004. Globalization and the university: Myths and realities in an unequal world. *Tertiary Education and Management* 10:3–25.

Altbach, P. G., and T. Umakoshi, eds. 2004. *Asian universities: Historical perspectives and contemporary challenges.* Baltimore: Johns Hopkins University Press.

Arishie, M. 2006. Keeping the profs in funds. *Egyptian Gazette* (Cairo), March 16, 2.

Chait, R. P., ed. 2002. *The questions of tenure.* Cambridge, MA: Harvard University Press.

Douglass, J. A. 2000. *The California idea and American higher education: 1850 to the 1960 Master Plan.* Stanford, CA: Stanford University Press.

Enders, J., ed. 2001. *Academic staff in Europe: Changing contexts and conditions.* Westport, CT: Greenwood.

Geiger, R. L. 2004. *Money and knowledge: Research universities and the paradox of the marketplace.* Stanford, CA: Stanford University Press.

Hutchins, R. M. 1995. *The higher learning in America.* New Brunswick, NJ: Transaction. Originally published in 1936.

Kerr, C. 2001. *The uses of the university.* Cambridge, MA: Harvard University Press.

Kirp, David. 2003. *Shakespeare, Einstein, and the bottom line: The marketing of higher education.* Cambridge, MA: Harvard University Press.

Lewis, H. R. 2006. *Excellence without a soul: How a great university forgot education.* New York: Public Affairs.

Liu, Nan Cai. Forthcoming. Research universities in China: Differentiation, classification, and world-class status. In *World class* worldwide: *Transforming research universities in Asia and Latin America*, ed. P. G. Altbach and J. Balán. Baltimore: Johns Hopkins University Press.

Lyall, K. C., and K. R. Sell. 2006. *The true genius of America at risk: Are we losing our public universities to de factor privatization?* Westport, CT: Praeger.

Ma, W. Forthcoming. The flagship university and China's economic reform. In *World class worldwide: Transforming research universities in Asia and Latin America*, ed. P. G. Altbach and J. Balán. Baltimore: Johns Hopkins University Press.

Odorika, B. and B. Pusser. Forthcoming. La maxima casa de estudios: Universidad Nacional Autónima de México as a State-Building University," in *World class worldwide: Transforming research universities in Asia and Latin America*, ed. P. G. Altbach and J. Balán. Baltimore: Johns Hopkins University Press.

Perkin, H. 2006. History of universities. In *International handbook of higher education.*, eds. J. J.F. Forest and P. G. Altbach, 159–206. Dordrecht, the Netherlands: Springer.

Pocha, J. S. 2006. Internet exposes plagiarism in China, but punishment of professors rare at universities. *Boston Globe*, April 9.

Rosenzweig, R. M. 1998. *The political university: Policy, politics, and presidential leadership in the American research university*. Baltimore: Johns Hopkins University Press.

Schuster, J. H., and M. J. Finkelstein. 2006. *The American faculty: The restructuring of academic work and careers*. Baltimore: Johns Hopkins University Press.

Slaughter, S., and L. L. Leslie. 1997. *Academic capitalism: Politics, policies, and the entrepreneurial university*. Baltimore: Johns Hopkins University Press.

Slaughter, S., and Gary Rhoades. 2004. *Academic capitalism and the new economy: Markets, state, and higher education*. Baltimore: Johns Hopkins University Press.

Task Force on Higher Education and Society. 2000. *Higher education in developing countries: Peril and promise*. Washington, DC: World Bank.

Trow, M. 2006. Reflections on the transition from elite to mass to universal access: Forms and phases of higher education in modern societies. In *International handbook of higher education*, ed. J. J.F. Forest and P. G. Altbach, 243–80. Dordrecht, the Netherlands: Springer.

Vucinich, A. 1984. *Empire of knowledge: The Academy of Sciences of the USSR (1917–1970)*. Berkeley: University of California Press.

6

Higher Education's Landscape of Internationalization: Motivations and Realities

The international activities of universities have dramatically expanded in volume, scope, and complexity over the past two decades. This essay examines the nature of internationalization, the motivations for it, and the international activities of universities worldwide. Internationalization, especially commercial cross-border education, is big business, earning considerable income for universities and other providers. International programs offer opportunities for students to study abroad and to learn about other cultures. International initiatives also provide access to higher education in some countries where local institutions cannot meet the demand for access.

International initiatives range from traditional study abroad programs, branch campuses in other countries, franchised foreign academic programs or degrees, independent institutions based on foreign academic models in specific countries, and other models. Other approaches stress upgrading the international perspectives and skills of students on campus, enhancing foreign language programs, and providing cross-cultural understanding. In this essay, we are concerned with all of these aspects of internationalization—especially the cross-border provision of higher education programs and the commercialization of international higher education.

Globalization is often confused with internationalization (Altbach 2004). For our purposes, globalization means the economic, political, societal, and other forces that are pushing 21st-century higher education toward greater international involvement. These factors include the growing integration of research, the use of English as the lingua franca for scientific communication, the growing international labor market for scholars and scientists, and, especially, all aspects of information technology (IT). IT facilitates communication, permits efficient storage, selection, and dissemination of knowledge at all levels and makes it possible to offer academic programs of all kinds through e-learning. The emergence of multinational publishing, technology, and communications firms has to some extent been exacerbated by the current wave of globalization.

Global capital has become interested in higher education and knowledge industries generally and has, for the first time, invested heavily in various aspects of education and training worldwide. The emergence of the "knowledge society," the rise of the service sector, and the dependence of many societies on knowledge products and highly educated personnel for economic growth are new phenomena (Castells 2000; Friedman 2005; Odin and Mancias 2004). These are some of the elements of globalization—the inevitable forces that are shaping the world of the 21st century—that underlie much of our analysis.

We will outline specific programs, institutions, innovations, and practices in higher education that academic institutions and systems, other organizations involved in the academic enterprise, and for that matter individuals create to cope with globalization and to reap benefits from this new environment. While globalization is a largely unalterable element of contemporary society, there are many choices involving internationalization.

Just as globalization has tended to concentrate wealth, knowledge, and power in the hands of those already possessing these elements, international academic mobility has favored already well-developed education systems and institutions. Significant elements of inequality exist in the expanding world of international higher education. Initiatives come largely from the North and are focused on the South. Ownership of knowledge, knowledge products, information technology infrastructure, and the like is almost exclusively in the hands of Northern institutions, corporations, and interests. Student flows tend to move from South to North. Other initiatives and programs flow mainly from North to South, although we are seeing increasing numbers of South to South activities, especially in Asia and Africa. While internationalization is much more than a one-way street and serves important needs in the developing world, it is largely controlled by the North.

We will stress the cross-border flows of students, academic personnel, and programs—including the flows of students from one country to another, the growing international market for academic and scientific personnel, curricular internationalization, cross-border academic programs and institutions, the growing influence of the new for-profit higher education sector in internationalization, and other trends. We will not focus on one key aspect of higher education—e-learning or the use of IT to deliver academic programs across borders. E-learning is, without question, one of the fastest-growing elements of internationalization and thus deserves a separate analysis.

The Free-Trade Context
International academic mobility is stimulated and facilitated by the contemporary stress on free trade. The World Trade Organization (WTO) exemplifies this trend and has considerable relevance for our analysis. The WTO is currently negotiating GATS, the General Agreement on Trade in Services. GATS will, when it is fully implemented and agreed to by WTO member countries, provide the parameters for international trade in education and other service-related industries. While this essay will not discuss GATS and its implications in detail, it is worth noting the major targets of GATS because they correspond to many of the central themes of international mobility of higher education. The GATS framework includes the following:

Mode 1: *cross-border supply*. This factor may include distance education (e-learning), franchising of courses or degrees, and other arrangements. This mode does not necessarily require the physical movement of the consumer or provider.

Mode 2: *consumption abroad*. The consumer moves to the country of the provider. This element includes traditional student mobility from one country to another.

Mode 3: *commercial presence*. The service provider establishes facilities in another country to provide the service. This phenomenon includes branch campuses and joint ventures with local institutions.

Mode 4: *presence of natural persons*. This includes persons traveling to another country on a temporary basis to provide educational services, including professors, researchers, and others (OECD 2004, 35; National Education Association 2004).

We mention GATS and the WTO here because they are catalysts for current thinking about international higher education and because GATS will play a significant direct role in providing an international regulatory framework that encourages trade in education services. At present, GATS remains under negotiation, and individual countries have considerable leeway concerning what aspects of GATS they agree to in the formal negotiations.

The free trade context is influenced by current thinking about higher education as a commodity to be freely traded internationally and the idea that higher education is a private good rather than a public responsibility. These powerful contemporary ideas place higher education much in the domain of the market and promote the view that commercial forces have a legitimate or even a dominant place in higher education (Kirp 2003; Altbach 2002).

The Motivations and Sources of Internationalization

There are many reasons for academic internationalization worldwide. By understanding the most important stimuli for internationalization, it will be possible to analyze the basic nature of the phenomenon.

PROFITS

Earning money is an important motivation for some internationalization projects. This aspect without exception involves the for-profit sector, as well as some traditional nonprofit universities that have sought to solve their financial problems by earning income from international initiatives. For-profit higher education providers such as Laureate Education (formerly Sylvan Learning Systems), Kaplan, Inc., the Apollo Group (the parent company of the University of Phoenix, now the largest private university in the United States), and others have entered the international market by establishing new institutions in other countries, purchasing existing institutions, and entering into partnerships with firms or educational institutions in other countries. Local private universities, some of them in the for-profit sector, with overseas links have also been started in many countries. Many of these institutions use an American, British, German, or other foreign curriculum, and many teach in English. They are in some cases accredited in other countries.

Traditional nonprofit universities have also entered the international market. According to a recent survey, the main motivations for internationalization are not financial gains but rather to enhance research and knowledge capacity, increase cultural understanding, as well as other related goals. But a significant number of universities, especially in countries whose governments have cut back on public funding and have encouraged international ventures (e.g., Australia and the United Kingdom). Among the initiatives are branch campuses, franchised degree programs, partnerships with local institutions, as well as others. Most of these efforts have been focused on developing and middle-income countries.

For many countries, the recruitment of international students is also seen as a way of earning profits, both direct and indirect. Many countries charge high fees for international students—including the United Kingdom, Australia, Canada, and the United States. International graduate students also provide much needed research and teaching services with modest compensation in some countries. International students also spend significant amounts of money in the host countries (Davis 2003). It is estimated, for example, that such students contribute some $12 billion to the US economy.

Quantifying the financial scope of academic internationalization in its many permutations is not possible. The sums are quite large. For a growing number of countries, knowledge industries now form a substantial part of the total economy, and higher education constitutes a significant element of that economy. It is also difficult to calculate the impact of international activities on academic institutions and firms actively engaged in them, but again the amount is large and growing rapidly.

ACCESS PROVISION AND DEMAND ABSORPTION

A significant part of the provision of international higher education services relates to providing access to students in countries without the domestic capacity to meet the access demand. Higher education is everywhere much in demand. With the advent of mass higher education worldwide, the proportion of young people entering postsecondary education has expanded dramatically. Even in countries that still enroll relatively few young people (under 20 percent)—such as India, China, and much of Africa—demand is rapidly growing. Domestic institutions, both public and private, often cannot fulfill the demand. Access provision is related to the profit motivation for the most part.

TRADITIONAL INTERNATIONALIZATION

Many universities have been engaged in international activities for decades and quite a few for a century or more, as a modest part of their traditional activities. In many countries these institutions, especially in the United States, use campus international programs as a way to provide an international and cross-cultural perspective to their own domestic students and to enhance the curriculum. Examples of initiatives include study abroad experiences, internationalizing the curriculum, and sponsoring students from other countries to study on campus. Colleges and universities that exercise kind this of internationalization tend to be the more prestigious and selective institutions, although programs are not exclusively limited to these schools. Campus-based internationalization can take many forms, including study abroad programs, the enhancement of foreign-language instruction, the introduction of international studies majors or area studies, and others (Siaya and Hayward 2003). Traditional internationalization is not seen as a profit-making activity, except from the perspective that it might enhance the competitiveness, prestige, and strategic alliances of the institution.

EUROPEAN INTERNATIONALISM

Related to the economic and political integration of Europe, academic internationalization has been actively pursued by European Union authorities for more than two decades. At first, the primary goal was to provide academic experiences outside the home country within the EU for university students, and such programs as ERASMUS were lavishly funded and promoted. Large numbers of European students studied elsewhere in the EU (Huisman and van der Wende 2005). Over the years, the scope of European regional integration was expanded. Now, the Bologna process is harmonizing entire academic systems so that degree structures will be compatible, credits transferable, and academic qualifications equal throughout the EU. Students are still encouraged to study abroad within the EU. European internationalization focuses mainly on the countries of the EU, although several non-EU member states have joined as well.

An additional aspect of European internationalization involves efforts by the EU to expand Europe's international programs in other parts of the world. These efforts are particularly active in Latin America and the Asia/Pacific regions. Regional and institutional linkages, scholarship programs, and other initiatives have been established.

DEVELOPING-COUNTRY INTERNATIONALIZATION

Although they produce a large majority of the total flow of students worldwide, developing countries host only a small proportion of the world's international students. Some of these countries are seeking to attract foreign students to their universities for a variety of reasons—including improvement of the quality and cultural composition of the student body, prestige, and especially the desire to earn income. India and the Philippines, for example, are significant host countries for students from developing countries. India hosts more than 8,000 students from abroad, 95 percent from developing countries (Bhalla 2005). China, Malaysia, and India are developing strategies to attract students from other countries and to export educational programs and institutions.

INDIVIDUAL INTERNATIONALIZATION

Often forgotten in the debate about the internationalization of higher education is the fact that individuals make many of the key decisions—and pay for it as well. Most of the world's more than 2 million international students are self-funded. Their academic work is paid for by the students themselves and their families—not by governments, academic institutions, or philanthropic sources. Students make the basic decisions on destinations and fields of study. With the constraints concerning immigration regulations, students decide whether or not to return home following their academic work or stay at home and enroll in the programs offered by foreign education providers. Students are the largest source of funds for international education.

Growth Areas for Cross-Border Higher Education

While international higher education initiatives exist in almost every country, the dominant forces that influence programs and institutions and the sources of international higher education services are in the developed countries—especially the large English-speaking nations and, to a lesser extent, the larger countries of the EU. Middle-income countries in Asia and Latin America and, to a lesser extent, the poorer nations of the developing world constitute the "buying" countries. A small number of developed countries reap the main financial benefits and control academic and other programs, given such factors as flows of international students, institutions or providers that franchise academic programs to foreign providers, countries that provide international accreditation or quality assurance, or controlling partners in "twinning" arrangements.

The markets for international higher education are varied and segmented. The largest programs may be called "demand absorbing"—initiatives that provide access to students who would otherwise not be able to attend a postsecondary institution. In most cases, lack of capacity to meet growing demand in many countries is the reason for this trend. In a few cases, such as Malaysia, government policies favoring particular ethnic groups over others play a role. Generally, demand-absorbing programs tend to be at the less prestigious end of the higher education system. Foreign providers may link up with local providers—entrepreneurs or academic institutions in the public or private sectors—or may establish their own branch campuses. In almost all cases, the motivation for the foreign provider is to earn a profit.

Some international initiatives rank at the upper end of the hierarchy as well. Many top European and American institutions have set up branch campuses in Singapore and Qatar at the invitations of those countries. The University of Chicago business school was established in Spain (and recently relocated to the United Kingdom). These prestigious institutions offer degree programs that may include a period of study at the home campus, or they may offer the entire academic program offshore.

The market for international higher education initiatives thus attracts students who cannot otherwise obtain access at home and thus seek almost any means to study as well as high-quality programs carefully targeted at a small and able elite group. Some students from the North also seek an overseas cultural or academic experience as part of their undergraduate studies. While predominantly an American phenomenon—175,000 US students went to other countries—other industrialized countries also send significant numbers of their students abroad, both in the context of EU programs and through other means.

While we are mainly concerned here with the physical movement of students, programs, and providers—and to some extent academic staff—across borders, the internationalization of the curriculum and other efforts to provide an effective cross-cultural educational preparation for university students also constitute an expanding area. Initiatives, mainly in the industrialized nations, to prepare students for a globalized world, are a widespread phenomenon.

The Landscape of International Education

The increasing demand and call for international education is changing the face of internationalization and emphasizing the mobility of students, programs, and providers. It is not known to what extent the greater demand will result in student mobility, but clearly there will be significant growth in the movement of programs and education providers across national borders. New types of providers, forms of delivery, and collaborative partnerships are being developed to take education programs to students in their home countries.

A fascinating but complex world of international academic mobility is emerging. The last five years have been a hotbed of innovation and new developments. A review of some of the more interesting developments illustrates the variety of providers, both traditional private and public higher education institutions as well as the so-called "new providers"—commercial IT and media companies, corporate universities, professional associations, and international conglomerates that are delivering education to other countries. Both face-to-face and virtual modes are being used to deliver programs through twinning, franchising, articulation, validation, and joint- or double-degree arrangements. Institutions and providers show more interest in establishing a physical presence through branch campuses, independent institutions, teaching and testing centers, and acquisitions or mergers with local higher education institutions.

This section outlines recent developments in program and provider mobility. The examples include all regions of the world and have been taken from the breaking news service of the Observatory on Borderless Higher Education, which tracks and reports trends in borderless education (Observatory on Borderless Higher Education 2004).

Only initiatives announced or established in the last two years are described here to illustrate the most recent developments. While examples from conventional higher education institutions outnumber those from commercial company providers or from corporate universities, the increase from these new types of providers should not be underestimated in terms of volume, innovation, and impact.

MIDDLE EAST

The diversity of new developments in the Middle East makes it a relevant region to examine. For example, Poland has been approved to establish a new private medical institute in Israel where students will study for three years before moving to the Medical University in Gdansk for an additional three years of clinical study and then returning to Israel for an internship. Saudi Arabia is in the process of establishing new private universities with the involvement of foreign institutions and investors. For instance, the Prince Sultan Private University is being established in cooperation with the University of Arizona and UNESCO. In addition, the Dar-AL-Faisal University is being founded in cooperation with the Stevens Institute of Technology in the United States and with financial investment from the Boeing Company and Thales, the French defense firm. It is also noteworthy that Harvard is planning to set up a branch campus in the United Arab Emirates.

In Bahrain, a new Euro University is being planned in affiliation with the University of Hanover (Germany). Egypt is home to the American University established more than 80 years ago. In the last three years the German University in Cairo and the L'Université Française d'Egypte have been established, and a new British University is under development. Slightly different types of partnerships are being established between local and foreign partners, thus illustrating the creativity and diversity of new forms of collaboration. An interesting example is the franchise agreement through which the distance MBA program of Heriot-Watt University from the United Kingdom is being offered at the American University in Egypt.

ASIA PACIFIC

Vietnam is an emerging center of activity, with the development of a fully foreign-owned branch campus of RMIT from Australia. The International College of IT and Management, established by Troy State University from the United States is another example of a foreign branch campus. The number of active partnerships between local and foreign institutions is steadily expanding. For instance, the University of Hue in Vietnam recently developed a franchised and joint-degree bachelor's program in tourism with the University of Hawaii. Hanoi University of Technology is currently offering master's and bachelor's degrees with higher education institutions from Belgium (1), France (8), Germany (1), Singapore (2), and the United States (1). The Vietnamese government recently announced the development of the "International University in Vietnam" as another initiative to increase the national capacity for higher education. It is expected that half the university teaching staff will be Vietnamese and the other half from foreign universities. The involvement of foreign institutions will build on and expand from the current links of Ho Chi Minh City National University.

Thailand is another country increasingly active in cross-border education and is an appealing destination for institutions and providers from Egypt, China, Australia, and the United States. For example, the Egyptian Al-Azhar University and Jinan University from China both plan to open a branch campus in 2005. Swinburne University of Technology (Australia) has been operating a branch campus since 1998, although it is changing its focus to industry training alone. Troy State University from the United States has a teaching site in Bangkok for its MBA program, and students can transfer to the United States depending on funds and visa requirements. Other institutions operating in Thailand include the Thai-German Graduate School of Engineering as well as 13 Australian and 9 UK universities.

In Singapore, the University of New South Wales (Australia) will establish the first 100 percent foreign-owned higher education institution. New South Wales, which received full approval to do so from the Singapore government, plans to offer undergraduate and graduate-level programs and to develop a strong research capacity. Other well-respected foreign institutions offering education and training programs in Singapore through joint ventures, exchanges, and branch-campus models include the University of Chicago Graduate School of Business, Shanghai Jiao Tong University, Stanford University, Johns Hopkins University, the German Technische Universität München, and the Technische Universiteit Eindhoven from the Netherlands.

It is also interesting to note the exporting activities of Singapore institutions. For example, the National University of Singapore has developed a joint MBA with Fudan University, aimed at both Chinese and Singapore students. It is also embarking on a new graduate school initiative for Chinese students to be located in Suzhou Graduate Town, which is part of the Suzhou Industrial Park.

Raffles LaSalle Ltd. from Singapore is a publicly traded company active in providing programs in fashion and design in many Asian countries. It has a number of innovative partnership arrangements and spans many countries. It is described by Observatory on Higher Education as "a remarkable instance of international partnership, combining a Singapore firm with branches in Australia, China, Malaysia and Thailand, accreditation from an Australian state and a Canadian province, degrees from an Australian and a UK university, and a number of in-county university and college partners" (Observatory on Higher Education 2004).

The speed of change and innovation in India's higher education sector is unprecedented and includes both the import and export of programs and services. One of the more interesting initiatives is the partnership between the Caparo Group—a UK firm with interests in steel, engineering, and hotels—and Carnegie Mellon University in the United States to set up a new campus in India.

AFRICA

While Africa, with the partial exception of South Africa, is the least affected region in terms of international and cross-border initiatives, there is some activity. The Universiteit Nienrode (Netherlands Business School), a private institution, has recently established a new branch campus in Nigeria in partnership with the African Leadership Forum, a nonprofit organization founded in 1988. This is one of the first such initiatives on the continent outside South Africa. In South Africa, in the last few years, there have only been a handful of foreign institutions with branch campuses—including Monash and Bond from Australia, De Montfort (United Kingdom), and the Netherlands Business School. As a result of the recent review of all MBA programs offered in South Africa, three of the foreign institutions are leaving because of accreditation-related issues. Monash will remain (it does not offer an MBA program) as well as the British-based Henley Management College, which is primarily a distance provider. South Africa is one of the countries that have experienced a decrease in the number of foreign programs offered, due largely to strict new government regulations and accreditation processes. Kenya is home to two private nonprofit univer-

124 PHILIP G. ALTBACH

sities. Pakistan's Aga Khan University opened a branch university campus in Kenya in 2002 that specializes in nursing education, and Alliant International University from the United States provides education in social sciences and the humanities.

Mauritius is taking some bold new steps as it tries to establish itself as a "cyber-island" by attracting foreign IT firms from the West and from India. A "knowledge centre," described as a world-class integrated education and training complex is a key aspect of its plans. To date, there are already more than 50 foreign universities and professional bodies offering programs locally. These programs tend to be at the diploma or certificate level and in specialized fields. The concept of attracting foreign education providers to support the education and training needs of a new cyber-island may have positive consequences in terms of stemming brain drain or even stimulating brain gain, but the impact on local education institutions is as yet unclear.

EUROPE

Russia is an example of a country undergoing major economic reform with important implications for the higher education sector. Many higher education institutions—for example, the Moscow International Slavonic Institute and the Moscow State University of Industry—are operating programs abroad, such as in Bulgaria. However, Russia is not only a sending country, it is also a receiving country through joint and double degrees, twinning, and franchise arrangements. For instance, the Higher School of Economics has a double degree program with the London School of Economics. The Stockholm School of Economics is operating in St. Petersburg and the University of Oslo's Centre for Medical Studies in Moscow. The British Open University is active through 80 business training centers across the country. The University of Southern Queensland is partnering with Far Eastern National University in Vladivostok for program delivery. The Pune (India)–based International Institute of Information Technology plans to offer its master's and PhD programs through the newly established Russian-Indian Centre for Advanced Computer Research in Moscow.

In Greece, the University of Indianapolis has been active for more than a decade, first through an articulation program whereby students would start their studies in Athens and then go to the United States for completion of the program. This model has now evolved into a campus in Greece called the University of Indianapolis Athens.

In terms of activities by private companies, Laureate Education owns a part of or all of the Universidad Europa de Madrid in Spain, Les

Roches and Glion Hotel School in Switzerland, and the L'ecole Superieur du Commerce Exterieur de Paris in France. Apollo International is offering its courses in the Netherlands, and Raffles La Salle from Singapore has recently signed an agreement with Middlesex University to offer their bachelor's and master's programs in fashion and design.

NORTH AMERICA

To report on US-led cross-border activities is a challenge because of the volume, diversity of providers, and types of partnerships (de Wit 2002). A review of the previous regional sections shows that US colleges and universities and private companies are probably the most active and innovative in program and provider mobility around the world. One of the more interesting recent developments is that George Washington University is giving serious consideration to opening a branch in South Korea in 2006, now that the government of South Korea has changed its regulatory system to permit foreign providers. There are several examples of US program mobility into Korea through partnerships with local institutions and companies. For instance, Syracuse University, in conjunction with Sejong University in Seoul, offers a specially designed MBA program for Korean students. Duke and Purdue Universities are also offering MBAs in Korea, and Stanford University is delivering online graduate and postgraduate courses and uses alumni as local tutors. These types of cross-border activities from US higher education institutions can be found in many Asian countries—for example, China, Vietnam, Thailand, Malaysia, Singapore, Philippines, and more recently India as well as the Middle East. For instance, the University of Missouri at St. Louis has been involved in the establishment of the first private university in Kuwait—the Gulf University of Science and Technology—and has a similar relationship with the Modern College of Business and Science in Oman.

An important feature of the US cross-border activity involves private and publicly traded companies. The Global Education Index, developed by the Observatory on Borderless Higher Education, is a system of classifying many of the largest and more active publicly traded companies that are providing education programs and services. A scan of more than 50 companies shows that the United States is home to the majority of these companies (Garrett 2004). Some of the better-known ones include Kaplan (owned by the *Washington Post*), the Apollo Group, DeVry, Career Education Corporation, and Laureate Education. Kaplan owns 57 colleges in the United States but now owns the Dublin Business School—Ireland's largest private undergraduate institution.

This is likely to be the first of many future purchases of foreign institutions. The Apollo Group owns the University of Phoenix, now the largest American private university, and is aggressively seeking to broaden its foreign investments and holdings. Since 1995, Apollo has also owned Western International University, which runs a branch campus called Modi Apollo International Institute in New Delhi through a partnership with the KK Modi Group, an Indian industrial conglomerate. Through its three business schools in Beijing, the Canadian Institute of Business and Technology offers Western International University programs. Another smaller but nonetheless interesting initiative has been the establishment of Northface University by Northface Learning Inc., which offers degree programs in IT and business and has the backing of IBM and Microsoft. This will be a company to watch in terms of future international expansion. The University of Northern Virginia is another small private university offering programs in business and IT and has recently opened a branch campus in the Czech Republic and has created delivery partnerships in China and India. These are only a few examples of the hundreds of new initiatives that US higher education institutions and companies are undertaking to deliver education courses and programs to other countries of the world.

In early 2004, the Canadian International Management Institute, a private postsecondary institution that represents the recruiting interests of 10 Canadian universities and colleges, signed a memorandum of understanding with the Chinese Scholarship Council to offer a foundation and credit transfer program to students in China wanting to gain Canadian university degrees. It is a five-year program during which students will be based in China for foundation studies, cultural adjustment, and language training for the first three years. If students meet grade requirements, they can continue their studies either in Canada or China for the final two years.

The Al-Ahram Canadian University in Egypt is Canada's first and, to date, only example of Canadian universities directly supporting the establishment of a new foreign university. The Al-Ahram Organization is a large company that owns the Egyptian daily newspaper. It is cooperating with McMaster University, Ecole Polytechnique de Montreal, and the Université du Quebec in Montreal to establish a new private university that opened in 2005.

The Serebra Learning Corporation is a publicly traded Canadian company offering generic and tailor-made software plus more than 1,800 courses mainly in IT. Serebra is working with the Consortium for Global Education—a group of 45 Baptist higher education institutions in the United States to provide quality-assured IT training in the developing world. Serebra also played a key role in the creation of the Pakistan Virtual University.

LATIN AMERICA
In Mexico, the University of the Incarnate Word, a private American institution in San Antonio, Texas opened a new campus in 2003. Other American institutions with Mexican campuses include Endicott College and Alliant Intentional University, as well as Texas A&M, which has a "university center" in Mexico City. In 2000, Laureate Education purchased the Universidad del Valle de Mexico and is expanding to Guadalajara. It also owns Universidad Interamericana, a private university with campuses in Costa Rica and Panama, and part of three private universities in Chile. Bologna University from Italy is one of the few foreign institutions with a branch campus in Argentina. In terms of exporting, the Technical Institute of Monterrey in Mexico is well known for its online education programs, especially the MBA, delivered to many countries in Latin America.

This section examined the diversity of educational activities by both conventional higher education institutions and new commercial providers. The initiatives demonstrate the range of countries and types of partnerships being formed to promote, exchange, link, and predominantly sell higher education across borders. Another trend is the domination of developed countries—especially Australia and the United States and the emerging interests of India and China. New opportunities and potential benefits and risks can be identified in this international tour of recent cross-border activities.

Quality Assurance and Recognition Issues
Several issues related to quality assurance and the recognition of providers, programs, and credits or qualifications at national and international levels warrant closer attention.

The first issue concerns the licensing or registering of institutions and providers who are delivering cross-border courses or programs. A fundamental question is whether the institutions, companies, and networks that are delivering award-based programs are registered, licensed, or recognized by the home (sending) country and by the receiving country. The answer to this question varies. There are many countries that do not have the regulatory systems in place to register or evaluate out-of-country providers. Several reasons account for this, including lack of capacity or political will. If providers are not registered or recognized it is difficult to monitor their performance. Usually, if an institution or provider is not registered as part of a national system, regulatory frameworks for quality assurance or accreditation do not apply. This is the situation in many countries around the world, and hence foreign providers (bona fide and rogue) do not have to comply with national regulations.

Numerous questions and factors are at play in the registration or licensing of foreign providers. For instance, do providers who are part of and recognized by the national education system in their home country face criteria and conditions that differ from those that apply to other types of providers? Does it make a difference if the provider is for-profit or nonprofit, private or public, an institution or a company? What conditions apply if in fact the provider is a company without home-based presence and only establishes institutions in foreign countries? How does one track all types of partnerships between local domestic institutions or companies and foreign ones? Clearly, there are challenges involved in trying to establish appropriate and effective national or regional regulatory systems.

The second issue addresses the quality of the courses or programs offered and of the academic experience of students. The increased provision of cross-border education by institutions and commercial companies has introduced a new challenge to the field of quality assurance. Historically, national quality-assurance agencies have generally not focused their efforts on assessing the quality of imported and exported programs, with some notable exceptions. Hong Kong, Malaysia, South Africa, and Israel as receivers of cross-border education have developed regulatory systems to register and monitor the quality of foreign provision. The United Kingdom and Australia are sending countries that have introduced quality assurance for exported cross-border provision by their recognized higher education institutions. The sector now must somehow deal with the expansion of cross-border education—in particular, from the new private commercial companies and providers that are usually not recognized by nationally based quality-assurance schemes.

The role of accreditation is the focus of the third issue. Market forces are highlighting the profile and reputation of an institution or provider and their programs. Marketing and branding campaigns are undertaken to earn name recognition and to increase enrollments. The possession of some type of accreditation is part of the campaign and assures prospective students that the programs and awards are of high standing. This situation is introducing an internationalization and commercialization dimension to accreditation practices.

It is interesting to note the increase in the number of bona fide national and international accreditation agencies that are now working in over 50 countries. For instance, the US national and regional accrediting bodies are providing or selling their services in over 65 countries. The same trend is discernible for accreditation bodies of the professions such as ABET (engineering) from the United States and EQUIS (business) from Europe.

Furthermore, self-appointed networks of institutions and new organizations engage in accreditation of their members. These are positive developments in terms of trying to improve the quality of the academic offer. However, some concern exists that these networks and organizations are not totally objective in their assessments and may be more interested in contributing to the race for more and more accreditation "stars" than in improving quality. Another related and more worrisome development is the growth in accreditation mills. These organizations are not recognized or legitimate bodies, and they more or less "sell" accreditation status without any independent assessment. They are similar to degree mills that sell certificates and degrees with no or minimal course work. Different education stakeholders—especially the students, employers, and the public—need to be made aware of these accreditation (and degree) mills, which are often nothing more than a web address and are therefore outside the jurisdiction of national regulatory systems.

The fourth issue addresses the recognition of the actual awards or qualifications offered for the goals of employment and further study. Specifically, students, employers, and the public need to be made aware of the quality and validity of the programs and awards provided. Mechanisms are required that recognize the academic and professional qualifications gained through domestic or international delivery of education. The key questions are who awards the qualification, especially in partnerships and network arrangements, whether the provider is recognized (and, if so, by what kind of accrediting or licensing body), and in what country that body is located? Given the importance of both student mobility and professional labor mobility, within and between countries, the mechanisms for qualification recognition have to be national, regional, and/or international in nature and application.

The fifth issue focuses on the need for a review of the policy and regulatory environments in which program and provider mobility is operating. Of current interest and debate is the question of whether national-level accreditation and quality-assurance systems (where they exist) are able to address the complicating factors of education mobility across countries, cultures, and jurisdictional systems. A fundamental question is whether countries have the capacity to establish and monitor quality systems for both incoming and outgoing education programs, given the diversity of providers and delivery methods. Should national quality-accreditation systems be complemented and augmented by regional or international frameworks? Is it advisable and feasible to develop mutual recognition systems between and among countries? Would an International Code of Good Practice be appropriate or strong enough to monitor quality? These are key questions for the education sector to address.

As the discussion moves forward it will be of strategic and substantive importance to recognize the roles and responsibilities of all the players involved in quality assurance—including individual institutions and providers, national quality-assurance systems, nongovernment and independent accreditation bodies, professional associations, and regional or international organizations. It will be important to work in a collaborative fashion to build a system that ensures the quality and integrity of cross-border education and maintains the confidence of society in higher education.

It would be wrong if one was left with the impression that these issues do not have implications for individual providers and especially higher education institutions. Quality assurance starts with the provider who is delivering the program—domestically or internationally. Many higher education institutions have adequate quality assurance processes in place for domestic delivery, but these processes do not cover all the aspects of delivering abroad. The challenges inherent in working cross-culturally, in a foreign regulatory environment and, potentially, with a foreign partner raise new issues. These include academic entry requirements, student examination and assessment procedures, workload, delivery modes, adaptation of the curriculum, quality assurance of teaching, academic and sociocultural support for students, title and level of award, and other issues. Quality issues must be balanced with the financial investment and return to the source provider. Intellectual property ownership, choice of partners, division of responsibilities, academic and business risk assessments, and internal and external approval processes are only some of the issues the higher education providers need to analyze.

The Future of Internationalization
Universities have, from their medieval European origins, been international institutions, attracting students and faculty from many countries. The rise of nationalism and the nation-state in the period following the Protestant Reformation focused academe inward. Later, the emergence of the Third World from colonialism in the mid-20th cen-

tury also stimulated the establishment of national universities. Now, in the 21st century, academe is increasingly international in scope and direction. Information technology; the knowledge economy; increased mobility for students, faculty, programs, and providers; and the growing integration of the world economy all impel this internationalization. Without question, internationalism will continue to be a central force in higher education in the coming period.

QUESTIONABLE TRENDS

Australian experts have argued that about 15 million students will study abroad by 2025—up from the current 2 million. This prediction might, however, be overly optimistic. Australia itself, after expanding the number of international students studying in the country dramatically for a decade, has experienced a certain decline. The United States, the leading host country, has also declined modestly in 2004—although totals again modestly increased in 2005 and 2006. While the basic trends are strong and stable, there are a variety of uncertainties that may affect internationalization.

Political realities and national security. Terrorism and the reactions to it in many countries may affect international higher education in significant ways. The tightening of visa requirements in the United States and other countries, national security restrictions on what subjects can be studied in certain countries, fear on the part of potential international students to come to some countries, and other problems may affect the flows of students across borders and other aspects of international higher education.

Government policies and the cost of study. Policies concerning the cost of tuition, fees for visas and other documents, and in general the changing policies of the host countries may affect international initiatives in different ways.

Expansion of domestic capacity. As countries build up their own local access to higher education, and especially as they develop master's and doctoral programs, there may be less interest in going abroad to study or in enrolling in international programs within the country.

English. The growing use of English as a medium of research and instruction, especially at the graduate level, may stimulate interest in international programs, offered by universities in English.

The internationalization of the curriculum. As the curriculum is harmonized worldwide—moving largely toward models developed in the United States and other large industrialized countries—students may find international programs useful.

The expansion of e-learning. As degrees offered through distance education expand and become more widely accepted internationally, these degrees are likely to grow in size and scope and become a more significant part of the higher education system worldwide. It is not clear if international e-learning degrees will become more widespread or if domestic e-learning programs will continue to dominate. It is worth noting that most of the largest distance-education universities are located in developing or middle-income countries.

The private sector. At present, private higher education is the fastest-growing segment of higher education worldwide. A small part of this sector is international. It is not clear if private higher education providers will find the international market sufficiently profitable—although it seems quite likely that there will be some expansion of private sector institutions in the international market.

Quality assurance and control. Quality assurance is a major concern within countries and it is even more of a problem internationally. It is as yet unclear how quality can be measured in international higher education programs. Many international programs have been criticized for low standards.

European policies. It is not yet clear how the Bologna initiatives and the harmonization of higher education in the European Union will affect international patterns within the EU or between the EU and the rest of the world. Will the EU build walls to protect is own "European higher education space," or will it welcome students and programs from the rest of the world? Will tuition and other fees be imposed on non-EU students? The answers to these and other questions are largely unanswered.

Our focus in this essay is to understand both the underlying motivations and patterns of international higher education and the landscape of international programs and institutions. We believe that international higher education will play an increasingly influential role in providing access in some countries and will become a "niche market" in others. At present, numerous uncertainties exist about both the realities and the future of international higher education. Our concern is to ensure that international higher education embodies a force for the public good and not simply a means for earning profits. We are at an international crossroads—the programs and practices that are emerging now will shape the realities of international higher education for years to come.

References

Altbach, Philip G. 2002. Knowledge and education as international commodities. *International Higher Education*, no. 28:2–5.

———. 2004. Globalization and the university: Myths and realities in an unequal world. In *The NEA 2005 almanac of higher education*, ed. National Education Association, 63–74. Washington, DC: National Education Association.

Bhalla, Veena. 2005. International students in Indian universities. *International Higher Education*, no. 41:8–9.

Castells, Manuel. 2000. *The rise of the network society*. Oxford: Blackwells.

Davis, Todd M. 2003. *Atlas of student mobility*. New York: Institute of International Education.

de Wit, Hans. 2002. *Internationalization of higher education in the United States of America and Europe: A historical, comparative, and conceptual analysis*. Westport, CT: Greenwood.

Friedman, Thomas L. 2005. *The world is flat: A brief history of the twenty-first century*. New York: Farrar, Straus & Giroux.

Garrett, Richard. 2004. The global education index, 2004 report. *Observatory on Borderless Higher Education*. London: Association of Commonwealth Universities.

Huisman, Jeroen, and Marijk van der Wende, eds. 2005. *On cooperation and competition II: Institutional responses to internationalization, Europeanization, and globalization*. Bonn: Lemmens Verlag.

Kirp, David. 2003. *Shakespeare, Einstein, and the bottom line: The marketing of higher education*. Cambridge, MA: Harvard University Press.

National Education Association. 2004. *Higher education and international trade agreements: An examination of the threats and promises of globalization*. Washington, DC: National Education Association.

Observatory on Borderless Higher Education, ed. 2004. *Breaking news stories service 2002–2004*. London: Association of Commonwealth Universities.

Odin, Jaishree K., and Peter T. Mancias, eds. 2004. *Globalization and higher education*. Honolulu: University of Hawaii Press.

Organization for Economic Cooperation and Development. 2004. *Internationalization and trade in higher education: Opportunities and challenges*. Paris: OECD.

Siaya, Laura, and Fred M. Hayward. 2003. *Mapping internationalization on U.S. campuses*. Washington, DC: American Council on Education.

The Academic Profession

7

Centers and Peripheries in the Academic Profession: The Special Challenges of Developing Countries

The academic profession worldwide is united by its commitment to teaching and the creation and transmission of knowledge. Yet, as pointed out by Burton Clark, it is also composed of "small worlds" and "different worlds" divided by discipline, role, and other factors (Clark 1987). This chapter examines the conditions of the academic profession and workplace in developing countries. A growing proportion of the world's postsecondary students are found in developing countries, and the rate of expansion of higher education is greatest in this part of the world. By 2000, more than 44 million of the world's 80 million plus postsecondary students were in developing or middle-income countries—despite the fact that only 6 percent of the population in these countries has earned postsecondary degrees, while 26 percent in high-income nations have similar qualifications (Task Force on Higher Education and Society 2000, 111 and 115). Further, many developing countries are building up large and complex academic systems, including research universities. Yet very little is known about the professionals responsible for teaching and research in these universities.

What is known about the conditions of the academic profession and of academic work in the developing world is not positive. The conditions of work and levels of remuneration are inadequate, involvement in institutional governance is often very limited, and the autonomy to build both an academic career and academic programs in the university is often constrained.

While some of these circumstances exist in middle-income nations such as the countries of the former Soviet Union, this chapter is mainly concerned with developing countries—nations with low-level per capita income. There are major variations among the developing countries and, indeed, within the academic systems of these countries. Larger countries, such as India and China, have some universities and specialized postsecondary institutions with excellent facilities that operate at international levels—although they have not yet achieved the status of top world-class institutions. However, these higher education systems are overall of fairly low quality. A number of the smaller countries do have some academic institutions with high standards of teaching and research. Certain countries have given a higher priority to higher education than others or have higher literacy rates or per capita income than others. Cuba, for example, has a high literacy rate and educational attainment although its per capita income is low. Botswana, which benefits from some mineral wealth, has built several quite good academic institutions. In Latin America, Mexico, Chile, Brazil, and Argentina are no longer classified as developing countries and have relatively high income levels and large and sophisticated academic systems. Yet some of the conditions common to poorer nations are found throughout Latin America. As with most comparative analyses, the generalizations presented here do not fully apply to all of the countries or higher education systems discussed in the chapter.

Worldwide Trends

Many of the conditions affecting the academic profession in developing countries are central realities worldwide. For example, G. R. Evans (2002) points out that the British academic profession has been drawn away from its traditional values and that in many ways this has weakened the country's universities. As she points out, these trends are observable worldwide. The central realities of higher education in the 21st century—massification, accountability, privatization, and marketization—affect universities everywhere and academics, to differing degrees. Massification has led, among other things, to an expanded academic profession and an academic community that is increasingly fragmented. Accountability has limited the traditional autonomy of the profession, more tightly regulating academic work and eroding one of the major attractions of the academic profession. Privatization has, in some contexts, placed pressure on academics to generate income for themselves and for the university through consulting and other non-teaching activities. Marketization has forced academics to become more aware of students' curricular interests. Professors have also been encouraged to engage in entrepreneurial activities. The sad fact in the era of mass higher education is that the conditions of academic work have, for most academics, deteriorated everywhere.

There has been a major shift in the nature of academic institutions and academic work in many countries and for a substantial part of the academic profession. These changes have implications for the career structure of the professoriate, choices for research and teaching, the relationship of academic staff to administration, and the participation of academics in the governance of institutions—to mention a few factors. In industrialized nations, the top segments of increasingly differentiated academic systems have thus far managed to retain the ability to engage in high-level teaching and research and to protect the central values of the university. While the problematic trends described earlier affect academics everywhere, the impact may be especially severe in developing countries, where the traditional roles of the professoriate are often less well established, financial and other resources less adequate, and the pressures greater.

Centers, Peripheries, and Dependency

The professoriate in the developing countries of the South is a profession on the periphery (Altbach 1998). With few exceptions, research is undertaken at the major universities in the industrialized countries of the North, and the norms of academic work at these institutions set the standard everywhere. The academic world is itself hierarchical, and research universities in the industrialized countries are at the center of an international knowledge system (Shils 1972). These institutions produce most of the research and control the key international journals and other means of communication. They train researchers and top scholars, and in most countries educate the elites (Geiger 2004). Academics in teaching-oriented universities in the North are peripheral to those at the major research universities in the North. The academic profession in developing countries is also peripheral to the international centers.

The academic systems of developing countries are, without exception, imported from the North. Indeed, all contemporary universities are based on the medieval University of Paris model, with the exception of the al-Azhar University in Cairo. In part, the European model was imposed by the colonial powers, but even in Ethiopia, Thailand, and Japan, where foreign academic patterns were not imposed, European models prevailed over existing indigenous academic traditions. Following independence, when developing countries had the chance to change the nature of the university, none of them chose to do so.

Indeed, in many cases, even the language of the colonial power was retained for instruction and research. The major European languages remain dominant in many developing countries; for example, English and French are still entrenched in Africa. Indeed, no African languages (unless one classifies Arabic and Afrikaans as African languages) are used at African universities. Although India uses many of its regional languages for instruction, English remains important and preferred by students because it is more advantageous in the marketplace. The European and increasingly the American academic models—based on departments, competition among academic staff, institutional hierarchy, and specific definitions of science and scholarship—continue to prevail throughout the Third World.

Language is one element of the peripherality of the academic profession in developing countries. In the 21st century, English is the main language for academic communication—in journals and Internet networks, as well as at international meetings (Crystal 1997). Major Western languages—such as French and to a lesser extent German and Spanish are also widely used. Other languages may be used for teaching and perhaps local publications, but have little international relevance for scientific research. This is as true for Danish or Hungarian as it is for Chinese or Swahili. A significant number of developing countries use English or French for instruction—permitting the use of textbooks and curricular materials in those languages, but also weakening the connection to local cultures and realities.

The long-established academic communities of the North are larger and wealthier than their counterparts in the South, with resources that permit them to maintain leadership in all areas of academic work. Universities in the North also have close relationships with multinational corporations and other consumers of research. These links provide further funding sources and outlets for research and other academic work. This combination of wealth, resources, and position ensures the centrality of the universities of the North.

The contemporary dominant position of the academic communities at the center is an immutable reality of the world knowledge system. Universities in developing countries, and their academic communities, must function in the unequal world of centers and peripheries. Peripherality does not mean that academics in the developing world cannot undertake creative scientific or intellectual work or that they will forever be relegated to a subordinate status in academe. It does mean that they will seldom stand at the frontiers of world science or achieve any control over the main levers of academic power worldwide.

Related to peripherality is dependency. Third World academics often perceive themselves to be dependent on the main centers of knowledge and the world scientific networks. The vast inequality in wealth, size, and access to resources and institutional infrastructure contributes to dependency. The policies and practices of academic systems in the North also play a role in the power imbalance. For example, scholarly journals select articles based on the interests as well as the methodological and scientific norms that prevail in the North, which often places Third World researchers at a disadvantage in getting their work published and recognized internationally. In many developing countries, funding for research, participation in international conferences and programs, and access to academic collaboration is often dependent on external support from the North. The decision-making structures are based in the North and reflect the interests and concerns of the dominant academic communities. The situation is most extreme for Africa, where almost all research and funding for international linkages come from external sources—foreign governments, multilateral agencies such as the World Bank, philanthropic foundations, and so on. African scholars and scientists are dependent on foreign funds and must comply with the particular priorities and programs of the funders for their research (Teferra and Altbach 2002).

The fact is that most academics work in the "small worlds" of their departments and universities, spend most of their time teaching, and are thus unaffected in their daily lives by the trends in international scholarship. While research and knowledge communication at the top of the system are directly involved in the peripherality and dependency discussed here, the daily lives of most academics operate at a different level—less directly affected by academic globalization. Academics in developing countries function in a world of peripherality and, depending on the country and region, dependency but at the same time are deeply embedded in national realities.

The Domination of External Values
The universities of the developing world are in many ways dependent on the Northern-dominated system. Not only is the institutional model and, often, language of instruction adopted from the North but many of the norms and values of the academic profession as well. The Third World also looks to the North for validation of academic quality and respectability. For example, academics are expected to publish in Northern academic journals, and promotion sometimes depends on such publication. Even where local scholarly publications exist, many academic decision makers do not consider them of sufficient quality. While it is understandable that in small and relatively new academic

systems there may be the desire to implement external validation of the work of scholars and scientists, relying on foreign journals has implications for the professoriate. For example, internationally circulated journals are often highly competitive, but they may not place much value on research topics relevant in developing countries. Moreover, it is always more difficult for authors to write in a language that is not their own. Journal editors, for their part, must be guided by the methodological and topical predilections of their colleagues and are as a result less interested in work done by Third World authors, who are disadvantaged by the lack of access to the library and laboratory facilities available at the major universities of the North.

Third World academic systems, however, rely on the North to give legitimacy to their academic work. China and other developing countries measure the research productivity of academics in part by relying on the Science Citation Index (SCI) and, to a lesser extent, the Social Science Citation Index (SSCI)—both of which are published by the Institute of Scientific Information in Philadelphia, Pennsylvania. This measurement of the impact of scholarly work counts the citations in a group of internationally circulated journals. The number of journals covered is only a small proportion of those published, and almost all of them are edited and published in the North. Thus, the scientific work produced in the developing countries is largely overlooked. The SCI and SSCI are the only major scholarly citation indexes available. Their prominence augments the power of international scientific networks, further undervaluing scientific work carried out in developing countries. While Third World academics strive to keep abreast of world science, they are at a distinct competitive disadvantage. The way in which the world of scientific publishing is organized discourages national and regional scientific communities from emerging in the Third World. While understandable and probably necessary for universities seeking to engage in research and teaching at the highest international levels, an overreliance on these external norms distorts academic development and introduces unrealistic expectations for institutions and for the academic profession.

The Impact of Globalization
The globalization of higher education has had a broad structural impact on systems everywhere (Scott 1998), and certain elements are specifically affecting the academic profession. The most visible aspect of globalization is the emergence of a worldwide market for academic talent, stimulated in part by the large numbers of students who study abroad. It must be emphasized that the international labor market for scholars

and scientists and most of the flows of foreign students are South-to-North phenomena. In 2006, more than 2 million students were studying outside the borders of their own countries—the vast majority of these students are from developing countries, and their destinations are in the industrialized nations. The United States is the host country for close to 600,000 students, with Western Europe, Australia, and Canada absorbing most of the rest. The flow of students from North to South is tiny, although there is some South-South flow. A large majority of international students from developing countries study for advanced degrees—in contrast to patterns from the industrialized nations, where students tend to study for their first degree or spend just a semester or year abroad. A significant number of students who obtain their degrees abroad do not return home, and those who do return and join the academic profession bring the values and orientations of the country in which they studied back with them.

While foreign study has received considerable attention, its impact on the academic profession has not been analyzed. In many developing countries, academics with foreign degrees constitute a significant part of the professoriate. Furthermore, these returnees are clustered at the top of the profession and dominate the research-oriented universities. They are the "power elite" of the academic community. These trends are linked to a number of factors. Foreign academic degrees are valued not only because of the perceived quality of the training and the exposure to the best facilities and professors available but also because foreign study is deemed to be more prestigious than receiving training at home. Scholars returning from abroad often wish to employ the values they absorbed during their studies to upgrade local standards, whether or not such replication is practical or desirable in local conditions. These academics follow the latest international academic developments and seek to maintain links with the countries in which they studied, often importing scientific equipment as well as ideas. Conflicts between foreign-returned academics and their locally educated colleagues are common.

There is also an increasingly important flow of academic talent around the world. Again, the flow is almost exclusively from South to North. It takes many forms, including migration from one country to another on a permanent basis, stints as visiting scholars or postdoctoral fellows, or temporary work assignments abroad. Statistics are difficult to obtain, but some 80,000 visiting scholars were at American universities in 2000. It is a well-known fact that there is a large flow of academics from a number of African countries to North America and Europe—for example, more Ghanaian medical doctors are practicing outside of Ghana than at home. There is now a flow from sub-Saharan African nations to South Africa, while at the same time South African academics are taking jobs in the North.

What used to be called the "brain drain" has evolved into a much more complex phenomenon. For academic and scientific personnel, settling in another country no longer means permanent emigration. In some cases, people from developing countries employed in the North return home when attractive opportunities open up once domestic circumstances have improved in terms of living conditions, academic infrastructures, and the intellectual and political climate. As Taiwan and Korea developed in the 1960s and became stable democracies, academics and scientists who had settled abroad began returning home to take jobs in universities. More common is the phenomenon of scientists and scholars from developing countries who have emigrated maintaining active relationships with their countries of origin (Choi 1995). They serve as consultants, visiting professors, lecturers, or advisers to universities, governments, and sometimes companies in their countries of origin. In this way, they act as important links between centers and peripheries. Migrants understand conditions in their countries of origin and regularly participate in academic life there as well as their new homes.

In the 21st century, the diaspora of professors, scientists, and intellectuals from developing countries who study or live in the North represents a significant factor in the academic culture of the developing world. Globalization makes this human flow possible. An international academic culture, the willingness of universities worldwide to accept students and in many cases faculty members from abroad, and immigration policies that permit migration all contribute to this diaspora. While the bulk of the flow is from South to North, there is also significant movement among the industrialized countries. Academics move from countries with relatively low salaries and poor working conditions to those with greater resources. For example, large numbers of academics from the former Soviet Union have moved to Western Europe and North America in recent years. Smaller numbers have gone from the United Kingdom to the United States and Canada because of deteriorating salaries and working conditions in the United Kingdom. There has also been a modest South-South flow—Indians can be found teaching in a number of English-speaking African countries, and South Africa has attracted academics from other African countries. Egyptians and Palestinians staff universities in the Gulf and Saudi Arabia. The costs and benefits of this massive international migration are considerable—with most of the benefits accruing to the wealthier academic systems.

Information technology (IT) is also closely related to globalization and is beginning to affect universities and the academic profession in many ways. Two basic elements are of concern here—the use of IT for scientific communication worldwide and for pedagogical purposes both through distance education and for improving instruction and learning in traditional universities. The IT revolution has yet to fully unfold and will increase its impact on higher education everywhere. It is likely to be especially influential in developing countries, where the demand for access is greatest.

IT is a new phenomenon in much of the developing world—Africa, for example, has been connected to the Internet for just a few years, and even now many African academics have only sporadic access to it (Teferra 2003). The issue of access is central. In the academic context of developing countries, many academic staff do not have their own computers and must rely on spotty access and service. Personal e-mail accounts are by no means universal. Connectivity is unreliable and often slow, due to inadequate and poorly maintained telephone systems—meaning that many sophisticated databases will not run well. Prices are often high, and this means that individuals cannot afford their own accounts, and universities may ration access. Despite these serious problems, IT has provided many academics in developing countries with unprecedented access to current scientific information, which to some extent makes up for the inadequate libraries that exist in virtually all developing countries. Just as important, the Internet has permitted academics to communicate with colleagues worldwide, dramatically decreasing traditional isolation.

While IT has given access to knowledge on a scale hitherto unknown, it has in some ways increased the peripherality of developing-country academics (Castells 2000). Studies show that developing countries use information from the North but contribute relatively little to the total flow of knowledge. Developing countries are, in sum, users of knowledge produced by others.

Developing countries are making use of IT-based distance education—indeed, 7 out of the 10-largest distance-education providers are located in developing countries—in countries such as Turkey, India, and China. With the exception of the few academics who have been involved with developing and delivering curriculum in these distance-based universities, few individuals in developing countries have had their teaching affected by IT. Even fewer have been able to use IT to enhance classroom-based teaching, as they lack the necessary facilities, equipment, knowledge, and funds. It is likely that these constraints will continue for some time, and that IT use will be minimal in developing-country universities. Many of the worldwide IT "products" originated in the industrialized countries and are often available from media corporations. Designed for use in the North, these products may not be relevant for developing countries. They may also be too expensive. The new African Virtual University, for example, has had trouble finding "content" relevant for African countries. Creating courses with a developing-country perspective requires both money and technological skills, which are often in short supply.

The impact of the Internet and IT on the academic profession is in many ways similar to the patterns of inequality described earlier in the chapter. Academics in developing countries are dependent on outsiders for the technology, basic equipment, and content. These assets have helped developing-country academics to keep abreast of scientific research, communicate with international colleagues, and participate in scientific debates on a more equal basis. However, academics in developing countries are still peripheral in many ways in the Internet-based knowledge system.

The Shape of the Profession

The professoriate is changing in many parts of the world, and developing countries are not free from these changes. In developing countries, a higher proportion of academics work on part-time contracts or are subject to irregular hiring practices. In many developing countries, a large part of the profession is composed of part-time staff who teach a few courses and do not have regular academic appointments or real links to the university. This is the norm at most Latin American universities, where full-time permanent staff are a tiny proportion of the total academic labor force. In many countries, tenure is not guaranteed, and even full-time academics have little formal job protection, although, in fact, relatively few are actually fired. Clear guarantees of academic freedom or the assurance of a stable career are often missing.

There are curious contradictions in the nature of academic appointments. On the one hand, those hired in regular full-time positions are generally given de facto security of appointment, without much evaluation as to job performance, competence in teaching or research, or other attributes of a successful academic career. At the same time, while few appointees are in fact removed from their academic posts, many academic systems do not offer a formal tenure system that protects academic freedom or inhibits interference by university authorities in the intellectual life of academic staff.

In many Latin American countries, the pattern of academic appointments includes periodic "contests" for academic posts, which require each professor to defend his or her position publicly and permit others to apply for the post. Often, contests do not occur due to the inability of university authorities to organize open competitions on a regular basis. In reality, few faculty are removed from posts they already hold, but the possibility of removal remains a fact. In many developing countries, the terms and conditions of academic appointments are not clearly spelled out, leaving considerable latitude for administrative or governmental interference in an academic career.

The requirements for academic appointments vary greatly in developing countries and are in general less rigorous than is the case in most industrialized nations. In the North, the standard requirement for an academic appointment includes holding a doctoral degree or the equivalent—the highest degree possible in the country. In Germany, Russia, and other countries following the German academic model, a second doctorate—the habilitation or its equivalent—is required for appointment to a full professorship.

It is probably the case that a majority or a significant minority of academics in virtually every developing country hold just a bachelor's degree. Those in senior academic positions almost always have higher academic qualifications, but much of the academic labor force has modest qualifications for their jobs. A number of countries, including India and Brazil, have engaged in successful efforts to increase the qualifications of their academic staff by providing opportunities for study to those already in academic positions and increasing the minimum qualifications for appointments. The lack of qualifications has meant that academic upward mobility is limited for many junior staff. It also means, of course, that the level of expertise possessed by many teachers is quite modest, affecting the quality and depth of the instruction provided to many students.

It is unlikely that, on balance, the qualifications of academic staff will improve dramatically in the coming period. Continued expansion throughout the developing world means that large numbers of new teachers will be required, and selectivity will be minimal. The bulk of enrollment growth worldwide will be in developing countries—in India, for example, enrollments will almost double in the next two decades. The challenge of providing teachers to instruct these students will place severe strains on the limited capacities in most developing countries for advanced training in the universities.

The mixed qualifications of academic staff have resulted in a highly differentiated academic profession. The small minority of well-qualified professors, many of whom hold foreign doctoral degrees, are located at the top of the system. The large majority of poorly qualified teachers at the bottom possess few possibilities for mobility. Missing is a successful middle rank of scholars. A wide gulf exists between the thin wedge of highly qualified personnel and the large, poor, and marginally qualified group of teachers.

In spite of the limited data on the socioeconomic backgrounds of the academic profession in developing countries, some generalizations can be made. The involvement of women in the profession varies and is surprisingly high in some countries. In many Latin American nations and in South Asia, the proportion of women holding academic positions is high—often higher than in industrialized countries. As of 1993, more than one-third of academics in three large Latin American countries (Brazil, Mexico, and Chile) were women (Boyer, Altbach, and Whitelaw 1994). Only a few industrialized nations have reached that level. In developing countries, academics tend to come from well-educated, urban families, although the majority of the population remains largely uneducated and rural. Academics do not, however, come mainly from elite families, due in part to the fact that salaries are not high and chances for mobility are limited.

The academic profession in developing countries differs significantly from the professoriate in the North. In developing countries, there are more part-time staff. Full-time professors have less job security and are sometimes subject to insecure terms of appointment; they are not as well qualified; and they come from more modest backgrounds. While there have been efforts to upgrade academic skills in some developing countries, massification has meant that qualifications have not kept up with the need for more teachers in the classrooms of the Third World.

Developing Country Realities

While the basic roles of academics everywhere are similar—teaching, research, and service—in all countries most academics are mainly teachers, with research and service a minor or negligible part of their work. Academics worldwide have recently suffered from a deterioration in income, working conditions, and, in some cases, prestige (Altbach 2002). Working conditions for academics in developing countries are, in general, significantly less favorable than for their colleagues in the North—and there is less emphasis on the research and service roles of the profession.

INSTITUTIONAL ENVIRONMENT

The working environment for most Third World academics is far different than what is the norm in the industrialized nations. While this chapter is not intended as an analysis of the infrastructures of academic institutions, it is necessary to point out that conditions vary considerably across and within countries. For example, India has a few academic institutions—such as the Indian Institutes of Technology, several management schools, and the Bhabha Atomic Research Centre—with facilities comparable to average institutions in the North, although not the very best. But the vast majority of Indian universities, colleges, and other academic institutions fall far below the level of the average postsecondary institutions in the North. While precise figures do not exist, it is probably the case that 95 percent of Indian academics work in an environment that is well below international levels (Jayaram 2003). The situation is somewhat better in China, which has a growing number of academic institutions that seek to compete on a global level in terms of research and teaching but where the large majority of academics work in substandard conditions; and most staff teaching in postsecondary education do not hold an advanced degree. In many developing countries, especially smaller nations, no academic institutions exist that even approach international standards in terms of facilities or quality. Even large countries, such as Ethiopia or Nigeria, have few if any academic institutions that can offer working conditions permitting scholars and scientists to function competitively on an international basis. Even in fairly well-developed academic systems in relatively affluent countries such as Argentina, the physical facilities available to most academics are quite limited. What is surprising in the developing world is the ability of many academics to work effectively under such difficult circumstances.

The academic environment is characterized by inadequacies at all levels. The cost of maintaining up-to-date facilities and resources has increased with the escalating prices of journals and books and the complexity and sophistication of scientific equipment. In the 21st century, it is increasingly costly to stay competitive in world science. Further, all of these scientific products would have to be imported at unfavorable exchange rates and in an environment of financial scarcity.

As noted earlier, access to the Internet, while expanding in the developing world, remains inadequate. The infrastructure is antiquated and poorly maintained. Access to some of the major databases is limited by the high cost of accessing them. Few academics have work stations for themselves, and computer use is rationed at many institutions.

In fact, many academics lack even a desk on which to place a computer, even if one were available. Office space is in short supply, limiting the possibility for academic work and consultation with students and colleagues. Many academics have nothing but the books they use as texts or perhaps a few related publications. The physical infrastructure available to most academics is inadequate for scientific research and scholarship and barely adequate for teaching. Indeed, in much of the developing world, facilities are actually deteriorating due to financial shortages and the pressures of ever-increasing numbers of students.

BUREAUCRACY AND POLITICS

Universities everywhere are bureaucratic institutions. In the North, the concept of shared governance is the norm, with the professoriate sharing or controlling (decreasingly) the key governing structure of universities. Professorial power has weakened everywhere as academic institutions expand and demands for accountability mount. However, academics' control over key aspects of the curriculum, the hiring of new faculty members, issues of instruction and evaluation, and related issues remains largely intact.

The same cannot be said for many universities in developing countries. First of all, the tradition of professorial power and shared governance is weak. In countries formerly under colonial rule, universities were founded with strong bureaucratic structures and firm controls to ensure loyalty and adherence to the norms of the colonial authorities. In other countries, academic institutions, which were often directly established by government, also lacked the traditions of faculty power. Governments have been concerned about institutional stability, student political activism and unrest, and the risk that universities could become sources of dissent in society. These factors led to the buildup of strong bureaucratic controls and prevented the growth of professorial autonomy and strong faculty governance. Even in Latin America, with its long tradition of formal autonomy for the universities, the academic profession has attained less control over working conditions and over institutional structures.

Many universities in developing countries have become politicized, which has directly affected the academic profession. In developing countries, universities are important political institutions—not only do they train elites but they also play a direct political role as a forum for student political activism, dissident perspectives, and even mobilization of opposition activities. Especially in societies with unstable governments, universities often serve an oppositional political function.

In developing countries, two kinds of politics affect higher education: academic politics within the university and societal politics. Academic politics can be found everywhere—in departments, among colleagues, and in the university at large. In the North, while factions may be present in departments, institutions and units within them are generally not disrupted by politics or governed by political considerations. Seldom does the partisan politics in broader society intrude into the on-campus operation of the institution. In developing countries, politics is more prevalent at universities and is not infrequently a motivating force in academic policy decisions, the hiring or promotion of academic staff, and other areas.

A number of factors explain the intrusion of politics into academe. In the developing country context, the university is an institution with considerable resources. In such a resource-scarce environment, the decisions made on campus—including the hiring of staff (faculty and administrators), student admissions, the creation of new programs, and so on—have broader implications. Universities in developing countries have a tradition of being politicized, the result of a long history of involvement in independence movements or other struggles. Politics has continued to be an element of campus life in the absence of the norms in the North that keep partisan politics away from the university.

In Latin America, for example, party politics sometimes determines the election of academics to administrative posts. Candidates for rector or dean may stand for election backed by a political party or a campus faction. Political partisanship is often felt in the appointment of professors and other staff. Occasionally, even student admissions or examination results may be influenced by political considerations.

Universities are complex bureaucratic institutions. In developing countries, bureaucratic control, government involvement in academic decisions, and the politicization of all elements of higher education have been detrimental to the academic profession and the strength of academic norms and values in higher education.

ACADEMIC FREEDOM

Not surprisingly, given the realities discussed here, academic freedom is often not well protected in developing countries (see chapter 3). The institutional protections common in the North are often missing—such as tenure or civil service status, as well as academic freedom. A number of factors have combined to put professors in developing countries in a more vulnerable position than their counterparts in the North. The history of higher education in developing countries, as noted, is one of governmental oversight and bureaucratic control. Colonial regimes as well as postindependence governments worried about the political loyalty of the professoriate and of the university. To a certain extent, a tradition of subservience exists in the academic profession of developing countries (Gilbert 1972). Academic freedom is often more highly contested in developing countries because the work of professors can have direct political relevance—that is, their writings can have an immediate impact on society. The campus environment is often highly volatile, and professors may contribute to dissent on campus and in society. Protecting professorial freedom of expression and academic work does not receive a high priority from governments.

These limitations on academic freedom damage the professoriate, creating problems for expression and research. When professors step over an often undefined line, they can suffer serious consequences—ranging from mild sanctions to loss of their positions, or imprisonment. In some countries, research, especially in the social sciences, is restricted. Publications are closely monitored, and professors who express views in opposition to government policy face problems. Most academics, however, do not perceive the situation regarding academic freedom as problematic. In the sciences few restrictions are imposed. Most academics are in any case involved exclusively in teaching, and classroom expression is seldom monitored. However, the lack of a respected culture of academic freedom has an impact on the intellectual atmosphere of the university.

WORKING CONDITIONS

It is clear that, in general, the professoriate in developing countries works under much less favorable conditions than what is standard in the North. Again, there are significant variations—with a small proportion of academics at the top universities enjoying conditions similar to the North. Few classrooms have anything more than the most rudimentary teaching aids. Class size tends to be large, and in any case the almost universally accepted method of instruction consists of the lecture, with little opportunity for discussion or questions. In some countries, the lack of laboratories and equipment deprives students of an essential component of scientific training. Rote learning constitutes the norm in many places.

Teaching loads, even for senior professors, are high by international standards, and academic staff typically spend more time in the classroom than do their peers in the North. There are some exceptions, such as China, where teaching loads are less onerous. The trend, with enrollment pressures and financial shortfalls, is toward ever higher teaching loads. The practice of assigning advanced graduate students to assist professors is virtually unknown. Academic staff may spend 20 or more hours per week in direct teaching. Little time remains for research, course preparation, advisement, or other academic activities. Academic staff often possess little control over what courses are taught. Differences do exist by country, rank, and institution, with academics at the most prestigious universities teaching less than their colleagues further down on the academic hierarchy. Junior staff often teach more than senior academics.

In a growing number of countries, academics are expected to engage in remunerative activities unrelated to their basic teaching. Consulting; extra instruction in the form of revenue-producing, noncredit courses, or other programs; extramural service; and other activities increasingly constitute part of the academic workload. These forms of work produce additional income for universities as well as for individual faculty members. The traditional job of the professor is expanding to include entirely new kinds of responsibilities.

REMUNERATION

Without adequate salaries, professionals would be hard pressed to perform their best-quality work. The gulf between the industrialized nations and the developing countries with regard to salaries is immense. Of course, academics everywhere earn less than people with similar qualifications in the rest of the labor force, but people do not become professors to get rich. Nonetheless, in most industrialized countries, it is possible for academics to achieve a modest middle-class standard of living based on their salaries. With variations by country, discipline, and rank, academic salaries are usually sufficient to live on in the North. In developing countries, however, with rare exceptions, this is not the case.

In many developing countries, a full-time academic salary cannot support what is considered to be a middle-class standard of living. This is almost universally the case for junior academics but is also true of senior professors in many countries. Thus, in many countries, academics must hold more than one job. Their main appointments provide a portion of their income, but they must earn additional income from teaching at other universities, consulting, or even holding jobs in business or in service occupations unrelated to their academic work. In many countries, academics provide tutoring or other ancillary teaching in order to boost their income, even when such activities are proscribed by the university. In the industrialized world, professors also take on outside consulting in order to earn extra income. The difference in developing countries is that, without this additional income, academics could not survive, and many cannot be the sole breadwinners in their families.

Salaries do, of course, vary significantly across and within institutions. Private universities often pay higher salaries than public institutions—the majority of academics in developing countries work at public universities. Income is linked to rank, but in some countries professors engaged in research and graduate teaching can earn higher salaries. In a few countries, professors receive additional payment for publications and other evidence of academic productivity. In Mexico there is an elite cadre of research-active professors who receive additional remuneration in recognition for their work. Salaries tend to be higher at the most prestigious institutions, in business schools, and other specialized schools. In some countries, academic salaries are not paid regularly, placing great strains on the affected academics, civil servants, and other public officials. The many part-time professors earn much less than full-time professors, in some cases just a token payment.

As a general rule, the low academic salaries in developing countries are unlikely to improve. Salary structure produces a significant impact, as the poor salary levels have led to brain drain. The best scholars and scientists in developing countries can earn many times their local salaries by relocating to the North, and many take this option. Few academics in developing countries are able to devote their full attention to their academic work because of the need to supplement their incomes. Thus, an academic career in the Third World is less than a full-time occupation, even for academics who hold regular full-time positions. This has negative consequences for research and academic productivity, generally. When combined with the structural impediments discussed earlier, it is hardly surprising that the research productivity of academics in developing countries is so low. Salary structure also negatively affects morale.

Future Prospects

This overview of the academic profession in developing countries has provided a generally gloomy perspective. Although the outlook for improvement is not promising, some specific changes may enhance morale, productivity, and, perhaps most importantly, the quality of universities and other academic institutions. These suggestions are not complex—in some instances stating the obvious—but implementation will be a challenge in many countries.

- Adequate salaries and a stable career path should be provided to at least a key segment of the professoriate that holds full-time positions at the main universities.
- At the top academic institutions, university facilities need to be

upgraded sufficiently so that the most-well-qualified professors are able to pursue research and offer excellence in teaching.

- Procedures for involving the professoriate, along with administrators (and in some cases students), in academic decision making are essential to ensure that the academic staff have a significant role in the governance of the institution.
- In some countries, the academic profession must be depoliticized—this would involve links between political parties and academics, close ties between the professoriate and student activists, and the partisan nature of academic decision making and elections.
- Academic freedom must finally become a recognized part of university life, with guarantees protecting freedoms regarding research and publications, teaching, and reasonable expression in the public sphere.
- The academic profession itself must develop a sense of responsibility with regard to expression and publication, especially on controversial topics.
- The academic profession must receive adequate training—the doctorate, for those involved in research as well as teaching; the master's degree, for those who are exclusively teachers; and for all, some exposure to training in pedagogical methods.
- Academics must be provided with the means to keep up with current trends in their fields.
- Great care needs to be taken to ensure that part-time and temporary academic staff are well qualified and provided with appropriate benefits.

Conclusion

This chapter has presented an almost unremittingly pessimistic picture of the current state of the academic profession in developing countries. Yet, what is surprising is that so many people who are working in higher education institutions freely chose the academic life and persevere under difficult circumstances. Fortunately, academic work in developing countries does have many rewarding aspects. Scholars are generally held in high regard, and a professorship, even if poorly paid, is an occupation with high status. Learning is respected, and those who possess knowledge are held in high esteem. Despite the circumstances described here, university life holds considerable attraction. It is, after all, the life of the mind, and those who are inspired to heed the call for intellectual pursuits will put up with many hardships to pursue an academic career.

Yet, as is clear from this analysis, the profession is truly in crisis. The continued deterioration in the conditions of the professoriate has not only had a negative impact on one of the most highly educated and potentially productive segments of the population but has also weakened higher education as well, since academic institutions cannot perform well without a committed, well-trained, and stable academic profession. In the context of globalization, developing countries require access to the wider world of science and technology, and the academic profession represents a central link to the international knowledge network. As the primary educator of future generations, the academic profession is in many ways the linchpin of development.

References

Altbach, Philip G. 1998. Gigantic peripheries: India and China in the world knowledge system. In *Comparative higher education: Knowledge, the university and development*, 133–46. Greenwich, CT: Ablex.

———. 2002. How are faculty faring in other countries? In *The questions of tenure*, ed. Richard P. Chait, 160–81. Cambridge, MA: Harvard University Press.

Boyer, Ernest L, Philip G. Altbach, and Mary Jean Whitelaw. 1994. *The academic profession: An international perspective*. Princeton, NJ: Carnegie Foundation for the Advancement of Teaching.

Castells, Manuel. 2000. *The rise of the network society*. Oxford: Blackwell.

Choi, Hyaeweol. 1995. *An international scientific community: Asian scholars in the United States*. Westport, CT: Praeger.

Clark, Burton R. 1987. *The academic life: Small worlds, different worlds*. Princeton, NJ: Carnegie Foundation for the Advancement of Teaching.

Crystal, David. 1997. *English as a global language*. Cambridge: Cambridge University Press.

Evans, G. R. 2002. *Academics and the real world*. Buckingham, UK: Open University Press.

Geiger, Roger. 2004. *Knowledge and money: Research universities and the paradox of the marketplace*. Stanford, CA: Stanford University Press.

Gilbert, Irene. 1972. The Indian academic profession: The origins of a tradition of subordination. *Minerva* 10:384–411.

Jayaram, N. 2003. The fall of the guru: The decline of the academic profession in India. In *The decline of the Guru: The academic profession in developing and middle-income countries*, ed. Philip G. Altbach, 199–230. New York: Palgrave.

Scott, Peter, ed. 1998. *The globalization of higher education*. Buckingham, UK: Open University Press.

Shils, Edward. 1972. Metropolis and province in the intellectual community. In *The intellectuals and the powers and other essays*, 355–71. Chicago: University of Chicago Press.

Task Force on Higher Education and Society. 2000. *Higher education in developing countries: Peril and promise*. Washington, DC: World Bank.

Teferra, Damtew. 2003. *Scientific communication in African universities: External assistance and national needs*. New York: RoutledgeFalmer.

Teferra, Damtew, and Philip G. Altbach. 2002. Trends and perspectives in African higher education. In *African higher education: An international reference handbook*, ed. D. Teferra and P. G. Altbach, 3–14. Bloomington: Indiana University Press.

8

The Deterioration of the Academic Estate: International Patterns of Academic Work

Despite their common roots in medieval Europe and the mission of teaching and research, universities have evolved quite different patterns of organization and structure. While academics worldwide teach, and in some cases have a role in research and institutional governance, their terms of employment and working conditions vary considerably. This chapter discusses the following questions: How have increased enrollments, diversified faculties, and reduced funding impacted higher education worldwide? What changes are taking place internationally with respect to tenure, academic freedom, types of appointments, and faculty salaries? And, finally, what do the evolving, and largely deteriorating, conditions of faculty work ultimately mean for the global academic enterprise?

The professoriate has become a large and complex profession—with at 3.5 million professionals involved in postsecondary teaching worldwide, serving more than 80 million students (Task Force on Higher Education and Society 2000). The professoriate sits at the heart of the academic enterprise. Without a committed faculty, no university can succeed and provide effective teaching and learning. Yet, despite the great presence of higher education in the technological world of the 21st century, the academic profession finds itself under increasing pressure. Working conditions have deteriorated as traditional values of academic autonomy has diminished. Increased enrollments have not been accompanied by commensurate growth in faculty appointments or salaries. At present, there are unprecedented changes taking place in the terms of appointment, working conditions, and management of the academic profession. It is an opportune time to look at how the professoriate is changing internationally.

The Context

While the professoriate necessarily works within contemporary realities and within institutional and national settings, it is tied to universal historical traditions. The academic profession's conservative views of the university result from a sense of history. Most universities possess common roots in the medieval University of Paris and other European universities of the period (Ben David and Zloczower 1962). Ideas about the autonomy of teaching and research, the rightful place of the professoriate in institutional governance, and the role of the academic profession in society have existed for centuries and continue to have salience. Academics have always perceived themselves as standing apart from society, with special privileges and responsibilities, which has led to the concept of the academic profession as a calling. Many academic traditions have ebbed as universities have developed and become more professionalized. But there is still a historical residue of academic traditions that remains relevant.

Higher education exists in both a national and international context. The many national variations in the organization and management of academe are accompanied by an important international element. Academe's common historical roots, along with contemporary forces, are making higher education ever more influenced by global trends. Perhaps more than at any time since the Middle Ages, when universities functioned in a common language (Latin) and both faculty and students were highly mobile, academe operates in a global environment. Now, English is in some ways the Latin of the new era. There is again an international labor market for the professoriate, and more than one million students are studying outside their own countries. New regulations concerning comparability of degrees in the European Union and the ease of communication and the establishment of joint-degree and other collaborative programs among universities in different countries illustrate the increasing globalism in higher education.

Contemporary Realities

In higher education, the central event of the past half century has been expansion. In country after country, higher education, once the preserve of the elite, has been transformed into a mass, and now almost universal, phenomenon (Trow 1972). This massification has given rise to more diverse and powerful administrative structures and diminished the sense of community among the professoriate. Increasingly, academics work in large organizations and are constrained by bureaucratic procedures.

Now that higher education institutions have diversified, academe is no longer a preserve of the elite. Most academic systems now contain institutions with a variety of missions. Universities themselves now vary more in the level of academic quality. Today, postsecondary education is comprised of a diversity of institutional types—including vocationally oriented community colleges, polytechnic schools, undergraduate colleges, and specialized schools in both the public and private sectors. The traditional ideal, and self-concept, of the professor is no longer valid for the academic profession as a whole. Diversification of institutions has meant diversification of the professoriate as well.

Patterns of institutional control vary considerably from country to country. The United States is unusual for its decentralized higher education system. In contrast, throughout Europe, and much of the rest of the world as well, academic systems are much more tied to the central government, both in terms of control and financing. In addition, higher education is almost exclusively public. This means that the terms and conditions of academic work, including salary scales (which are often tied to pay scales in the civil service), patterns of appointment and promotion, and others are in many cases determined by government policy. Professors have traditionally valued their autonomy—the ability to control not only what happens in the classroom but also to determine the substance of their work. Few occupations have enjoyed the same level of freedom the professoriate enjoys to control the use of their time and the focus and range of productivity. In Europe, particularly, the ideals of professional autonomy, combined with academic freedom in the classroom and laboratory, have been hallmarks of the professoriate and remain primary values of the profession.

Traditionally, very little accountability was built into academic work. To this day, in much of the world, evaluation of teaching remains rare, and tracking faculty performance in research and other academic duties is not rigorous. Moreover, most academics around the world are not paid based on any concept of merit or productivity, but rather by rank and seniority. Again, this pattern is slowly changing as accountability and assessment become more entrenched. However, the fact is that academics have been trusted to perform at an acceptable level of competence and productivity for centuries without any serious measurement of academic work. Now, accountability is entering the vocabulary of academic life. As higher education consumes more resources because of expansion, government and private funders demand greater accountability. A culture of accountability has emerged and affected the academic profession. In many countries, assessment of academic work is becoming common practice, with evaluation of teaching, research, service, and administrative work all part of the new academic workplace in more institutions.

In many countries, fiscal constraints on higher education have had a negative impact on the professoriate. Even in the United States, Britain, and other countries with currently favorable economic climates, higher education has not generally benefited from increased support. Student enrollments have risen faster than the size of the teaching staff. Funds, usually from public sources, have not supported the costs of expansion. The working conditions of academe have suffered, with increasing class size and deteriorating facilities. Academic salaries have largely not kept up with inflation or with salaries in related occupations. The financial problems faced by universities in industrialized countries stem from public policies concerning higher education rather than underlying economic difficulties. In Britain, for example, fiscal cutbacks have occurred at the same time that student numbers have increased. In Germany, students have protested against deteriorating conditions of study caused by inadequate funding.

The fiscal crisis has hit developing and middle-income countries differently, with such regions as sub-Saharan Africa especially affected because of the combination of expanding enrollments and economic and political crises. India, chronically strapped for funds and with expansion continuing, has for several decades seen declines in the quality of higher education. The transitional economies of Central and Eastern Europe and the former Soviet Union have experienced pressures for expanded access while at the same time facing the challenges of economic transformation. Very few countries, rich or poor, can claim favorable economic circumstances for postsecondary education.

In most countries, problems abound in the employment market for academics. With fewer career-track positions available, new entrants to the profession face difficulties in obtaining full-time appointments. Promotions have become more problematical, and many countries have imposed quotas on promotions to senior ranks. This means that many faculty are kept in poorly paid junior positions under poor working conditions. Although many senior professors hired in the 1960s and 1970s are now retiring, they are often not being replaced by full-time junior staff. In many countries, a surplus of disaffected doctoral degree holders exists, many of whom take jobs outside of academe. Some exceptions to this bleak picture exist—for example, fields such as computer science or management studies offer good academic employ-ment prospects. While nations differ greatly in terms of the academic employment market, in no country does the system offer ample prospects for either junior staff or promotion opportunities for senior professors.

The professoriate has come in for some criticism. Popular maga-zines such as Germany's *Der Spiegel* have printed articles highly critical of German professors. A number of books published in the United States claim that professors do not work hard enough and have too much autonomy (Anderson 1992; Sykes 1988). However, there is no groundswell of popular discontent with higher education or with the professoriate evident anywhere. Still, the professoriate has lost some of its luster as a profession in recent years, although most sociological studies of occupational prestige show that academics continue to rank among the most highly esteemed groups in society.

Appointments, Promotions, and Tenure

Academic appointments are at present undergoing a period of consid-erable ferment and change. For purposes of analysis, it may be useful to consider systems that offer the equivalent of tenure, or permanent appointment of academics, as well as those that do not. Despite the nonuniversality of permanent appointments, considerable stability exists in academic careers even without formal guarantees. Traditionally, in many countries, academics hired in the lowest rank after finishing graduate studies were "confirmed" after two or three years of satisfactory performance, without undergoing a major evalua-tion. Confirmation meant either a de jure or de facto assurance of per-manent appointment. Until Margaret Thatcher's reforms in the 1980s, British universities worked this way. Confirmation as a lectur-er did not guarantee promotion, but it did assure a permanent position at that rank.

Now that tenure has been abolished in the United Kingdom, the sit-uation has changed. Current British arrangements are worth examin-ing, since other countries have looked to them as models. Permanent tenure for academic staff at Britain's universities was abolished for sev-eral reasons. One of the key objectives was ending the binary system, with its distinctions between the traditional universities and the voca-tionally oriented polytechnics. The latter sector did not have the right to confer academic degrees and never had a formalized tenure system. The polytechnics were upgraded to university status, and the terms of academic appointments in the reformed system reflected the preexist-ing practices at the polytechnics.

The Thatcher administration introduced external accountability into teaching and research and encouraged competition among academic institutions and individual academics. Measures were established for periodic evaluations of both teaching and research and the ranking of institutions. These rankings have implications for budgetary allocations as well as research emphasis (Schuller 1991). Now, British academics at all ranks hold term appointments with periodic evaluation and reappointment procedures. This arrangement is not unlike proposals for post-tenure review in the United States; terms of appointment are generally around five years and evaluation seldom lead to the loss of a position, although no guarantees are included of continuing appointments in British higher education. The professoriate working at traditional British universities strongly opposed the changes, but in the end the reforms were reluctantly accepted and caused neither major unrest nor disruption of academic life (Halsey 1992; Farnham 1999). In fact, few individuals lost their positions, and academe continued without major structural change. Academics holding positions at the time of the changes kept their tenure so long as they were not promoted or did not take a position at another university (Evans 1999). Most observers see the abolition of tenure as more of a symbolic loss than a practical one.

In the United States, tenure is awarded by individual academic institutions, rather than by government authorities or university systems. At least in the upper tier, the American tenure system has one of the most rigorous processes for evaluation and consideration of junior faculty anywhere in the world. The "six-year-up-or-out" process of evaluation provides for careful review of each candidate for tenure. Tenure can be abrogated by the university for reasons of financial exigency, program reorganization, or other institutional issues. Holders of tenure can also be terminated for specific dereliction of their responsibilities or for violations of university policy. While abrogation of tenure is quite unusual in the United States, it is by no means unprecedented.

In Europe, tenure has different legal and institutional roots and provides stronger guarantees to those who hold it. In much of Western Europe—including Germany, Italy, France, and Spain—tenure is a right granted to senior members of the civil service as a result of their appointments. University professors as well as most civil servants are protected (Mora 2000). Professors are also paid according to civil service scales, and there is little variation in salaries through the academic system. Under German law, *Beamte* status, for example, provides iron-clad job security regardless of financial or other problems facing the university, including program abolition or reorganization (Enders

2000a). In France, the faculty's civil service status protects senior academics at all universities. Faculty members may be, but seldom are, transferred from one university to another, but they cannot be fired. Along with the guarantees of employment and other rights, civil service appointments are highly valued in societies where they have traditionally been symbolic of elite status. Not surprisingly, senior academic staff fiercely guard their civil service appointments. Countries with this system have been slow to change due in considerable part to the opposition of the academic profession.

Senior academics still have significant prestige as well as power in society. In Italy, for example, many senior academics serve in Parliament, and several have been prime ministers. French professors and secondary school teachers constitute a significant proportion of the national assembly and have traditionally enjoyed considerable influence (Chevaillier 2000).

Tenure is given to senior members of the professoriate, and appointments to senior faculty positions are carefully monitored and competitively awarded. Senior academics in those European countries with a civil service system have the strongest guarantees of tenure and job security—until the age of compulsory retirement—of any faculty members in the world. Certain other academics are given permanent contracts as well. The proportion of academics with permanent contracts varies among European countries. For example, in Germany and Finland, the proportion of tenured staff stands at between 40 and 50 percent. In Austria, the Flemish parts of Belgium, the Netherlands, Norway, and Spain, between 50 and 60 percent are tenured; in France and Ireland, 80 percent; and in Italy, 90 percent (Enders 2000b, 16). At present, there are discussions concerning abolition or modification of civil service appointments for academics, but so far only the Netherlands, in the mid-1990s, has changed the system. Professors and other academic staff are now appointed directly by the universities and are no longer part of the state service.

In general, appointments in senior faculty ranks take place in Europe after considerable scrutiny of the individuals. In some countries, such as Germany, appointments to senior professorships come only after national searches. The American pattern of promoting junior academics up the ranks differs from the pattern in much of Europe, where a wide gulf exists between junior positions and senior professorships. The American system provides more continuity. In some European countries, a junior appointee commonly enjoys the security of tenure, but without guaranteed promotion.

At Japan's public universities, and many of the private institutions as well, employment arrangements are procedurally somewhat less secure than is the case in Europe, although full-time academic jobs in Japan are basically permanent. As in Europe, promotion up the academic ranks in Japanese higher education is more difficult, in part because of the rigid "chair" system that permits just one very powerful full professor for each department. While it has become more open, the system is criticized for the lack of accountability and assessment as well as for the difficulties that faculty members have in proceeding up the career ladder. The Japanese appointment system works, in part because it is so similar to the employment pattern in the rest of society. Faculty members, recognizing the likelihood of lifelong employment at a single university.

In China, much as in Japan, academic staff receive permanent appointments at the time of hiring to a regular faculty position, regardless of rank. Academics have job security until the age of retirement. Full-time academics are rarely removed from their positions for any reason, although in a small number of instances individuals have been fired for involvement in dissident political activity. Despite low academic salaries, by international standards, many Chinese faculty members traditionally received subsidized housing on campus, access to low-cost food, and other benefits. The situation is rapidly changing both on campus and in society as the economy becomes more market oriented. For example, faculty members have had to purchase their apartments from the universities, and newly hired professors do not usually receive housing.

The Latin American pattern of academic appointments stands in sharp contrast to that of continental Europe. Tenure, as it is known in Europe and North America, does not exist in most of Latin America. The academic profession is sharply divided between part-time instructors, who are paid a modest fee to teach a course or two and constitute the majority of those teaching throughout Latin America, and the minority of full-time faculty. Full-time faculty are responsible for the governance of the university. They are appointed and have their contracts renewed on the basis of periodic "contests" in public institutions. Academic posts are publicly announced, applicants are considered, and one candidate is chosen. Renewal of appointments is on the basis of a further "contest," which is announced and open to anyone. The incumbent may have to compete against other applicants. This system was established as a result of the reform movements of 1918 in Latin America to ensure the objectivity of academic appointments and a democratic environment in the universities. With the expansion of higher education, the system no longer works well in many countries, resulting in less frequent reliance on "contests," which are both expensive and time consuming. The actual turnover rate in the senior academic ranks is in fact very low. Types of appointments in the growing private sector in Latin America vary but rarely include permanent appointments.

Many countries in Latin America and Asia have "de facto" tenure arrangements. Even in higher education systems without formal tenure, most full-time academics spend their careers in a single institution. The legal or contractual guarantees in Europe and North America do not constitute standard practice elsewhere. In South Korea, India, and a number of other Asian countries, for example, while it is presumed academics will have lifelong full-time positions, only limited procedural guarantees exist. Few individuals are terminated, even when academic institutions face difficult challenges. In India, faculty members at the undergraduate colleges, who make up the large majority of the profession, do express fear of possible dismissal by management even though few are actually fired.

Academic Freedom
In much of the world, little legal protection of academic freedom is offered in the form of meaningful employment guarantees. Nonetheless, a 14-country study found that faculty members felt fairly confident about their academic freedom (Altbach and Lewis 1996, 31). During periods of political crisis, academic freedom is frequently violated, especially where traditions of autonomy and academic freedom are not well developed. Examples include China in the aftermath of the events at Tienanmen Square, Serbia and Croatia during ethnic and civil conflicts, and Indonesia during the Suharto dictatorship (Human Rights Watch 1998). Conditions have since improved markedly in these countries. In much of the Middle East, academics feel constrained from freely expressing their views or engaging in research on sensitive topics. Similar constraints exist in some African countries. In Ethiopia government pressure on professors resulted in some dismissals, and the jailing of faculty members at Addis Ababa University. In Singapore and Malaysia academic researchers, especially in the social sciences, feel pressured not to do research on sensitive topics such as ethnic relations. During the 1950s, the United States, which has a strong tradition of protecting academic freedom and a recognition of the connection between tenure and academic freedom, experienced problems in this area during the McCarthy anticommunist period. A small number of faculty members were fired for political reasons, and many people feared that the tradition of academic freedom

was being threatened (Schrecker 1986). Academic freedom disappeared in Germany during the Nazi period and was greatly restricted in the former Soviet Union and Central and Eastern Europe during the communist era.

Despite occasional problems, academic freedom in Western industrialized countries is secure. Faculty members are usually free to conduct research, express their views in the classroom, and participate in public debates on topics relating to their areas and expertise on broader social and political issues. Academic freedom is defined more narrowly in many parts of the world than is the case in the United States. Since the end of the 19th century, the American ideal of academic freedom has encompassed the classroom, laboratory, and public arena. The more restrictive European concept stems from the Humboldtian commitment to freedom of teaching and research within the university and areas of faculty specialization (Shils 1991). These disparities in definitions and traditions complicate the making of direct comparisons. Nonetheless, academic freedom has now evolved into a more robust form in Central and Eastern Europe, although there are problems in Belarus and some backsliding in Russia. Several of the former Soviet central Asian countries do not have much academic freedom. While frequently violated during periods of political unrest, the idea that professors deserve considerable freedom of research and expression in the classroom and laboratory is gaining acceptance, even in parts of the world where the concept is not entrenched.

In few countries does academic freedom play a role in formulating the terms and conditions of academic appointments. The United States is, in fact, one of the few countries where the system focuses on academic freedom. Elsewhere, tenure and other aspects of appointments follow employment practices, civil service procedures, and other administrative policies. The fate of academic freedom is not seen as being linked to the terms and conditions of professorial appointments.

A worldwide survey of academic freedom would likely produce a diverse set of results. In much of the world, restrictions are placed on academic freedom, both in the classroom and laboratory and even more in the public forum. In much of the world, progress has been documented, but one might estimate that one-third of the professoriate feels some restrictions, and in a few countries the situation remains perilous. Unfortunately, no one monitors the state of academic freedom.

Appointment Trends
In response to the pressures referred to earlier—budgetary problems,

accountability, changing patterns of enrollments, and so on—academic hiring has changed to a considerable degree. Most importantly, diverse types of appointments to teaching and research posts have been introduced. The development with the greatest impact on the academic profession is the growing percentage of academic staff without permanent appointments, even in countries that retain tenure arrangements, and the greater use of part-time teachers. The two most common worldwide trends are the growth in part-time appointments and the expansion or creation of full-time, nontenured posts that have specific time limits.

In the United States, it is estimated that less than half the new appointments are now on the tenure track. A growing proportion of classes are taught by part-time teachers (Schuster and Finkelstein 2006). Latin American higher education has traditionally been dominated by part-time faculty, and, despite a consensus that greater numbers of full-time staff will raise academic standards in universities and create a research culture, little has changed. Part-time teaching is less entrenched in other parts of the world, although the phenomenon is growing as institutions struggle to cope with ever-expanding enrollments and inadequate funding from government.

Part-time faculty provide some advantages to higher education. They are typically professionals experienced in their fields and able to bring practical knowledge and experience to their teaching. Especially valuable in applied fields where links between theory and practice are central, these faculty may be able to guide students toward the knowledge that will be useful in obtaining jobs after graduation. Part-time staff are always much less expensive to employ than full-time staff, receiving only modest stipends for their teaching, often at an hourly rate of remuneration and, with no other benefits. With no commitment to part-time staff, the university has complete flexibility in hiring. As dictated by budgets, curricular interests, and student demand, adjustments can be made in the number and specializations of the part-time teachers. Part-time staff seldom get offices or laboratory space, thus saving scarce university resources.

The disadvantages, often overlooked, are also significant. Part-time faculty have a minimal commitment to their institutions. These faculty simply teach their classes and leave, which is why in Latin America they are referred to as "taxicab" professors. Part-timers do not participate in research and are not involved in campus or departmental governance. Further, they are unlikely to be knowledgeable about current intellectual trends or research in their fields. They seldom have links to the increasingly important world of international scholarship and do not participate in the knowledge networks in their fields. The implications are especially severe for research-oriented universities, where the need for full-time researchers is especially strong, but even postsecondary institutions not much engaged in research will feel the negative implications of an overreliance on part-time staff.

Part-time faculty lack the opportunity to be fully involved in an academic community. In most universities, existing rules do not permit this, and in any case the time commitments of part-timers preclude such engagement. It is difficult, if not impossible, to build an academic institution or culture on the basis of part-time faculty, nor is it possible to develop a research base.

In a way, academic systems that rely increasingly on part-time staff, including the United States, are becoming "Latin Americanized." The realities of higher education in much of Latin America provide a disconcerting look into what may lie ahead for universities, and for individual teaching staff, if part-time employment becomes the dominant model. With a few exceptions—such as Campinas University in São Paulo, Brazil—which has a high proportion of full-time professors—universities do not produce much research. Universities offer low-cost instruction to large numbers of students.

The new private universities, which now absorb a majority of enrollments in a growing number of Latin American countries, including Brazil and Chile, rely mainly on part-time faculty to save money. Their budgets do not, in general, permit the appointment of many full-time professors. Analysts in Latin America have pointed out that fully effective universities can emerge only when a critical mass of full-time faculty are appointed, creating a cadre of academics who work in the disciplines, engage in the governance of the university, and attend to the development of both teaching and research (Albornoz 1991).

Alternative Appointment Patterns
One of the most dramatic systemic changes in terms of academic appointments took place in Britain in the 1980s, when the traditional tenure system was abolished for new entrants to the profession (Shattock 2000). The other European country that has undergone the most comprehensive change in academic appointments is the Netherlands, where professorial appointments were taken devolved from the government onto the universities, annulling the civil service status of the professoriate (de Weert 2000). This significant change in the legal basis of appointments increased the universities' power to make their own decisions. However, the working conditions and terms of appointment of the professoriate changed very little.

The more predominant trend has been toward the appointment of full-time academic staff not eligible for permanent positions. In continental Europe, this category of appointment has existed for more than a century, as codified in the German Humboldtian university model in the early 19th century. The Humboldtian chair system, while modified in recent years, remains the central organizational principle of academic appointments in Germany. The chair system is rigidly based on seniority, elevating one senior professor as the chairholder in each discipline. Junior staff hold term appointments and cannot proceed up the ranks at a single university to a professorship. Rather, they must compete for available openings at other universities; or on the completion of their term appointments, they must move on to a similar position elsewhere.

In Germany, 72 percent of the teaching staff are on limited-term appointments without professorial rank and without tenure—the greater portion on full-time contracts. Nonprofessorial appointees commonly do not have the possibility of promotion up the ranks to a tenured professorship. Most of these appointees must complete a second research-based dissertation (the *Habilitation*) and then compete for the few available professorial positions, but not at the university where they earned their *Habilitation*. These academic employees, many of whom have completed their *Habilitation*, have limited-term appointments. Although their contracts may be extended by the university, these junior staff cannot expect to be promoted without moving to another institution This forced mobility creates a high degree of instability in the German academic system.

In a recent liberalization in the structure of senior professorial ranks, several new ranks have been added and at least the possibility exists of having more than one senior professor in a department or discipline. Yet, the system remains hierarchical, with a great divide between the senior professors, who have completed the *Habilitation* and hold civil service rank, and the rest of the teaching and research staff. While there has been some discussion of modifying or even eliminating the *Habilitation*, there has been no change so far in this requirement. Most academic systems in Central and Eastern Europe followed the German chair model. The Japanese national universities also retain the chair system, with a rigid hierarchy of academic appointments, although without requiring faculty to move from one university to another (Arimoto 1996). Reforms in the early 2000s are in the process of modifying the appointment system in the national universities.

Some European countries have also coped with rising enrollments and tight budgets by expanding nonprofessorial appointments. Italy recently started to reform its academic system to cope with massification (Moscati 2000). The expansion in student numbers resulted in deteriorating conditions of study, higher dropout rates, and a growing time-to-degree problem. Teacher-student ratios have ballooned to 1:30, despite recent reforms permitting research appointees (who have limited-term positions) to teach. The tradition that reserved control over teaching and design of courses for senior professors has recently been modified. The ranks of full and associate professors have been expanded as well, especially at the bottom where there are no permanent appointments.

France has tried a somewhat different approach to deal with rising enrollments. Rather than stock the universities with temporary staff, the Ministry of Education transferred large numbers of secondary school teachers to universities to provide instruction in the courses. Since both secondary and tertiary teaching staff share civil servant status and have similar academic credentials, this arrangement has been widely accepted. Secondary school teachers are accorded considerable respect in French society. Moreover, academic secondary schools provide instruction at a level not dissimilar from that in the first year or two of university. It is possible to shift teachers back to secondary education if they are no longer needed in the universities.

Worldwide, higher education systems are increasing the number of junior staff appointments that lack the prestige, job security, career track, and perquisites of the traditional professorship. These appointments often specify a term of appointment that may or may not be extended. A kind of caste system has evolved, with the senior professoriate at the top and growing numbers of proletarian part-time and term-appointed full-time staff below. The proportion of upper-caste senior academics is decreasing, as institutions alter their hiring policies in response to fiscal and other pressures.

Remuneration Levels
Traditionally, the full-time professoriate could expect a salary guaranteeing its members a middle- or upper-middle-class standard of living. While few people enter the academic profession to reap great financial rewards, they do expect to earn an appropriate middle-class salary. The 1994 14-country Carnegie study of the academic profession found that most academics (except for respondents from Hong Kong) were dissatisfied with their salaries, with large majorities of respondents in all of the countries describing the levels as only fair or poor (Altbach and Lewis 1996, 10). The professoriate in the industrialized countries still commands a middle-class salary, although academic salaries vary wide-

ly. Academic salaries have not kept up with inflation or with comparable salaries in the private sector. For much of the rest of the world, salary levels have deteriorated to the extent that remuneration no longer supports a middle-class lifestyle.

Across Europe, pay scales for the highest professorial ranks differ considerably by country. In absolute terms, without taking relative costs of living into account, the highest salaries are paid in Belgium, Italy, and the Netherlands, followed by France, Germany, and Ireland. The lowest top levels of remuneration are found in Finland, Portugal, and Spain. Salaries in Norway, Sweden, and the United Kingdom are considered relatively low and/or declining. In these countries, there is considerable discontent among academic staff (Enders 2000b). A 2000 article encouraged British academics to earn extra money by "moonlighting" through consultancies, evaluating manuscripts, and related income-producing activities (Sutherland 2000, 20). In Japan, academic salaries at the national universities seem to be similar to mid-range European countries, with a number of the well-established private universities paying somewhat more. For comparison, the average salary for full professors in American doctoral-level universities is considerably higher than in almost all European countries ("More Good News" 2000, 25).

Salaries vary within countries by seniority, rank, type of institution, and other factors. In Western Europe, it is estimated that the widest internal variations can be found in Austria, France, Germany, and Ireland; the lowest starting salaries for academics in these countries are about half as much as the highest senior salaries. In contrast, salary differentials are relatively flat in Finland, Norway, Portugal, and the United Kingdom (Enders 2000b, 18). In the United States salary differentials are similar to those of European countries with the greatest gaps—when instructors and assistant professors are included.

The highest academic salaries in the world are found in Europe, North America, and Australia. Some exceptions exist, such as Hong Kong, Singapore, and a few of the Arabian Gulf states. Yet, even countries with well-developed university systems and relatively high income levels—such as South Korea, Taiwan, Argentina, and Malaysia—have lower levels of academic remuneration. Throughout Latin America, the small number of full-time professors barely earn enough from their university jobs to maintain middle-class social status. In most of the region, academic salaries for senior professors are frequently only one-third of average levels in Europe, and while the cost of living may be somewhat lower, it by no means fully compensates for the difference. Typically, professors in Latin America and much of the rest of the developing world must supplement their academic salaries through consulting, additional teaching, or other remunerative activity.

The situation in South Asia is worse, especially for the large majority of teachers at undergraduate colleges. Indian academics have, however, seen several increases in salaries in recent years, and college teachers with reasonable seniority can aspire to a middle-class life style. Professors in university departments do better financially. Salary increments are awarded on the basis of seniority, and there is little, if any, performance evaluation.

Most Chinese academics are full-time, and while academic salaries are quite low by international standards, most teaching and research staff were traditionally provided with housing and other benefits that, to an extent, offset the low pay. In the past decade, universities have cut back or eliminated these perquisites, creating financial problems for the academic profession. While incentives were provided to purchase apartments, neither benefits nor salaries have kept up with China's economic growth and increasing prosperity, with the result that Chinese academics must do consulting, teach in the new private institutions, or in other ways supplement their income. While salary increases were traditionally based on seniority, new performance measures have been introduced.

Academic salaries in much of Africa, which at one time provided middle-class status, are no longer adequate. Indeed, the deterioration of salaries has contributed to an exodus of the best scholars on the continent. Others moonlight in the new private sector or do consulting for international organizations or private businesses. In the transitional economies of Central and Eastern Europe and Russia, academic salaries have not kept up with the cost of living, and no longer provide adequate remuneration. Many people have left academe, while others have taken jobs abroad, and fewer of the brightest young people are attracted to the professoriate.

Throughout the world, academic salaries have failed to keep pace with inflation or with rising incomes in other professions. Even in the United States, where remuneration has generally grown slightly faster than inflation for the past seven years, academic salaries have nonetheless remained stagnant over the past three decades (Bell 1999, 20). In Western Europe, academic salaries, which were acceptable while a small professoriate served an elite student population, are adequate but no longer considered attractive. Wherever academic salaries cannot compete with those in other sectors, higher education struggles to attract and retain the best minds and talent.

The emerging international academic job market causes academic salaries and working conditions in one country to have an impact in other marketplaces. Despite inadequate statistics, evidence exists of a substantial flow of academics across national borders—a trend likely to continue. The world of science and scholarship has always been an international one, and the growing use of English as the primary language of academic discourse enhances this sense of an international academic community. European Union regulations requiring degree recognition have eased mobility within the EU. Differences in the availability of laboratory and research facilities, salary structures, terms and conditions of appointments, and academic freedom, among other factors, may stimulate academics to seek better positions in other countries.

Patterns of migration are evident, with a trend from the developing countries in the South to the industrialized North. This has caused extreme imbalances in some cases—for example, it is estimated that as many highly trained African scholars are working in the North as in Africa itself, representing a serious loss of academic talent. Likewise, many scientists from such countries as India, Pakistan, and Taiwan have made their careers working elsewhere. The United States, Canada, and Australia have received an influx of academic talent from Europe, and especially from the United Kingdom.

Salary levels and other issues relating to remuneration have a substantial effect on the academic profession. In China, the government's effort to make the universities more self-sufficient meant that professors were asked to do consulting and engage in a range of nonteaching activities. Especially at the top-ranking universities, academic culture has been affected, and professors spend more time and energy on nonuniversity activities. The government's goal is to encourage the professors to generate a portion of their income instead of paying them more. Latin American professors, even those with full-time appointments, must find additional income elsewhere. The fact is that academic salaries have deteriorated worldwide, and there is no sign of a reversal of this trend.

Conclusion

This chapter has presented an overview of the terms and conditions of academic work in an international context. A number of trends emerge from this analysis. A gradual change has occurred in the nature of academic appointments. The traditional idea of the professor who holds a lifelong job focused on teaching and research and carries a responsibility for institutional governance, is giving way to changes. Despite the changes, a commitment to permanent or at least long-term academic appointments remains. However, fewer new full-time, permanent appointments are being made, and limited-term categories and more part-time positions are being created.

Accountability and assessment of academic work are slowly becoming part of the academic career. The specific measurement of academic performance, particularly research and teaching, is central. Although these policies have attracted great interest, it is surprising how limited their actual implication has been worldwide.

The traditional power of the senior faculty over the governance of the university has diminished. More authority now resides with external bodies, governing boards that are no longer dominated by professors, and other arrangements.

In a few countries, such as the United Kingdom and the Netherlands, systemic reforms have included significant modifications of the traditional terms and conditions of academic appointments and academic work. It is likely that other countries will eventually implement changes of similar scope. For example, whether to continue the civil service status of the academic profession is now under discussion in several European countries. The conditions of academic work are worsening. Salaries are not keeping pace with inflation, promotion is becoming more difficult, accountability places more restraints on the traditional autonomy of the profession, and academic facilities in many countries are inadequate.

Even after the reforms, the essential structure of academic appointments is unlikely to be altered in any revolutionary way. The academic ranking system will remain, although new titles and nomenclature are being introduced in some places. Full-time professorial appointments, with job security, will remain the "gold standard," although it is likely that fewer academics will achieve this level.

In their organization, higher education institutions and systems and the academic profession are moving in a somewhat "American" direction. Having developed the first mass comprehensive higher education system, the United States has provided a model that other countries have carefully considered. American approaches to academic organization—the course-credit system, the structure of academic ranks, performance-based salaries, periodic review of productivity, and other aspects—are often incorporated into plans for the reform of academic appointments into other countries.

From the perspective of the academic profession, these changes have had an almost entirely negative effect—deterioration of salaries and working conditions, increased bureaucratization, and decreased professional autonomy. Academics worldwide, when asked how they feel about their work, express pessimism. Yet, they feel a strong commitment to the basic elements of the profession—teaching and research (Altbach and Lewis 1996). The challenge will be to ensure that the academic profession is attractive to intelligent and motivated teachers, scholars, and researchers. Paradoxically, at a time when there is universal agreement concerning the importance of higher education for the future of knowledge-based societies, the academic profession finds itself in a beleaguered state.

References

Albornoz, Orlando. 1991. Latin America. In *International higher education: An encyclopedia*, ed. Philip G. Altbach, 853–67. New York: Garland.

Altbach, Philip G., and Lionel Lewis. 1996. The academic profession in international perspective. In *The international academic profession: Portraits of fourteen countries*, ed. Philip G. Altbach, 3–48. Princeton, NJ: Carnegie Foundation for the Advancement of Teaching.

Anderson, Martin. 1992. *Imposters in the temple.* New York: Simon & Schuster.

Arimoto, Akira. 1996. The academic profession in Japan. In *The international academic profession: Portraits of fourteen countries*, ed. Philip G. Altbach, 149–90. Princeton, NJ: Carnegie Foundation for the Advancement of Teaching.

Bell, Linda A. 1999. Ups and downs: academic salaries since the early 1970s. *Academe* 85 (March-April): 12–21.

Ben-David, Joseph, and A. Zloczower. 1962. Universities and academic systems in modern societies. *European Journal of Sociology* 3:45–84.

Chevaillier, Thierry. 2000. French academics between the professions and the civil service. In *The changing academic workplace: Comparative perspectives*, ed. P. G. Altbach, 75–104. Chestnut Hill, MA: Center for International Higher Education, Boston College.

de Weert, Egbert. 2000. Pressures and prospects facing the academic profession in the Netherlands. In *The changing academic workplace: Comparative perspectives*, ed. P. G. Altbach, 105–33. Chestnut Hill, MA: Center for International Higher Education, Boston College.

Enders, Jürgen. 2000a. A chair system in transition: Appointments, promotions, and gate keeping in German higher education. In *The changing academic workplace: Comparative perspectives*, ed. P. G. Altbach, 25–50. Chestnut Hill, MA: Center for International Higher Education, Boston College.

Enders, Jürgen. 2000b. Down by law? Employment and working conditions of academic staff in Europe. Paper presented at the International conference on Employment and Working Conditions of Academic Staff in Europe.

Evans, G. R. 1999. *Calling academe to account: Rights and responsibilities.* Buckingham, UK: Open University Press.

Farnham, David. 1999. The United Kingdom: End of the donnish dominion? In *Managing academic staff in changing university systems: International trends and comparisons*, ed. David Farnham, 209–36. Buckingham, UK: Open University Press.

Halsey, A. H. 1992. *Decline of donnish dominion: The British academic profession in the twentieth century.* Oxford: Clarendon Press.

Human Rights Watch. 1998. *Academic freedom in Indonesia: Dismantling Soeharto-era barriers.* New York: Human Rights Watch.

Mora, José-Ginés. 2000. The academic profession in Spain: Between the civil service and the market. In *The changing academic workplace: Comparative perspectives,* ed. P. G. Altbach, 165–92. Chestnut Hill, MA: Center for International Higher Education, Boston College.

More good news, so why the blues? The annual report on the economic status of the profession, 1999–2000. 2000. Academe 86 (March-April): 12–36.

Moscati, Roberto. 2000. Italian university professors in transition. In *The changing academic workplace: Comparative perspectives,* ed. P. G. Altbach, 133–64. Chestnut Hill, MA: Center for International Higher Education, Boston College.

Neave, Guy, and Gary Rhoades. 1987. The academic estate in Western Europe. In *The academic profession: National, disciplinary and institutional settings,* ed. Burton R. Clark, 211–70. Berkeley: University of California Press.

Schrecker, Ellen W. 1986. *No ivory tower: McCarthyism and the universities.* New York: Oxford University Press.

Schuller, Tom, ed. 1991. *The future of higher education.* Buckingham, UK: Open University Press.

Schuster, Jack H., and Martin J. Finkelstein. 2006. *The American faculty: The restructuring of academic work and careers.* Baltimore: Johns Hopkins University Press.

Shattock, Michael. 2000. The academic profession in Britain: A study in the failure to adapt to change. In *The changing academic workplace: Comparative perspectives,* ed. P. G. Altbach, 51–74. Chestnut Hill, MA: Center for International Higher Education, Boston College.

Shils, Edward. 1991. Academic freedom. In *International higher education: An encyclopedia,* ed. P. G. Altbach, 1–22. New York, Garland.

Sutherland, John. 2000. Double Your Money. *Times Higher Education Supplement,* June 16, 20–21.

Sykes, Charles J. 1988. *ProfScam Professors and the demise of higher education.* Washington, DC: Regenery.

Task Force on Higher Education and Society. 2000. *Higher education in developing countries: Peril and promise.* Washington, DC: World Bank.

Trow, Martin. 1972. The expansion and transformation of higher education. *International Review of Education* 18 (1): 61–83.

Themes and Variations

9

The Past and Future of Asian Universities

Notable in size and diversity, Asia has a majority of the world's population and several of the most dynamic and fast-growing economies—and some of the weakest. In higher education, Asia has not traditionally stood out as a leader in research or innovation. Asia is experiencing massive higher education expansion; indeed, a majority of the world's enrollment growth is taking place in Asia (Altbach and Umakoshi 2004). Further, Asian economies will increasingly require university-trained personnel to ensure the success of sophisticated economies. Research and development will inevitably become more important to Asian countries.

This chapter examines higher education trends in Asia, from India and Pakistan to China and Japan. While Asia's diverse academic systems do not lend themselves to easy generalizations, there are some common elements as well as shared experiences. Many challenges are facing Asian universities in the 21st century, when institutions will need to be part of the international knowledge system and play a central role in meeting national educational requirements. Universities are part of the global system of science and scholarship while at the same time being rooted in their own societies.

This chapter looks at both the potentials and the challenges in broad terms, as it would prove impossible to examine all of Asia in one chapter (Postiglione and Mak 1997). The focus will be on such factors as expansion, competition, and quality, as well as the role of research and the links between higher education and society in the Asian context. The central reality of the period since the 1980s in most Asian countries is expansion and coping with the effects of massification on higher education. Although much of this analysis revolves around the implications of expansion, a few Asian countries, such as Japan, face declining populations and the related problems of likely contraction of the higher education system. Between 1980 and 1995, enrollments in developing countries increased from 28 million to 47 million—a significant part of that growth taking place in Asia (Task Force on Higher Education and Society 2000, 27). Asian higher education will continue to expand rapidly, in large part because some of the largest Asian countries—such as China and India as well as Vietnam, Cambodia, Pakistan, Bangladesh, and several others—now educate relatively small proportions of their young people at the postsecondary level and face immense pressure to meet the popular demand for access and the economic needs of modernizing economies. Vietnam, for example, educates around 6 percent of the university age cohort, while Cambodia has half that proportion in higher education (Task Force on Higher Education and Society 2000, 104–07). India educates around 10 percent. China has recently boosted its enrollment rate to around 20 percent and now has the largest number of students in postsecondary education in the world—having recently passed total US enrollments, although the United States is educating well above half of the relevant age group.

Academic institutions have always been part of the international knowledge system, and in the age of the Internet they are increasingly linked to trends in science and scholarship worldwide. All Asian nations—even the largest and best developed, such as Japan, China, and India—remain largely peripheral internationally (Altbach 1998). The major Western universities retain scientific and research leadership. As Asian universities grow in stature, they will need to function in a highly competitive academic world. All elements of academic life, including research, the distribution of knowledge, students, and the academic profession, are part of an internationally competitive marketplace. Without doubt, the immediate future holds considerable challenges for Asian higher education, as it does for higher education in the rest of the world.

Colonial and Postcolonial Historical Patterns

Contemporary Asian higher education is fundamentally influenced by its historical traditions. No Asian university is truly Asian in origin—all are based on European academic models and traditions, in many cases imposed by colonial rulers and in others (e.g., Japan and Thailand) on voluntarily adopted Western models (Altbach and

Selvaratnam 1989). The fact that all Asian universities began as foreign implants has played a central role in how academic institutions have developed—with regard to academic freedom, institutional autonomy, the relationship of the university to society, and other factors.

It is significant that no Asian country has kept, to any significant extent, its premodern academic institutional traditions. Most Asian countries had pre-Western academic institutions. The Confucian academies in China, the traditional *pathashalas* or *madrasahs* in India, and similar institutions in Vietnam, Cambodia, Thailand, and elsewhere were largely destroyed or abandoned as Asian countries began the process of modernization in the 19th century. In India, for example, British academic practices came to dominate the system, although traditional patterns were never entirely eliminated (Ashby 1966; Basu 1989). Today, a small number of institutions provide education in traditional fields, such as ayurvedic medicine, but they are largely organized along Western lines.

The imposition of academic models by the colonial powers has had a profound impact. The British academic model was imposed on all of the countries under British colonial rule, and it remains a powerful force in such countries as India, Pakistan, Bangladesh, Sri Lanka, Malaysia, Hong Kong, Nepal, and several others. Even where the British model has been largely jettisoned, such as in Singapore, elements of it remain evident, and ties with the United Kingdom remain strong. Because of the extent of British colonial rule in Asia, the British model is probably the most important foreign academic influence in that whole region.

Other European colonial powers also exported their university ideas to Asia: the French in Indochina (Vietnam, Cambodia, and to a lesser extent Laos); the Dutch in the Dutch East Indies (Indonesia); Spain and, after 1898, the United States in the Philippines; and Russia in the central Asian republics that were part of the Russian empire and then the Soviet Union. Japan began its role as a colonial power at the end of the 19th century, and it had an active higher education policy in Taiwan and Korea, its main colonies. It is worth noting that, with the exception of the Americans in the Philippines, the other (European) colonial powers were not enthusiastic exporters of higher education. Even the British, in whose colonies higher education was the most developed, did not spend a great deal of effort or money in fostering universities. Indeed, the role of indigenous populations in establishing Western-model universities during the colonial era deserves more emphasis.

It is also worth noting that, with few exceptions, the colonial powers did not dismantle existing indigenous higher education institutions.

Rather, Western-style universities proved more popular because they were tied to the colonial administration and to emerging economic interests. Indigenous schools were simply left to atrophy. An exception to this generally laissez-faire approach was Japan, which had a more activist educational policy in Korea and Taiwan and actively repressed local institutions of higher education (Lee 2004).

The European powers felt that the implantation of higher education in their colonies would introduce a subversive institution. They were correct in this assumption since Western-educated intellectuals produced by the universities were everywhere the leaders of independence movements, and the universities themselves were important intellectual centers involved in the development of nationalism and dissent. Perhaps the most dramatic example of the impact of Western-educated university graduates is Indonesia, where the very concept of the Indonesian nation with a common language was created by a small group of intellectuals trained both at home and in the Netherlands. Despite the reluctance of the colonial authorities, there was a need for small groups of Western-educated people, literate in the language of the colonial administration, to staff the civil service and provide midlevel administration. The pressure for expansion came almost entirely from local people seeking the opportunities provided by a Western academic degree, and in some cases the colonial powers permitted modest expansion to meet these demands.

The role of Christian missionary work in the development and expansion of higher education in Asia is also significant. Missionaries devoted much effort to establishing higher education institutions to foster conversions to Christianity. In much of Asia, the establishment of early academic institutions was due to missionary work. This was especially the case in India, China, and Korea, where Christian organizations were among the early founders of colleges and universities, although in most Asian countries missionaries had less success in converting people to Christianity. A significant exception to this rule is the Philippines, which is largely Roman Catholic as the result of centuries of Spanish colonial rule. The Spanish colonial authorities gave the Catholic Church the full responsibility for higher education. South Korea also has a large Christian minority. Missionaries generally had the support of the colonial authorities although from time to time, as in India, there were disagreements concerning higher education policy. In some parts of Asia, Christian universities and colleges remain an important part of the academic landscape.

There are important common elements in the European colonial model in Asia. In all cases, instruction was offered exclusively in the language of the colonial power. Universities in the British colonies functioned in English, in the Dutch East Indies in Dutch, in Korea and Taiwan in Japanese, in the Philippines in English, and so on. The widespread use of European languages in higher education has had a profound impact on the development of higher education. It has been difficult, in some Asian countries, to use local languages in higher education. Indonesia is an example of a country that made an early and effective shift from a European language (Dutch) to an indigenous language (Cummings and Kasenda 1989). South Asia retains English as one of the languages of instruction. Thus, in much of Asia, the impact of colonial languages on academic development has been, and continues to be, central to higher education.

The colonial powers placed restrictions on the academic institutions they established in Asia; government control was strict and academic freedom limited. The purpose of the colonial universities was to train a loyal civil service and a small number of medical doctors, lawyers, and others to serve the colonizers—not to establish universities in the full autonomous sense of the term. Thus, the colonial university did not have all of the characteristics of the metropolitan model. This historical tradition of subservience and of a lack of full autonomy and academic freedom created problems for the emergence of modern universities in postindependence Asia.

The Asian countries that were not colonized (e.g., Japan, China, and Thailand) did not adopt European languages. Japan and Thailand are the most significant examples. China, while never formally colonized, was strongly influenced by Europeans, and also by Japan, along the coast where higher education became the most entrenched. In all of these cases, the noncolonized Asian countries chose Western academic models rather than relying on indigenous intellectual and academic traditions. In the second half of the 19th century, Japan and Thailand established Western-style academic institutions after careful consideration. In the Japanese case, the new Meiji regime adopted the German academic model along with some aspects of the American college as the pattern for the new universities. After some debate among policymakers concerning the appropriate language of instruction, during which the minister of education advocated the use of English, Japanese was chosen as the medium of instruction. In Japan, Thailand, and China, governments established Western-style higher education to assist in the process of modernization and industrialization.

Upon attaining independence, no Asian country chose to break with the academic models imposed by the colonial powers. Other links with the universities in the former colonial power were also

retained. In the former British colonies, English was retained to varying extents as a medium of instruction. As mentioned, Malaysia,
which moved from English to Bahasa Malaysia a few years after independence, has recently reintroduced English to some extent in its universities. Indonesia was the largest country to shift the language of
education, introducing Bahasa Indonesia immediately following independence. Korea and Taiwan stopped using Japanese and moved to
Korean and Chinese, respectively. In the decade following the 1949
Communist revolution in China, a variety of Western patterns yielded
to the Soviet academic model (Hayhoe 1996). For different reasons
and at different times, China and the central Asian republics, once
part of the Soviet Union, found the Soviet model to be inappropriate.
China dropped it in the 1970s, while the central Asian nations are now
in the process of change.

As Asian academic systems have grown and matured, countries
have not been inspired to develop new indigenous academic models.
Rather, Asian countries have looked abroad for ways to expand and
improve their universities. For the most part, the United States has provided the ideas and forms for academic development. There are several reasons for this "Americanization" of Asian higher education. The
US academic system is the largest in the world—the first to cope with
the challenges of enrollment expansion. The United States also has the
largest and most advanced academic research system. Moreover, many
Asian academic and political leaders studied in the United States and
absorbed American academic ideas during their student years.

Asian academic systems carry the baggage of their historical past.
The legacy of colonialism linked universities to government and gave
considerable power to governmental authorities over higher education.
Even in countries without a colonial past, notably Japan and Thailand,
the impetus for the establishment of modern universities came from
government. Asian universities have shallow roots in the soil of their
countries—the norms and values of academe are perhaps less well
entrenched than in many Western nations. On this point, however, it
should be remembered that German universities voluntarily suc-
cumbed to Nazi authority despite their rich historical tradition. Still,
historical traditions play an important role in all social institutions—
and no institution is more influenced by history than universities.

The Asian Economic Miracle
Nowhere in Asia have the early stages of contemporary economic development been dependent on higher education. Even in those countries
that have achieved impressive rates of growth and have joined the

ranks of the industrialized world—Japan, Taiwan, South Korea, China, and to some extent Thailand and Malaysia—development has not been based on knowledge industries or on higher education. The underpinnings of economic growth are varied. The typical pattern was industrialization based on an inexpensive labor force, with basic education and literacy skills, and a reliance on exporting relatively unsophisticated manufactured goods or the products of heavy industry. In some cases, raw materials (such as oil and rubber in Malaysia) or agricultural products were added.

Significant investment in education did play a role, but the focus was on primary and to some extent secondary education to provide the workforce for the emerging industries with the appropriate literacy and skills. The countries that had the most success—Japan, South Korea, Taiwan, and in recent years China—invested heavily in basic education and achieved very impressive gains in literacy and other educational skills. The South Asian countries, which invested less in education and still have much lower literacy rates, have done less well economically.

Higher education was not emphasized during the initial phases of industrialization, and most Asian academic systems remained small, enrolling a modest percentage of the age cohort. The universities largely served the elites, and there was only limited demand from other sectors of the population. Governments invested little in higher education. In a number of countries, private universities became an important part of the system (Altbach 1999).

As a middle class developed, as a growing segment of the population acquired some wealth, and as literacy levels and secondary schooling became more widespread, demand grew for access to higher education. For much of East Asia, these trends occurred in the 1980s and have continued today. Other parts of the region have moved more slowly. Moreover, in a few places, such as India, expansion was not directly linked to economic development. Universities and other postsecondary institutions were established to serve this growing demand, often in the private sector, given the frequent unwillingness of government to invest in higher education. Almost everywhere in Asia, university expansion was driven by demand from the increasingly articulate emerging middle classes and those seeking upward mobility in society. Only later, as governments recognized the role of postsecondary expansion in economic development, did the public sector invest significantly in higher education.

As countries such as Japan, South Korea, Taiwan, and Singapore developed, their economies became more sophisticated and wages rose, and they were no longer competitive with lower-wage economies.

These countries sought to develop more sophisticated industries and a service sector to remain competitive. In short, they were forced to move toward becoming "knowledge-based economies"—and higher education was seen as a key factor in national economic survival.

Investment in academic institutions and in a research infrastructure is taking place in many Asian countries, although the pace of investment and expansion varies considerably. Japan transformed itself first, starting in the 1960s, and it was followed by Taiwan, South Korea, Singapore, with Malaysia, Thailand, and others following somewhat later. Governments took more interest in higher education, and increased expenditures for both expansion and research. Although government expenditure on higher education in much of Asia remains modest by international standards, it grew during this period of expansion. Asia had the advantage of an active private higher education sector that paid for much of the expansion. Some Asian countries, including Cambodia, Laos, Burma, and to some extent Vietnam, remain at an early stage of economic development, with higher education still given a low priority.

One of the most interesting examples linking higher education to new economic policies has been Singapore (Tan 2004). Singapore, which until recently has had no private higher education sector, kept enrollment rates modest in its two universities. As the country redirected its economic growth strategies to such high-technology areas as biotechnology, medical and financial services, and related fields, there was a recognition that a larger proportion of the population needed academic qualifications. Academic institutions have been expanded and a growing segment of the age cohort is enrolling in postsecondary education. Singapore is developing links with some of the best universities abroad, and for the first time, private initiatives in higher education are being permitted. Malaysia now has a national policy of encouraging high-technology development and is linking this strategy with targeted higher education expansion.

The regional giants, China and India, after developing their economies in a fairly traditional pattern, now have elements of both "old" and "new" economic policies, and their higher education systems are adjusting in different ways to the new realities. While China has achieved much higher literacy rates and more impressive economic growth than has been the case for India, both countries are faced with the challenge of adapting their academic systems to meet the demands of growing numbers for access while ensuring that at least a part of the system serves the needs of a high-technology economy. Both countries show that it is possible to have at least a part of the higher education system operate at very high levels of quality and are involved with the international knowledge system. Such schools as the Indian Institutes of Technology and the key Chinese universities are examples of the best-quality academic and research institutions. India met the demand for access by permitting privately owned but government-subsidized colleges to expand, which has resulted in a decline in the overall quality of the academic system. China now seems to be moving in a similar direction, encouraging the private sector (which receives no government funding) to absorb demand for access and expanding enrollments in many of the public universities without commensurate increases in funding.

Higher education will inevitably become more central as Asian economies become more technology based, more heavily dependent on informatics, and more service based. Japan and Singapore have already been transformed into postindustrial information-based societies. China and India have moved partly into this realm, as have South Korea, Taiwan, and Malaysia. All these countries have recognized the importance of higher education in this transformation and are moving to ensure that at least part of the university system is prepared to function in the new environment. Japan's current structural reforms of the national universities are aimed in part at ensuring that higher education institutions will be prepared to play an active role in building the new economy. China is also in the process of ensuring that some of its top universities will have the training and research capabilities to assist in the economic changes needed for a research-based economy. Other Asian nations that recognize higher education's role in a knowledge-based economy are, in different ways, developing university structures that can serve the new economic realities. Poorer Asian countries— Cambodia and Burma are examples—have yet to grapple with these changes. Still others, such as Thailand and in the future perhaps Pakistan, have yet to think seriously about higher education's role in a changing economic structure.

As much of Asia moves toward a more sophisticated economic base, universities will become more central to the economy, research will receive more attention, and closer links will evolve between the universities and the economy. While the initial phases of Asian economic success did not depend on higher education and technology, it is clear that the next stages will rely on the universities for both training and research. Japan, Taiwan, and South Korea have already recognized this, and China and Malaysia are adapting to current realities. Other countries will inevitably recognize the importance of higher education for the next phase of development.

The Challenge of Massification

The central reality of higher education almost everywhere is the expansion in student numbers that has taken place since the 1960s. Worldwide, between 1975 and 1995, enrollments doubled, going from 40 million to over 80 million. While growth has slowed in many industrialized countries, expansion continues in the developing nations, and will remain the main factor in shaping academic realities in the coming period. The pressures for expansion will be most significant in the countries that still educate a relatively small portion of the age group— under 15 percent—and in Asia this includes such nations as India, Indonesia, Bangladesh, Burma, Vietnam, Cambodia, and Pakistan. Most industrialized nations educate from about 35 and to more than 50 percent of the age group—in Asia, only South Korea, Japan, and Taiwan have achieved this proportion, with Thailand, the Philippines, and Singapore catching up rapidly. By 2006, China was educating 23 percent of the age group and expanding access. These patterns of enrollment in Asia do not reflect the growing international trend to provide postsecondary education to "nontraditional" students—those who are older but have either missed out on an academic degree or who require additional skills for their jobs or professions. Few, if any, Asian academic systems cater to this significant population yet. This so far underserved segment of the population will also demand increasing access in the coming years.

Expansion is an inevitable and irresistible force. Ever-growing segments of the population demand access to postsecondary education because they know that it is necessary for social mobility and for improved salaries and standards of living in most societies. Countries need larger numbers of university-educated workers to support knowledge-based economies. As more young people gain access to secondary education, they naturally gravitate to higher education, having gained the qualifications to gain entry to universities. In addition, as a middle class grows in size and in political influence, it will also demand access to higher education. Few countries have been able to resist the social demand for access, and none can permanently block it.

Almost all Asian countries are currently coping with the implications of continuing expansion. This pressure makes it difficult to focus on other things—improving quality, upgrading research, enhancing the salaries and working conditions of the professoriate, among others. The inevitable result of expansion has been the development of differentiated systems of higher education, with institutions serving different roles and with varying levels of support and prestige. The traditional university remains at the pinnacle of a hierarchy but is no longer the main postsecondary institution. An overall deterioration in quality is also a result of massification. In most countries, there continue to be high-quality universities that maintain traditional academic standards and a commitment to research, but many of the institutions lower on the hierarchy offer an education that is more modest in quality—and in prestige as well. As in other parts of the world, mass higher education requires a differentiated academic system, with major variations in quality, purpose, and orientation. Massification inevitably has implications for the overall quality of the academic system as it creates a more diversified academic system with institutions of varying levels of quality.

Two of the most important challenges are funding the expansion and providing necessary physical facilities. The problem of funding is particularly acute for two reasons. Not only is it difficult to find public resources to support ever larger numbers of students, but there has also been a basic change in thinking in many countries concerning who should pay for higher education and other public services. Led by the World Bank and other international agencies, countries increasingly argue that higher education is mainly a "private good" serving the needs of individuals and less a "public" or social good. Therefore, the thinking is that the "user"—students, and perhaps their families—deserve to pay a significant part of the cost of higher education. This has led to the imposition of tuition and other fees for higher education in most Asian countries. Indeed, there may be no Asian country, with the exception of North Korea, that does not charge tuition. The two factors of a simple lack of sufficient public funds and a new perspective on higher education have combined to instigate a major rethinking of the financing of higher education as a private good in Asia. Even in countries that adhere to a socialist economic system—such as China and Vietnam—tuition has been introduced.

Without fully analyzing the nuances of the public- vs. private-good arguments here, it is clear that an effective higher education system will recognize that both are part of the academic equation. While it is certainly the case that earning a degree is a significant advantage to the graduate in terms of income and in other ways, it is also true that universities provide a considerable public good to society. Not only are there public benefits accruing from the individual graduate (such as a heightened civic consciousness and the ability to pay higher taxes because of higher earnings), universities provide other benefits to society: they are repositories of knowledge through their libraries and other databases. Further, they provide the basic and applied research that can help with development.

The Private Sector in Asian Higher Education

Another central reality of massification is increased reliance on private higher education institutions (Altbach 2000). Private higher education is the fastest-growing segment of postsecondary education worldwide. In Asia, private institutions have long been a central part of higher education provision. In such major countries as Japan, South Korea, Taiwan, the Philippines, and Indonesia, private universities enroll the majority of students—in some cases upwards of 80 percent. The large majority of Indian students attend private colleges, although these are heavily subsidized by government funds. The private sector is a growing force in parts of Asia where it was previously inactive—China, Vietnam, and the central Asian republics are examples.

In general, private universities are found at the lower end of the prestige hierarchy in Asia. There are a few exceptions—high-quality private universities, such as Waseda, Keio, and a few others in Japan; De La Salle and the Ateneo de Manila in the Philippines; Yonsei in Korea; and Atma Jaya in Indonesia. Generally, private institutions rely on tuition payments, receive little funding from public sources (although in Japan and several other countries some government funding is available to the private sector), and have no tradition of private philanthropy (in part because the tax structure does not reward private donation to nonprofit organizations such as universities), and as a result are unable to compete for the best students. However, the private sector plays a central role by providing access to students who would otherwise be unable to obtain academic degrees.

It is useful to disaggregate the Asian private higher education sector because of the significant differences among institutions and the divergent roles they play in society. As noted, there are a few very prestigious private universities in the countries in which a private sector operates. In some cases, these institutions are sponsored or founded by religious groups—largely but not exclusively Christian. Sophia and Doshisha in Japan, Yonsei and Sogang in South Korea, Santa Dharma in Indonesia, Assumption in Thailand, and De La Salle and Ateneo de Manila in the Philippines are examples. These universities are typically among the oldest in their countries, and they have a long tradition of training elite groups. Another category is the newer private institutions, often specializing in fields such as management or technology, established with the aim of serving a key but limited market with high-quality academic degrees. The Asian Institute of Technology in the Philippines and its sister institution in Thailand and the new Singapore Management University are examples of such schools. These prestigious private universities have been able to maintain their positions over time and rely largely on tuition payments for survival.

Most Asian private universities serve the mass higher education market and tend to be relatively nonselective. Many are small, although there are some quite large institutions, such as the Far Eastern University in the Philippines, which has a large student population and was for a time listed on the Manila stock exchange. Some are sponsored by private nonprofit organizations, religious societies, or other groups. Many are owned by individuals or families, sometimes with a management structure that masks the controlling elements of the school. This pattern of family-run academic institutions has received little attention from analysts and is important to understand as it is of growing importance worldwide. Even in countries that do not encourage for-profit higher education institutions, family ownership has become common.

The emerging for-profit sector is a growing segment of private higher education in some Asian countries. In 2002, China passed legislation that permits private higher education institutions to earn an "appropriate" profit. Two for-profit higher education patterns have emerged in India: several quite large and successful postsecondary trade schools and a number of colleges (mostly focusing on professional and medical training) that charge high fees and are intended to provide a return on funding to investors although the legal status of these institutions has come into question. While a number of Asian countries have not as yet opened their doors fully to for-profit higher education, there are already semi-for-profit enterprises operating; and before long this trend will prevail.

Many Asian countries have long experience in managing large private higher education sectors, while others are seeking to establish appropriate structures. The main challenge is to allow the private sector the necessary autonomy and freedom to establish and manage institutions and to compete in a differentiated educational marketplace, while at the same time ensuring that the national interest is served. In India, where the large majority of undergraduate students attend private colleges, these institutions are largely funded by the state governments and are closely controlled by the universities to which most are affiliated. University authorities, for example, determine and administer examinations and award academic degrees, stipulate the minimum qualifications for entry, and supervise the hiring of academic staff. Japan and South Korea have a long tradition of rigidly controlling the private institutions—going to the extent of stipulating the salaries of academic staff, the numbers of students that can be admitted, approving the establishment of new departments or programs, and supervising the appointment of trustees. In recent years, these two countries have moved toward allowing private institutions more autonomy and freedom. Other countries have imposed less strict supervision.

As in other parts of the world, private higher education is expanding throughout Asia, and the countries that are moving toward a large private sector would be well advised to look at the experience elsewhere in Asia for guidance. There is a dramatically growing private sector in China, with more than 500 private postsecondary institutions, most of which are not accredited or approved by the government. Vietnam and Cambodia also have rapidly growing private sectors, as do the central Asian nations. The challenge will be ensuring that the emerging private sector is effective, well managed, and serving national goals.

Distance Higher Education

Of the world's 10-largest distance higher education institutions, 7 are located in Asia—in Turkey, China, Indonesia, India, Thailand, South Korea, and Iran. These institutions have enrollments of more than 100,000 each. A variety of distance methodologies are used to deliver academic programs. These institutions, which are all public universities, were established to meet the growing demand for higher education, especially in regions not served by traditional academic institutions.

The potential for expansion of distance higher education is fueled by a variety of trends. Access to technology is rapidly expanding in many Asian countries, which enables growing numbers of people to take advantage of distance delivery programs. Distance institutions can reach students in places without traditional universities—a relevant factor in much of Asia, where transportation is difficult and people lack the funds to relocate to study in major urban areas. Distance higher education, as developed in the Asian context and in most developing areas, is less expensive to deliver than are traditional academic degree programs. Distance higher education does not require the facilities needed for traditional academic institutions.

While claims are made that Asian distance universities provide an acceptable level of academic quality, there have been few evaluative studies. It is likely that foreign providers will seek to enter Asian markets, especially if the academic doors are forced open should Asian countries enter into agreements under the General Agreement on Trade in Services, a part of the World Trade Organization (see chapter 2).

Trends and Challenges

Asian higher education faces considerable hurdles in the coming period. While there are significant differences among Asian countries in size, historical patterns of academic development, wealth, and other factors, it is nonetheless possible to highlight trends that are common in most of the region. Since the problems are similar, it may be useful for countries to examine the experience of other Asian countries rather than always looking toward the West for answers to pressing questions of higher education development. The following issues seem to be of special relevance for Asian academic development.

MASSIFICATION

The challenges of mass higher education have been considered in this chapter. It remains a central reality for most of Asia (Japan and South Korea are exceptions, with their well-established academic systems and falling populations). Massification will place continuing strains on public funds, and at the same time will shape academic decision making. Massification requires differentiated academic systems able to serve different segments of the population and fulfill different purposes—with varying levels of funding and resources.

ACCESS

Directly related to mass higher education is the question of access—providing higher education opportunities for all sections of the population able to take advantage of them. In most Asian countries, educational opportunities lag behind for women, rural populations, the poor, and some minority groups. It will be a challenge to provide access to previously disenfranchised groups.

DIFFERENTIATION

Mass higher education requires a clear differentiation of goals and purposes among academic institutions so that resources are efficiently managed and the various purposes of higher education served. This means that there must be a coordinated system of higher education loosely managed by an authority that has both power and responsibility for a system of higher education. Such a management arrangement need not be under the direct control of the state but can be a joint effort by public authorities, the academic community, and other participants. Systems require clear definitions of institutional goals and responsibilities, as well as appropriate funding. The private sector should be treated as part of the national higher education system. Small as well as large countries will necessarily need to develop such systems because even small populations will need a range of academic preparation to meet the new economic realities.

ACCREDITATION AND QUALITY CONTROL

Large academic systems require transparency in terms of quality of academic programs and institutions and assurance that minimum standards are being met. This is necessary not only to provide students with appropriate information about institutions but also to ensure that public resources are being effectively spent. It is sometimes argued that the market will ensure effective quality control. While the market might ensure the quality of some products, it will not be effective for higher education because the measurement of quality is complex and far from obvious to students or to employers. Accreditation and quality control arrangements can provide this information and ensure that appropriate standards are maintained. There are many models available, and these can be adapted to specific Asian circumstances—some accreditation systems are supervised by government while others are the responsibility of the academic system itself, other nongovernmental organizations, or a combination of several stakeholders.

RESEARCH

Not all universities need to be focused on research—for example, most American universities are mainly teaching institutions—but almost every country needs some universities that engage in top-quality research in relevant fields or that at least are able to interpret research done elsewhere. This does not mean that countries without the financial resources or infrastructure need to have a full-fledged research university, but all need to have at least some academic staff capable of interpreting and using research. Supporting research universities is neither easy nor inexpensive. Yet, for most countries, it is necessary, for research is at the heart of the modern knowledge-based economy. Further, only universities can engage in basic research since this requires a long-term commitment and resources that industry cannot support. While a few Asian countries adopted the Soviet-style "research institute" model, most have realized that universities can better serve as the basis of a culture of research.

THE ACADEMIC PROFESSION

At the heart of any university is the academic profession. Yet, in many countries, the professoriate is in crisis—inadequately paid and suffering from ever higher workloads and low morale. In order to attract the "best and brightest" to academe, appropriate conditions must be created. In many Asian countries, there is too little evaluation of academic work—an evaluation system is needed that combines attractive working conditions and accountability to ensure productivity by the professoriate. Current trends toward a part-time teaching force (as is common in Latin America) contribute to a lack of professional commitment to academe. Research-oriented universities especially need a highly motivated and well-trained professoriate. In many Asian countries, few university teachers hold advanced academic degrees. An essential part of ensuring the necessary conditions for teaching and research is the presence of an academic environment based on academic freedom and an appropriate balance between autonomy and accountability for the professoriate. The academic profession requires careful attention and support in a modern university system.

GLOBALIZATION AND INTERNATIONALIZATION

Universities worldwide are becoming part of a global academic environment, and this has implications for Asian universities. Distance education and information technology are parts of globalization—students, staff, and academic institutions themselves are affected by the ease of communication and the access to information provided by information technology. Academic programs offered through distance education from abroad will have some impact on Asian countries as well. These are new realities that will require careful planning and adjustment in each system. Students and staff are increasingly part of an international academic community. Asian students are by far the largest group of students studying abroad worldwide, and more Asian scholars now work outside their own countries. The flow of academic talent is from Asia to the industrialized West for the most part (although Australia and Japan are also attractive destinations for Asian students and staff). India and China are the largest "exporters" of students and probably of staff as well; and Malaysia, South Korea, Taiwan, Hong Kong, and several other Asian countries also send significant numbers of students abroad. There is also a need for Asian universities to incorporate knowledge from abroad—and again the bulk of knowledge is imported from the "metropolitan" academic systems of the West. Asian academic systems cannot insulate themselves from the global academic system and will need to adjust positively to it.

TRANSNATIONALIZATION

Related to globalization is the trend for academic institutions and other education providers from one country to offer degrees or other academic programs in another country (Observatory on Borderless Higher Education 2004). Asia is already the largest world market for such transnational educational enterprises, and this phenomenon will grow rapidly. Malaysia is probably the world's largest transnational market at present. China has recently opened its doors to foreign providers, and other countries will no doubt follow down this path. In most cases, academic institutions from the industrialized nations—and especially from Australia and the United Kingdom, with the United States beginning to become involved—open branch campuses or develop partnerships or other arrangements in an Asian country. In some cases, distance methods are used to deliver all or part of the educational degree or other programs. The implications of transnational higher education enterprises are as yet unclear, for local higher education markets, quality, accreditation, and control of higher education.

Conclusion

Asian universities are shaped by their historical traditions and have to face the complex realities of the 21st century. They enter this new era from a position of some weakness. With the exception of a few Japanese universities, Asian academic institutions are seeking to catch up with their counterparts in the West in an environment where entering the "big leagues" is both difficult and expensive. Yet, many Asian countries have some features that work to their considerable advantages as well. Well-educated populations, traditions of scholarship, and a high respect for learning are part of virtually every Asian society. Asian countries also have the opportunity to shape their relatively new university systems to meet the needs of the 21st century in ways that the more entrenched universities of the West may have difficulty doing. What is clear is that universities are an essential part of the knowledge economies of the future. Unless they are able to build effective universities that can educate a growing proportion of the population while competing globally for research and knowledge products, Asian countries will be doomed to peripheral status.

References

Altbach, P. G. 1998. Gigantic peripheries: India and China in the world knowledge system. In *Comparative higher education*, 133–46. Greenwich, CT: Ablex.

———. 1999. *Private Prometheus: Private higher education and development in the 21st century*. Westport, CT: Greenwood.

———, ed. 2000. *The changing academic workplace: Comparative perspectives*. Chestnut Hill, MA: Center for International Higher Education, Boston College.

———, and V. Selvaratnam, eds. 1989. *From dependence to autonomy: The development of Asian universities*. Dordrecht, Netherlands: Kluwer.

———, and T. Umakoshi, eds. 2004. *Asian universities: Historical perspectives and contemporary challenges*. Baltimore: Johns Hopkins University Press.

Ashby, Eric. 1966. Universities: *British, Indian, African*. Cambridge, MA: Harvard University Press.

Basu, Aparna. 1989. Indian higher education: Colonialism and beyond. In *From Dependence to Autonomy: The Development of Asian Universities*, ed. P. G. Altbach and V. Selvaratnam, 167–86. Dordrecht, Netherlands: Kluwer.

Cummings, William K., and Salman Kasenda. 1989. The origins of modern Indonesian higher education. In *From dependence to autonomy: The development of Asian universities*, ed. P. G. Altbach and V. Selvaratnam, 143–66. Dordrecht, Netherlands: Kluwer.

Hayhoe, Ruth. 1996. *China's universities, 1895–1995: A century of cultural conflict*. New York: Garland.

Lee, Sungho H. 2004. Korean higher education: History and future challenges. In *Asian universities: Historical perspectives and contemporary challenges*, ed. P. G. Altbach and T. Umakoshi, 145–74. Baltimore: Johns Hopkins University Press.

Observatory on Borderless Higher Education. 2004. *Mapping borderless higher education: Policy, markets, and competition*. London: Association of Commonwealth Universities.

Postiglione, G. A., and G. C. L. Mak, eds. 1997. *Asian higher education: An international handbook and reference guide*. Westport, CT: Greenwood.

Tan, Jason. 2004. Singapore: Small nation, big plans. In *Asian universities: Historical perspectives and contemporary challenges*, P. G. Altbach and T. Umakoshi, 175–99. Baltimore: Johns Hopkins University Press.

Task Force on Higher Education and Society. 2000. *Higher education in developing countries: Peril and promise.* Washington, DC: World Bank.

10

African Higher Education: Challenges for the 21st Century

Africa higher education, at the beginning of the new millennium, faces unprecedented challenges. Not only is the demand for access unstoppable, especially in the context of Africa's traditionally low postsecondary attendance levels, but higher education is recognized as a key force for modernization and development. The dawning of the 21st century is viewed as the knowledge era, and higher education must play a central role. This chapter reflects on some of the key problems facing African higher education.

Generalizing about a continent as large and diverse as Africa is difficult, although there are some common elements. Given the complex challenges facing higher education on the continent, our optimism for the future is quite guarded. African universities currently function in difficult circumstances, and the road to success will not be an easy journey.

If Africa is to succeed economically, culturally, and politically, it must have a strong postsecondary sector. Universities are essential institutions for a knowledge-based economy, and to educate the people needed to build a successful economy. Basic literacy is not enough for contemporary development. After being shunted to the side by national governments and international agencies alike for almost two decades, higher education is again recognized as a key sector in African development.

Africa, a continent with 54 countries, has no more than 300 institutions that fit the definition of a university. By international standards, Africa is the least-developed region in terms of higher education institutions and enrollments. While a few countries on the continent can claim to have comprehensive academic systems, most have just a few academic institutions and have not yet established the differentiated postsecondary systems required for the information age (Task Force on Higher Education and Society 2000). Nigeria, Sudan, South Africa, and Egypt have 45, 26, 21, and 17 universities, respectively; and each country has many additional postsecondary institutions as well. A few countries, including Cape Verde, Djibouti, Gambia, Guinea-Bissau, Seychelles, and Sao Tome and Principe have no universities; but even in these countries, preparations have been under way to create one or more major postsecondary institutions. Other countries—including Somalia, Angola, and the Democratic Republic of Congo—have lost university-level institutions as the result of political turmoil and are trying to rebuild a postsecondary sector.

Generalization is difficult because of the tremendous diversity evident in Africa, with exceptions regarding almost every rule. For example, sometimes the extent of postsecondary education is underestimated by ignoring the nonuniversity sector. Zambia has only two universities, but it also has about 50 or so colleges for "further education." The distinction between universities and colleges is based on how they are perceived at the local level, irrespective of their size and programs. The overall state and direction of higher education in northern Africa is considerably different from the rest of sub-Saharan Africa. Even in sub-Saharan Africa, a few countries, such as Botswana, Namibia, and South Africa are not fully consistent with our generalizations. Diversity in function, quality, orientation, financial support, and other factors are evident in Africa; national circumstances and realities vary significantly. Nonetheless, generalizations can be made, and it is important to understand the broader themes that shape African higher education realities at the beginning of the 21st century.

The overall reality of inadequate financial resources combined with unprecedented demand for access, the legacy of colonialism, long-standing economic and social crises in many countries, the challenges of HIV/AIDS in parts of the continent, and other significant issues present a particularly difficult reality. This chapter will seek to provide a broad portrait of African higher education realities as a backdrop for further analysis and future change.

African Higher Education in Historical Perspective

Higher education in Africa is as old as the pyramids of Egypt, the obelisks of Ethiopia, and the Kingdom of Timbuktu. The oldest university still existing in the world is Egypt's Al-Azhar, founded as and still representing the major seat of Islamic learning. Indeed, Al-Azhar is currently the only major academic institution in the world organized according to its original Islamic model. All other universities in Africa and the rest of the world have adopted the Western model of academic organization. While Africa can claim an ancient academic tradition, traditional centers of higher learning in Africa have in fact all but disappeared or were destroyed by colonialism. Today, the continent is dominated by academic institutions shaped by colonialism and organized according to the European model. As is the case in much of the developing world, higher education in Africa is an artifact of colonial policies (Altbach and Selvaratnam 1989; Lulat 2003).

A multitude of European colonial powers including Belgium, Britain, France, Germany, the Netherlands, Italy, Portugal, and Spain— have shaped Africa's route of development. These colonial legacies affect contemporary African higher education. The most important of the colonial powers in Africa, Britain and France, have left by far the greatest lasting impact on the organization of academe and the continuing links to the metropole as well as the language of instruction and communication.

Colonial higher education policy had some common elements. *Limited access* was the result of the colonial authorities' fear of widespread access to higher education. They were interested in training limited numbers of African nationals to assist in administering the colonies. Some colonial powers, notably the Belgians, banned higher education in their colonies. Others, such as the Spanish and the Portuguese, restricted enrollments. The French preferred to send some students from its colonies to study in France. Throughout all of Africa, the size of the academic system was small at the time of independence. A World Bank (1991) study reports that at independence less than one-quarter of all professional civil service posts were held by Africans; most trade and industry throughout the continent was foreign owned; and only 3 percent of high school–age students received a secondary education. With all its copper wealth, Zambia had only 100 university graduates and 1,000 secondary school graduates. In 1961, the University of East Africa (serving Kenya, Tanzania, and Uganda) turned out a total of only 99 graduates for a combined population area of 23 million. Zaire (now the Democratic Republic of the Congo), for example, reached independence without a single national engineer, lawyer, or doctor. Between 1952 and 1963, French-speaking Africa produced a mere four graduates in the field of agriculture, while English-speaking Africa turned out 150 (Eisemon 1982).

The *language of instruction* in every case was the language of the colonizer. In some countries, existing forms of local languages used in "higher forms of education" were replaced by the language of the colonizers. *Limits on academic freedom* and on the autonomy of academic institutions were the norm. Another common element of colonial higher education policy is the dramatically *restricted curricula* of universities in Africa at the time of independence. The colonizers tended to support disciplines such as law and related fields that would assist colonial administration but were not costly to maintain. Scientific subjects were rarely offered.

The legacy of colonialism remains a central factor in African higher education. Independence has been the national reality in most of Africa for less than four decades, and the ties to the former colonizers have, in general, remained strong. Significantly, no African country has changed the language of instruction from the colonial language. The impact of the colonial past and the continuing impact of the former colonial powers remains crucial in any analysis of African higher education.

This analysis is mainly concerned with contemporary higher education. The key elements of higher education in Africa include access, governance, the role of research and publishing, information technology, the academic profession, "brain drain" and migration of talent, and others. While these topics do not encompass all aspects of African higher education, they are central to any understanding of the continent's challenges.

Access

In virtually all African countries, demand for access to higher education is growing, straining the resources of higher education institutions. The institutions were originally designed for fewer students. Enrollments have escalated, although financial resources have not kept pace. In many countries, resources have actually declined due to inflation, devaluation of the currency exchange rate, economic and political turmoil, and structural adjustment programs—further undermining the financial stability of institutions and systems.

It is estimated that between 4 and 5 million students are currently enrolled in the continent's postsecondary institutions. A report by the Task Force on Higher Education and Society (2000) puts this figure at 3,489,000 students. Over 150,000 academic staff work in Africa's postsecondary institutions. Egypt has the highest enrollment in Africa, with over 1.5 million (including about a quarter of a million part-time) students. It also has the largest number of members of the academic profession, at about 31,000. The enrollment rate of the 18-to-22 age group is approximately 22 percent (Elmahdy 2003).

Nigeria is second in enrollments, with close to 900,000 students enrolled in its postsecondary institutions. It has 45 universities, 63 colleges of education (teachers colleges), and 45 polytechnics—the largest numbers in Africa. Of the total student population, 35 percent go to universities and 55 percent to colleges of education. However, the gross enrollment rate for ages 18 to 25 is only about 5 percent (Jibril 2003).

South Africa, with more than half a million students in its 21 universities and 15 technikons (postsecondary vocational colleges), is third in terms of the number of students on the continent. Of these, 55 percent go to universities (Subotsky 2003). Recent amalgamation of some universities and technikons may have altered these statistics somewhat. Tunisia and Libya have enrollments of close to 210,000 and over 140,000, respectively (Millot, Waite, and Zaiem 2003; El-Hawat 2003).

With a population of 32 million, the enrollment in Tanzanian higher education institutions for the year 2000 was under 21,000 (Mkude and Cooksey 2003). With a population of about 65 million, Ethiopia has no more than 50,000 students at its postsecondary institutions (Wondimu 2003). Today Guinea's enrollments amount to 14,000 students from the population of 7.66 million (Sylla 2003); Senegal has 25,000 students for 7.97 million inhabitants (Ndiaye 2003); and Côte d'Ivoire has 60,000 for its population of 13.7 million (Houenou and Houenou-Agbo 2003).

It should be noted that the number of institutions and student figures are not always directly correlated. Sudan, for example, with its 26 public universities and 21 private universities and colleges, has an enrollment of about 40,000 (El Tom 2003). In some countries, academic institutions may be quite small.

Enrollment in Ghana is less than 3 percent of the eligible age group, and in many countries the figure is under 1 percent of the student age cohort. For instance, in Malawi and Tanzania, the proportion is 0.5 percent and 0.3 percent of the eligible age group, respectively (Chimombo 2003; Mkude and Cooksey 2003). Less than 3 percent of the eligible age group have access to postsecondary education in all of Africa, which represent significantly the lowest percentage in the world. This is one of the reasons for the current surging demand for access to education as Africa seeks to catch up with the rest of the world.

Africa faces a significant challenge in providing access to higher education, not only to reach the levels of other developing and middle-income countries but also to satisfy the rising popular demand for opportunities to study, as a level of secondary education has been achieved that qualifies more persons for postsecondary study.

Funding and Financing

The central reality for all African higher education systems at the beginning of the 21st century is severe financial crisis. Academe everywhere, even in wealthy industrialized nations, faces fiscal problems, but the magnitude of these problems is greater in Africa than anywhere else. The causes are not difficult to discern and include a range of factors.

The pressures of expansion and "massification" have added large numbers of students to most African academic institutions and systems. The economic problems facing many African countries make it difficult, if not impossible, to provide increased funding for higher education. A changed fiscal climate has been induced by the World Bank, the African Development Bank, and the International Monetary Fund, which lend money for higher education and often impose conditions on these loans. Other facts include the inability of students to afford the tuition rates necessary for fiscal stability and, in some cases, constraints on institutions to impose tuition fees due to political or other pressures. Academic systems are affected by misallocation and poor prioritization of available financial resources, such as the tradition of providing free or highly subsidized accommodations and food to students and maintaining a large infrastructure and cumbersome number of nonacademic personnel. While these elements are not present in every African country and financial circumstances vary, overall funding issues loom large in any analysis of African higher education.

Higher education is a $4 to $5 billion enterprise in Africa. With Africa's largest student population, Egypt's higher education is a US$1.29 billion enterprise (Elmahdy 2003). Nigeria, with an estimated $0.5 billion budget (Jibril 2003), accounts for about a third of the remaining total figure. South Africa, Tunisia, Libya, and Algeria appear to dispense a significant portion of the remaining expenditures when compared to other countries of the continent.

For a continent of more than 700 million people, this expenditure is depressingly small. The annual spending for higher education in Africa as a whole does not even come close to the endowments at some of the richest universities in the United States. The budgets of individual universities in many industrialized countries exceed the entire national budgets for higher education in many African nations. These comparisons clearly illustrate the disparity between the financial situations of higher education institutions in Africa and in industrialized nations.

It comes as no surprise, then, that virtually all African universities suffer from the effects of scarce financial resources. Serious shortages of published materials of books and journals, the lack of basic resources for teaching, the absence of simple laboratory equipment and supplies (such as chemicals) to do research and teaching, and in some countries delays of salary payments for months are just some of the common problems faced by institutions across the continent.

The bulk of funding for higher education is generated from state resources. While small variations in the proportion of resources allotted to higher education by countries exist, African governments consistently provide more than 90 to 95 percent of the total operating budgets of higher education. The remaining portions come from fees for tuition, services, consultancy, renting facilities, and other sources. In addition, there is a growing trend toward funding from external sources. Research, for example, is largely funded by donor agencies, and this naturally has implications for the nature of the research and the impact on African higher education.

In many countries, governments pay stipends and living allowances to students, and this consumes a substantial proportion of university resources. In Guinea, for instance, scholarship money given to students accounts for as much as 55 percent of total government allocations to the universities (Sylla 2003). In most countries, student fees have traditionally not provided more than token support. There are some rare exceptions. In Lesotho, for instance, much of the income for the University of Lesotho comes from student fees. Students in Lesotho also repay student loans as soon as they have completed their studies and have secured jobs. The arrangements for loan payments are also contingent upon where graduates eventually work; that is, in public, private, regional, or international sectors (Ntimo-Makara 2003).

The enormous support for the provision of nonacademic activities and facilities—such as allowances, free accommodation, and catering—is now facing scrutiny in many countries. Such support not only consumes major portions of university budgets, which consequently undermine the raison d'être of higher learning institutions, but it may also serve as an incentive for students to take longer to complete their studies. In situations where jobs for graduates are not immediately available, students have been reported to delay the completion of their studies, which then blocks the opportunity for potential incoming students to enroll. Initiatives to curtail such support schemes are often precipitated by declining resources from governments and by multinational pressures on African governments to cut social services.

We can measure the scope of the financial challenges facing African higher education by examining what universities request from their governments and what they actually receive. In Ghana, according to Paul Effah (2003), five universities requested a total of $32 million in 2000. The government provided only $18 million—a mere 56 percent of what was requested; and the pattern is the same for the former poly-technic institutions whose statuses have been upgraded. In 1999/2000, the education sector in Uganda received 33 percent of the total government discretionary recurrent budget, and tertiary education accounted for only 18 percent of this total (Musisi 2003).

Without exception, African universities are under considerable financial pressure, with serious financial problems. That said, there are a few places where the financial situation appears to be less severe or even improving gradually. In Nigeria—a country that suffered serious social, economic, and political upheavals during the past military regimes—funds are expected to increase by 252 percent under the current elected government (Jibril 2003). Botswana, which has a small population and considerable mineral wealth, has provided its higher education sector adequate funding.

Over the last decade or so, the pressure to expand the revenue base of higher education has been clear. Universities have either taken it upon themselves or have been pressured by governments to expand the financial and resource base as expenses have risen with mounting enrollments and escalating demand. Various ideas to generate revenue and a variety of pilot programs have been implemented in many countries. While governments—sometimes with pressure from external donor agencies, specially the World Bank and International Monetary Fund—have been attempting to raise funds by imposing higher tuition and fees and through other means. There has often been resistance from the public and, especially, from students.

Some universities, such as Uganda's Makerere University, however, have been cited as models of successful transformation in funding higher education by moving away from the entrenched culture of government support as the sole funding source of universities. Musisi (2001) reports that in 1992/93, 5 percent of the students in Makerere paid their way; seven years later, 80 percent were doing so. In Tanzania, the new trend is to adopt policies to divide the costs between the government and those who use the university's services. The government is confining itself to funding the direct costs of education and leaving the remaining costs (such as residence fees, food, and the like) to be met by students, parents, and family members.

The complex dynamics that enabled fiscal reforms to succeed in some countries and to fail in others require careful analysis. The sustainability of such reforms; their perceived, real, and potential benefits and concealed drawbacks and ramifications; and the significance of external and internal forces toward such a change are interesting topics for further research.

In virtually all cases, researchers observe the ongoing decline of direct and indirect resources allocated for higher education by governments. The impact of this trend and how this over time has eroded the quality of teaching and research, the moral and physical well-being of the academic profession, and the general state of the universities as a whole remain a subject for more discussion and analysis.

Governance

Public higher education institutions predominate in Africa, and governmental involvement in university affairs is the norm. The current governance structure in most African universities reflects this legacy. Throughout much of Africa, the head of state holds the ultimate authority as the chancellor or president in appointing vice-chancellors and others down the administrative line; this is especially typical in Anglophone Africa.

In Anglophone countries, the chancellorship is a symbolic position. The vice-chancellor, who is equivalent to an American university president, has the executive power as furnished by the board of directors, which is composed largely of government-appointed members and, in some countries, students. The vice-chancellors have also been appointed by a minister of education with or without the approval of Parliament or even a chancellor. For example, in the Democratic Republic of Congo, under normal circumstances, university presidents are nominated by members of the academic community; however, it is the president of the republic who makes the final decision on the selection of the vice-chancellor upon the recommendation of the minister of education (Lelo 2003).

The chain of administrative power starts with the vice-chancellor and moves to deans and directors and then to department heads. The deans and directors in most cases are appointed either by the vice-chancellor, directly by government officials, or by boards of directors or trustees. In many cases, fellow members elect the department heads. In a few countries, a short list of candidates for the highest positions is submitted to the government as a compromise between the university community and the government. In most cases, professorial authority, which is typical in Western industrialized nations, is lacking in much of Africa. The academic profession has less power in the African context than it does in the West.

Excessive Nonacademic Staff

The teaching and research academic staff in many African institutions are fewer in number than the nonacademic and administrative staff.

The administrative bureaucracy in African universities is disproportionately large. A few examples illustrate this disparity.

At the National University of Lesotho, Matora Ntimo-Makara (2003)
reports, there are twice as many nonacademic support staff as there are
academics, and more than 60 percent of the institution's budget goes
to staff costs. The financial resources of the university are, therefore,
mainly used for nonteaching personnel. This imposes limitations on
the creation of additional teaching positions to enhance capacity in academic programs.

In Madagascar, James Stiles (2003) reports, the student-to-adminis-
trator ratio (6:1) remains high compared to other countries and high
compared to the ratio of students to teachers (47:1 in 1993 and 22:1 in
1996). This remains true even after the number of administrative staff
was reduced in 1997 by 5 percent while the teaching corps increased.

Togo, Emmanuel Edee (2003) reports, has 1,136 administrative and
technical staff in higher education, yet the academic staff number
fewer than 730, of whom only 55 percent are full time. While the number of nonacademic staff is high, they face several problems, including
overstaffing and lack of communication between the different services
and the students.

The number of nonacademic personnel and the proportion of
resources allocated to this sector are disproportionately high, and the
quality and performance of the administrative cadre leave much to be
desired. Bureaucracy and inefficiency are rampant. Training and skills
development for the nonacademic staff are rarities.

While the nonacademic staff at African educational institutions are
crucial, their disproportionate presence takes away the resources needed for the basic functions of universities: teaching and research. In
countries where such resources are very scarce, universities must consider minimizing this significant and unsustainable fiscal burden so as
to direct resources to the priority areas. While seldom discussed as a
key issue for academic development in Africa, the complex issues surrounding the administrative staff in African universities deserve careful attention.

Management Issues in Universities
Efficient management and administrative systems are of paramount
significance to the productivity and effectiveness of any enterprise; academic institutions are no exception. By and large, however, African universities suffer from poor, inefficient, and highly bureaucratic management systems. Poorly trained and poorly qualified personnel; inefficient, ineffective, and out-of-date management and administrative

infrastructures; and poorly remunerated staff are the norm throughout the many systems.

Accounts of serious corruption charges and embezzlement of funds in African universities are not common. Some blame misappropriation of funds and poor prioritization as factors in the financial difficulties in the universities. For instance, the fiscal crisis in Kenyan public universities, Charles Ngome (2003) observes, is worsened by the misappropriation of the scarce resources. As students continue living and studying under deplorable conditions, top administrators at the universities are regularly accused by the national auditor general's office of mismanaging funds and having misplaced priorities. During the 1995/96 financial year, it was reported that Maseno University lost over US$660,000 (kshs. 50 million), most of it through theft and false allowance payments. Even though the issues of mismanagement tend to be generally similar across nations and systems, it is important to note that the manner in which the university is governed and the leadership is appointed often contributes to the magnitude and scope of the problems.

Private Higher Education

In many African countries, the provision of higher education by private institutions is a growing phenomenon. When compared to other parts of the world, however, most African countries have been slow to expand the private sector in higher education (Altbach 1999). The trend toward private higher education has been enhanced by a number of factors: burgeoning demand from students for access, declining capacity of public universities, retrenchment of public services, pressure by external agencies to cut public services, growing emphasis on and need for a highly skilled labor force that targets the local market, and interest by foreign providers. In terms of numbers, there are now more private than public institutions in some countries, although the private schools are smaller and tend to specialize in specific fields, such as business administration. A number of examples showcase the development of private higher education in Africa.

Kenya has 19 universities, of which 13 are private (Ngome 2003). It is one of the few countries in Africa with a well-developed private university system, yet only 20 percent of the 50,000 enrolled students attend the 13 private universities (Ngome 2003).

In Sudan, Mohamed Elamin El Tom (2003) observes, the number of private higher education institutions increased from 1 in 1989 to 16 in 1996 and to 22 in 2001. The number of students enrolled at private higher education institutions increased nearly ninefold within four years—from under 3,000 in 1990/91 to close to 24,000 in 1994/95.

In the Democratic Republic of Congo, over 260 private institutions were operating in 1996, of which 28.9 percent were approved by the government, 32.3 percent authorized to operate, and 38.8 percent considered for authorization. Many newly established institutions, unfortunately, do not meet the required higher education standards because of their organization and the conditions within which they operate (Lelo 2003).

In Ghana, there has been an upsurge, especially among religious organizations, in the establishment of private higher education institutions. By August 2000, the National Accreditation Board had granted accreditation to 11 private tertiary institutions to offer degree programs. Ghana has 5 public universities and 8 polytechnics that have been upgraded in status (Effah 2003).

In Uganda, more than 10 private universities have been established or are being established. Currently, Uganda has 2 public universities; and the founding of 2 more public universities was also recently announced by the government (Musisi 2003). In Uganda, the total student population of the private institutions amounts to 3,600, while the 2 public universities enroll 23,000 students (Musisi 2003).

Togo—a country that has 1 major university and 4 other postsecondary institutions—has encouraged the creation of private institutions of higher education. Today, there are 22 private postsecondary institutions, of which 18 were created between 1998 and 2000 (Edee 2003).

Ethiopia, with a very small public academic sector, has recently seen the establishment of 20 private postsecondary institutions.

It is important to point out that most of Africa's private institutions are based in major capital cities and in cities where the student pool is robust and the infrastructure relatively good. Even though the number of private institutions on the continent has increased dramatically and appears higher in absolute numbers than the number of public institutions, enrollments in public institutions outnumber those in private institutions in nearly all countries. For instance, while enrollments in the 6 public universities in Madagascar were not more than 9,000, total enrollments in the 16 private institutions were less than 2,000, and none of the private institutions had more than 500 students (Stiles 2003).

Private institutions in Africa are secular as well as sectarian. In religious private institutions, institutional funding relies heavily on the founding religious organizations—based both locally and abroad—or their affiliates. Most other secular private institutions in Africa depend

on student tuition and fees to generate their revenue. As a consequence, the cost of education in these institutions is generally higher,
compared to other educational institutions.

In most African countries, governments do not give financial support to private institutions. In certain cases, however, private institutions receive direct government financial support. In Liberia, for
instance, the state provides subsidies to private and church-operated
postsecondary institutions and financial aid to students attending these
institutions to cover the cost of tuition and textbooks (Seyon 2003). In
Togo, private institutions that offer short-period technician-degree programs are subsidized by the state in the same way as other institutions
(Edee 2003). In Mozambique, some scholarships are also made available to private higher education students to help them pay their tuition
fees (Chilundo 2003).

Private for-profit higher learning institutions quickly offer high-
demand and relatively low-cost, skill-based courses. These institutions
are free from the obligations that constrain other public institutions
whose responsibilities cover wider and broader national objectives.
Private institutions also play an important role in serving as an immediate safety-net to meet the overwhelming need for higher learning on
the continent with a very low overall enrollment rate in higher education institutions by enrolling students who cannot find places in the
public sector, either because of their low scores on entry examinations
or because of limited space. In some countries, such as South Africa,
the private for-profit sector has come under scrutiny because of perceived problems of low-quality. Ensuring that the for-profit sector, and
private higher education in general, contributes to national goals for
higher education creates a considerable challenge given that few constraints are placed on the emerging institutions.

The courses taught at most private higher education institutions
are generally similar across the continent and narrow in their program
coverage. The most common ones are computer science and technology, accounting and management, banking, finance, marketing, and
secretarial training. The courses generally target the needs of the local
market.

Most private institutions hire academic staff from public institutions, most of whom continue to hold part-time positions at these public institutions. In some countries, the massive flow of academic staff
from public institutions to newly established private institutions has
seriously pressured certain departments in public universities. For
many academic staff, however, these private teaching positions have
become an important source of extra income.

The general trend, then, has been to moonlight at the newly established institutions while maintaining positions at the major public universities. In some cases, lured by highly lucrative salaries and benefits, academic staff have been reported to be joining private institutions full-time and abandoning their public institutions.

A public perception still looms across Africa that public institutions are academically superior to private institutions—even though a few of the private institutions hire the best academic staff and maintain new and up-to-date instruments, equipment, and facilities. This prevalent attitude may arise from the rigorous selection process prior to student admission and the fierce competition for admission to public universities. As enrollments escalate across the continent, the entrance requirements for the limited spaces in public institutions have become so rigorous that students who gain admission are clearly the nation's best. In general, private institutions primarily enroll students who cannot gain entry into public institutions—for many reasons—which continues to affect the general perceptions of private institutions as secondary to public institutions.

The emergence of private higher education as a business enterprise is plagued by a number of issues including legal status, quality assurance, and cost of service. The status of many private postsecondary institutions in Africa is low, with many operating without licenses, commensurate resources, or appropriate infrastructure. The quality of service at many of these institutions is also poor, even at a few of the institutions with better facilities and equipment and newer buildings than the countries' major universities.

The quality of education at many private postsecondary institutions has also been a concern. Many multinational businesses across the world provide educational services today driven by a profit motive. Multinational companies and a few foreign-based universities have established satellite campuses in countries where there is a big market for higher education. These transplanted institutions are often criticized for lack of accountability or social responsibility and for potentially threatening and eroding the cultural fabric of a nation.

Private higher education is a growing trend in much of Africa, and the forces behind this private diversification and expansion are both internal and external. A thorough examination of the process of diversification of private institutions must take into account national as well as international economic, political, and educational realities.

Gender

Gender imbalance is a common phenomenon in the continent's educational institutions. Cultural, sociological, economic, psychological, historical, and political factors foster these inequalities. While a number of efforts are now under way to rectify gender imbalance, much remains to be done across all education sectors. The gender imbalance in higher education is acute in virtually all African countries and in most disciplines. Various efforts and initiatives have been undertaken to increase the participation of female students in postsecondary institutions.

In Ethiopia, according to Habtamu Wondimu (2003), efforts have been made to improve the female enrollment rate—currently about 15 percent—by lowering the cutoff in the grade-point average required for admission. This "affirmative action," he notes, has improved the admission rate of female students. The higher attrition rate among women, however, continues to plague the overall status and numbers of women in Ethiopian higher education.

In Malawi, where only 25 percent of the student population is female, an affirmative selection policy for women has been implemented (Chimombo 2003).

In Mozambique, the proportion of female students has gradually increased since 1992. This improvement was partly due to the opening of private higher education institutions, where, on average, 43 percent of all students in 1999 were female; only 25 percent of students were female in the public sector (Chilundo 2003).

Most Tanzanian institutions have been taking steps to improve the participation of female students, who currently make up between 25 and 30 percent of enrollments. The Faculty of Arts and Social Sciences at the University of Dar es Salaam was able to register enough females to comprise 49 percent of students in the 2000/01 first-year intake. As in Ethiopia, the grade-point-average cutoff point for female candidates has been lowered to enable more females to qualify for admission (Mkude and Cooksey 2003).

Uganda's gender disparity is reported to have decreased in the past 10 years. Women constituted 27 percent of University of Makerere's total student intake in 1990/91 but today account for 34 percent of enrollments. Like institutions in Ethiopia, Malawi, and Tanzania, Ugandan universities are giving preferential treatment to female students. With awarding of additional points on entrance examinations, the proportion of female students enrolled has risen to 34 percent (Musisi 2003). In Zimbabwe, university entry qualifications for women have also been reduced, to increase female enrollments (Maunde 2003).

Significant gender disparities remain, however, in the more competitive faculties and departments and in the hard sciences, where female student participation is particularly low. In Kenya, for instance, female students make up about 30 percent of total enrollments at the public universities but only 10 percent of enrollments in engineering and technically based professional programs (Ngome 2003). The female student population in the natural sciences across African public higher education is consistently lower than that of male students. The pattern appears to be a universal phenomenon around the world, though the proportion of the disparity across countries can and does differ significantly.

There are, however, cases where female students outnumber their male compatriots in African countries. In Mauritius, even though overall enrollments show a more or less even gender distribution (47 percent female), enrollments do vary by gender across faculties, with a predominance of male students (76 percent) in engineering and a predominance of female students (68 percent) in the social studies and humanities (Baichoo, Parahoo, and Fagoonee 2003).

In Lesotho, more females than males are enrolled in education, the social sciences, and humanities (arts) programs. Overall, the total number of females represents about 56 percent of all students at the University of Lesotho (Ntimo-Makara 2003). In Uganda, the private universities, Uganda Martyrs and Nkumba, report female student enrollments of over 50 and 56 percent, respectively (Musisi 2003). In Tunisia, female student enrollments rose from 21.1 percent in 1987/88 to 50.4 percent in 1999–2000 and currently stands at 51.9 percent—the first time more women than men were enrolled at the university level (Millot, Waite, and Zaiem 2003).

Female academic staff are even smaller in proportion than female students in African institutions. In Guinea, of 1,000 academic staff members only 25—a mere 4 percent—are female (Sylla 2003). Out of 2,228 academic staff in Ethiopia, 137—or 6 percent—are female (Wondimu 2003). In Congo, Nigeria, and Zambia, no more than 15 percent of all university academic staff are female. In Uganda, female academic staff occupy fewer than 20 percent of the established academic posts (Musisi 2003). In a few countries, the figures are a little better: Morocco, Tunisia, and South Africa, have 24, 33, and 36 percent female academic staff, respectively (Ouakrime 2003; Millot, Waite, and Zaiem 2003; Subotsky 2003). The underrepresentation of female academic staff in higher ranks and qualification levels and in certain fields of study is particularly severe. For instance, in 1997, men in South Africa constituted 90 percent of professors, 78 percent of associate professors, and 67 percent of senior lecturers, but only about 47 percent of the junior ranks (Subotsky 2003).

Overall, gender disparities are common trends across the continent's higher education institutions. The disparity increases in magnitude as one climbs the educational ladder. The disparity is extreme in the academic ranks, with some variations in different fields and disciplines. Gender issues in African higher education are complex and require and deserve further study.

Research and Publishing

Long before the world entered into what is called the knowledge era, research was recognized as a central priority for higher education. Since the founding of the University of Berlin in 1810, research has been a defining element for many academic institutions and systems (Ben-David 1968, 1977). In the increasingly global world shaped by knowledge and information, establishing a strong research infrastructure has more than ever before become a sine qua non in this highly competitive environment.

Universities, as creators and brokers of these products, are situated at the center of the knowledge and information market. For all practical purposes, universities remain the most important institutions in the production and consumption of knowledge and information, particularly in the Third World. This is particularly so in Africa, where only a few such institutions serve as the preeminent and dominant centers of knowledge and information transactions.

By all measures, research and publishing activities in Africa are in critical condition. The general state of research in Africa is extremely poor and the research infrastructure inadequate. Scarcity of laboratory equipment, chemicals, and other scientific paraphernalia; a small number of high-level experts; poor and dilapidated libraries; alarmingly low and declining salaries of academic and research staff; a massive brain drain from the academic institutions; the "expansion" of undergraduate education; poor oversight of research applicability; and declining, nonexistent, and unreliable sources of research funds remain major hurdles to the development of research capacity across the continent.

Most countries in Africa have practically no funds allocated for research in the university budgets. Expenditures on research and development in Ghana, for example, show a declining trend from around 0.7 percent of the gross domestic product (GDP) in the mid-1970s to 0.1–0.2 percent of the GDP in 1983–1987. There is little evidence to suggest that this trend has changed. Paul Effah (2003) reports that the University of Ghana received only US$1.4 million to fund the operations of its 10 research institutes in 2000.

In Uganda, the amount earmarked for research at Makerere University for the 1999–2000 financial year was a mere US$80,000. As a consequence, research in the country has remained underdeveloped and heavily dependent on donor funding (Musisi 2003). In Malawi, a mere 0.7 percent of the whole University of Malawi budget was allocated to research and publications in 1999 (Chimombo 2003).

Tracking frontiers of knowledge is crucial for research and development. Having access to indicators of the knowledge frontiers such as journals, periodicals, and databases is a major prerequisite to undertaking viable, sustainable, and meaningful research. In much of Africa, these resources are either lacking or are extremely scarce. The escalating cost of journals and ever-dwindling library and university funds have exacerbated the problem. Many universities in Africa have dropped most of their subscriptions, while others have simply cancelled subscriptions altogether. Such extreme measures cannot be surprising in light of the fact that some of these universities cannot even pay salaries on a regular basis.

The local publishing infrastructure has traditionally been weak and, generally, unreliable. The paucity of local publications is complicated by many factors, including the small number of researchers with the energy, time, funds, and support needed to sustain journals; the lack of qualified editors and editorial staff; a shortage of publishable materials; a restrictive environment inhibiting freedom of speech; and a lack of commitment to and appreciation of journal production by university administrators.

It is remarkable that even though the state of research in much of Africa remains precarious, many researchers report that academic promotion depends to a large extent on publishing. Even in an environment unsupportive of research, publishing as a universal tool of measuring productivity remains a yardstick for academic promotion in Africa. It is a stark contradiction that African academics are expected to publish their work in an academic context that does not even provide them with access to journals, databases, and other publications vital in keeping abreast of international developments in science and scholarship (Teferra 2002).

Many of the research activities undertaken on the continent are largely funded—and, to a certain extent, managed and directed—by external entities, such as bilateral and multilateral agencies, nongovernmental organizations, and foundations. Estimates of the percentage of external support for research in Africa range from 70 percent to as much as 90 percent. The ramifications of this external funding, especially with regard to what is researched, are far reaching and have become the focus of discussions at numerous national, regional, and international forums.

Academic institutions in many countries are frequently linked by their participation in an international system of knowledge distribution. Universities in the large industrialized nations are the major producers and distributors of scholarly knowledge. Academic institutions in other countries, particularly in developing countries, are largely consumers of scholarly materials and research produced elsewhere.

It will be extremely difficult or even impossible for Africa to compete effectively in a world increasingly dominated by knowledge and information unless it consciously, persistently, and vigorously overhauls its potential and its most crucial institutions: the universities. Africa should and must do much more to develop its universities—the only institutions on the continent that generate and utilize knowledge and information. The international knowledge system has centers and peripheries in the production and distribution of knowledge. Africa, as a continent, finds itself on the very edge of the knowledge periphery (Altbach 1987) and appears to be increasingly isolated from the center.

Research and publishing must be strengthened. Governments, major donor institutions, nongovernmental organizations, and bilateral organizations should direct their policies toward prioritizing the revitalization of these important areas of African higher education. The current situation, in which donor agencies and international organizations fund the large proportion of Africa-based research, presents additional challenges. While it is unlikely that major research funding will be available from indigenous sources in the near future, it is important to ensure that the research taking place, regardless of the source of funding, meets the needs of African scientists and the broader interest of African societies.

Academic Freedom

Academic freedom makes it possible for new ideas, research, and opinions to emerge; for widely accepted views to be tested and challenged; and for critics to comment on and criticize the status quo. (See chapter 3). Academic freedom is an ideal that faces challenges all over the world. There is, however, little doubt that academic freedom is crucial in nurturing national academic and scholarly cultures. Ideally, academic freedom ensures that academics will be able to teach freely, undertake research of their own interest, and communicate findings and ideas openly and without any fear of persecution.

A civil society thrives on tolerance and freedom of expression. A country with robust freedom of expression allows a great variety of perspectives and views to be considered, entertained, and contested. Academic freedom is a crucial element of a civil society, and the development of a civil society is stunted in the absence of academic freedom and the broader freedom of expression.

Most African governments are intolerant of dissent, criticism, nonconformity, and free expression of controversial, new, or unconventional ideas. Aman Attieh (2003) notes that since 1992 serious violations of freedom of speech and expression by security forces, opposition groups, and militant groups in Algeria have silenced not only scholars but also the citizens as a whole. In Kenya, Charles Ngome (2003) states that unwarranted government interference and abuses of academic freedom have eroded the autonomy and quality of the higher learning institutions. The expulsion of over 40 university professors and lecturers from Addis Ababa University, in Ethiopia, in the mid-1990s (Wondimu 2003) also epitomizes a gross violation and intolerance of academic freedom on the part of governments in many African countries.

In such an environment, the academic community is often careful not to overtly offend those in power. This practice contributes to the perpetuation of a culture of self-censorship. Those who courageously speak their mind and express their views often find themselves facing dictators capable of using terror, kidnapping, imprisonment, expulsion, torture, and even death to silence dissident voices.

The stability of a culture of academic freedom is measured by a nation's tolerance of open and frank debate, criticism, and comment. As African countries slowly move away from one-party authoritarian and autocratic rule to elected democratic government and leadership, it is hoped that academic freedom will eventually improve in African academic institutions. African universities have a special responsibility to build a culture of academic freedom in teaching, research, and learning, as well as in societal expression. Developing such a culture in the postcolonial context of political instability and dictatorship will prove a daunting task.

Brain Drain and the Issue of Capacity Building

One of the most serious challenges facing many African countries is the departure of their best scholars and scientists away from universities. The flow away from domestic academe occurs with regard both to internal mobility (locally) and to regional and overseas migration. The term "brain drain" is frequently used to describe the movement of high-level experts from developing to industrialized nations. Much of the literature reflects this particular phenomenon—often pointing out its grave immediate and future consequences—within the context of capacity-building issues. Much of the literature on academic mobility concerns the overseas migration of academics. The movement of high-level expertise is an area of much discussion and debate.

The internal mobility of scholars can be best described as the flow of high-level expertise from the universities to better-paying government agencies and private institutions and firms that may or may not be able to utilize their employees' expertise and talent effectively. As the state of African universities has deteriorated, academics have sought employment opportunities outside universities, consequently draining institutions of their faculty members. Major public institutions in many countries have lost significant numbers of their key faculty members to emerging private higher education institutions and other commercially oriented institutions, perhaps not only in terms of the physical removal of those who leave but also in terms of the time, commitment, and loyalty of remaining academic staff. In many countries, academic staff often hold more than one job outside the university to help ends meet and as a consequence may spread themselves too thin to fulfill their university responsibilities of teaching, research, and service.

Academic staff are also lured away by a variety of government agencies, where salaries are often better and the working environment more comfortable. In many cases, the salaries and benefits in universities are lower than comparative positions in and outside of the civil service. For instance, a comparative salary analysis in Ghana in 1993 revealed that salary levels in sectors such as energy, finance, revenue collection, and the media were all higher than those of the universities (Effah 2003).

In many of the emerging private institutions, salaries and benefits are rather handsome when compared to salaries and benefits in academe. In Ethiopia, for instance, a private college is reported to be paying academic staff a monthly salary as much as three times greater than what a public university pays. In Uganda, the migration of senior staff from tertiary institutions, especially from Makerere University, was of paramount concern in the early 1990s. The relative improvement of employment conditions, salaries, the standard of living, and fringe benefits to the academic staff, Nakanyike Musisi (2003) argues, have combined to halt this exodus and brain drain from Uganda. However, the growing and better-paid private sector and the higher-level civil service continue to lure seasoned academicians away from tertiary institutions. The internal brain drain, though rarely discussed, is nonetheless an issue of great impact on higher education. It is especially important because it is something that African countries themselves could at least partly solve.

Civil strife, political persecutions, and social upheavals instigated the massive exodus of highly trained personnel from countries such as Somalia, Liberia, Ethiopia, Togo, Sierra Leone, and Nigeria. Rwanda and Algeria have also seen systematic killings of academics and intellectuals because of their ethnicity and religious predilections.

Regional migration—academic migration to regional and neighboring countries—has also brought about serious shortages of high-level academics in some countries. Many academic departments have lost their preeminent faculty members to regional universities in other parts of Africa. For instance, several senior scholars from Addis Ababa University, in Ethiopia, hold faculty positions at the University of Botswana. Southern African countries such as Zambia have also been complaining about the migration of their graduates and academic community to South Africa and Zimbabwe. Some have observed that expatriate Zambians staff entire departments in some institutions in these countries.

A 1998 study shows that in 1990, nearly 7,000 Kenyans with tertiary-level education migrated to the United States (Ngome 2003). In the same year, nearly 120 doctors were estimated to have emigrated from Ghana. Between 600 and 700 Ghanaian physicians, a number equal to about 50 percent of the total population of doctors remaining in the country, are known to be practicing in the United States alone (Sethi 2000); and yet, according to Paul Effah (2003), an analysis of existing vacancies in the tertiary institutions in Ghana indicates that about 40 percent of faculty positions at universities and more than 60 percent of those at the polytechnics are vacant. Munzali Jibril (2003) reports that two-thirds of the 36,134 faculty positions in Nigeria remain vacant.

Quoting several sources, Habtamu Wondimu (2003) describes the large number of Ethiopian academic staff who quit their teaching profession to take other jobs or go abroad for training or other reasons and do not return. Though the numbers vary from institution to institution, the estimate of the brain drain from Ethiopian universities might be as much as 50 percent. In Eritrea, one of the critical bottlenecks to a university's development plans, according to Cheryl Sternman Rule (2003), has been the shortage of qualified academic staff and the excessive dependence on expatriate staff.

In Rwanda, as Jolly Mazimhaka and G. F. Daniel (2003) report, skilled personnel and professionals have been either killed or have gone into exile, leaving a huge vacuum in the intellectual labor force, a phenomenon that has greatly affected every domestic sector and curbed the process of national development. Even before 1994, when the infamous genocide took place, many sectors of the national economy suffered from a serious shortage of professionals and management staff; the war and genocide have aggravated this situation.

Matora Ntimo-Makara (2003) points out that Lesotho's capacity to retain highly trained personnel is low, many of whom are attracted by South African's job market, which provides better salary packages. Lesotho's institutional capacity is eroded as a result. Students from Lesotho who study at and graduate from South African institutions seldom return home upon completion of their studies and instead take positions in South Africa. In Swaziland, according to Margaret Zoller Booth (2003), not only has the flight of schoolteachers created a negative climate for educational progress, but the university has also suffered from the exodus of professors seeking better positions in other countries, particularly South Africa. To curb this problem, a review is being considered to improve conditions for academics and staff.

Academics and other professionals in Nigeria have migrated to other countries, most notably the United States, South Africa, Botswana, Saudi Arabia, and member countries of the European Union. According to Munzali Jibril (2003), it is estimated that there are at least 10,000 Nigerian academics and 21,000 Nigerian doctors in the United States alone.

Reports indicate that many of the best and most experienced academics from South Africa are migrating to Australia, Britain, Canada, the United States, and other developed countries. It is ironic that while several countries complain about the loss of their highly skilled labor to South Africa, South Africa itself bemoans its loss of talent to other countries. It is useful to understand this "hopping" phenomenon in discerning the effects of brain-drain issues nationally, regionally, and internationally.

The causes of migration—whether regional or international—are a complex phenomenon. The reasons why scholars migrate or decide to stay abroad are products of a complex blend of economic, political, social, cultural, and psychological factors. The impact and chemistry of each factor varies from country to country and individual to individual and fluctuates over time—even for a single person (Teferra 2000).

While African countries and many major regional, international, and nongovernmental organizations have tried to stem massive movements of African expertise, the results of these efforts are far from satisfactory. Even though various attempts have been made to stem the brain drain, efforts were rarely made to tap the expertise of immigrant communities at their new places of residence. As communications technology is slowly expanding across Africa and physical distance is becoming a less serious obstacle, an active policy of mobilizing the remotely stationed intellectual capital and vital resource of migrated nationals needs to be given more emphasis (Teferra 2000).

Africa is not alone in seeking to stem the brain drain. Developing countries on other continents and, indeed, many industrialized countries have also sought to minimize the migration of talent in an increasingly globalized labor market. These efforts have largely been unsuccessful. Migration from poorer to wealthier countries is commonplace, as is migration from smaller and less cosmopolitan academic systems to larger and more central systems. At present, there is a small exodus from the United Kingdom to the United States and several other countries because of lower academic salaries in Britain. The international migration of highly educated people is by no means limited to Africa but is a worldwide and perhaps unprecedented phenomenon.

The challenges to capacity building in African institutions also emanate from health-related problems. Recent studies indicate that the impact of HIV/AIDS has taken its toll on the academics and students, and the scourge of this disease on African academic institutions is massive. The levels of sickness and death among faculty members from this disease have added to the teaching, financial, and administrative burdens already facing the rest of the academic community (Kelly 2001)

Social upheavals, political instabilities, economic uncertainties, real and perceived persecutions, and poor working and living conditions are often the most common variables facing the migratory community. Most African countries are as yet unable to rid themselves of these economic, social, and political hurdles that drive away many of their highly qualified and trained experts.

Language of Instruction

More than half a dozen languages are currently in use in African higher education. These include Afrikaans, Arabic, English, French, Italian, Portuguese, and Spanish. Only Arabic and, some would argue, Afrikaans are languages indigenous to Africa. Overall, Arabic, English, French, and Portuguese remain the major international languages of instruction at African higher learning institutions. At a time when globalization has become such a powerful force, the dominant position of European languages has become even more significant. English has become particularly powerful, even dominating other major European languages. The predominance of English is fueled by, among other things, the Internet and globalization.

In some African countries, languages struggle for dominance in the higher education sector. There is an interesting trend toward a transition regarding the language used as the instructional medium in Rwanda, for instance, where the core of leadership in government and power is changing. This is also the case in Sudan, where the political predilections are shifting, and in Equatorial Guinea and, to some extent, Somalia, where perceived socioeconomic benefits appear to be dictating the choice of language for instruction. South Africa is discussing the future of Afrikaans as a language of higher education in a context of English domination. Language remains a volatile social issue in many African countries.

The development of vernacular languages into an instructional medium in higher education will continue to be confronted by numerous issues, including:

- the multiplicity of languages on the continent;
- the controversy surrounding the identification and delegation of a particular language as a medium of instruction;
- the developmental stages of languages for use in writing and publications;
- a paucity of published materials;
- poor vocabularies and grammatical conventions of indigenous languages that make it difficult to convey ideas and concepts;
- a poor infrastructure for producing, publishing, translating, and developing teaching materials locally; and
- the pressures of globalization.

African universities rely on the knowledge system conceived, developed, and organized based on Western languages. The Western world produces the majority of knowledge conveyed in those languages. African universities do not have the capacity to generate enough knowledge of their own, nor do they have the capacity and infrastructure to process and translate existing information that comes largely from the Western world—yet. Most books, journals, databases, and other resources that are used in higher education institutions are imported, and these are communicated in Western languages. In the age of the Internet, globalization, and expanding knowledge systems, which are all driven by a few Western languages, no country can afford to remain shielded in a cocoon of isolation brought about by language limitations. Such isolation would prove both disastrous and, likely, impossible to achieve.

Many charge that the use of European languages in higher education in Africa has contributed to the decline of African higher education and the alienation of academe from the majority of the population. Others have argued that the use of metropolitan languages has contributed to national unity. Language conflict is by no means limited to

Africa but is a central issue in many developing countries as well as in a number of multilingual industrialized nations. Canada, for example, faced the possibility of the secession of the province of Quebec because of largely linguistic conflicts. Language also remains an issue of tension in Belgium, and it will remain one of the most significant challenges facing African academic development.

Student Activism

Student activism is prevalent in many African countries. Students have protested alleged social, economic, cultural, political, and personal injustices, and they are vocal in defending their interests and benefits. Student protests about poor student services, delay of stipends, and removal of perquisites and benefits are dominant confrontational issues in many African countries.

As universities have been forced to cut budgets and eliminate services, students have fought fiercely to maintain elements of the status quo. While students have been known to fight to ensure the continuation of their benefits or resist an increase in tuition and fees, they have not been much concerned about issues of academic quality or the curriculum. Self-interest seems to be the dominant force driving student unrest in Africa today.

University protests have led to government instability and have played different roles in political power shifts. In a few cases, they have even toppled governments. When such protests take place, officials conscious of their possible consequences take them seriously—often brutally crushing and suppressing them. Hundreds of students have been seriously hurt, imprisoned, persecuted, and even killed during protests in Africa. According to a study by Federici and Caffentzis (2000), there were over a total of 110 reported student protests in Africa between the years 1990 and 1998. This study demonstrates that government responses to student protests were "inhumane," "brutal," and "excessively cruel."

Student protests are generally perceived as a reflection of the grievances of the wider community. As civil societies are slowly developed and opposition groups become legitimized and tolerated in Africa, it will be interesting to track how these protests are perceived and how they are going to evolve.

Conclusion

That African higher education faces severe challenges is unquestionable. This chapter has provided a discussion of some of the key problems evident across the continent at the beginning of the 21st century.

The problems are difficult and may even be getting worse as the pressure for academic and institutional expansion confronts limited resources. Continuing political instability exacerbates the economic decline seen in many African countries, yet there are signs of progress as well. The emergence of democratic political systems and of a civil society is a positive development. The revival of academic freedom and the commitment by many in the higher education community to build successful institutions despite difficult circumstances reveal the viability of academic systems. A recent recognition—by the international community, particularly the leading donor agencies and major lending institutions—that African higher education is a vital area for development is also a positive step. African higher education is at a turning point. Recognition of the aforementioned problems can lead to positive solutions, with proper planning and effective leadership.

Note

Many of the insights and sources in this chapter come from the book, edited by Damtew Teferra and Philip G. Altbach, *African Higher Education: An International Reference Handbook*. Bloomington: Indiana University Press, 2003. This chapter is based on the introductory chapter in the book.

References

Altbach, P. G. 1987. *The knowledge context: Comparative perspectives on the distribution of knowledge*. Albany: State University of New York Press.

———. ed. 1999. *Private Prometheus: Private higher education and development in the 21st century*. Westport, CT: Greenwood.

Altbach, P. G., and V. Selvaratnam, eds. 1989. *From dependence to autonomy: The development of Asian universities*. Dordrecht, Netherlands: Kluwer.

Attieh, A. 2003. Algeria. In Teferra and Altbach, 151–61.

Baichoo, R., S. K. A. Parahoo, and I. Fagoonee. 2003. Mauritius. In Teferra and Altbach 2003,440–48.

Ben-David, J. 1968. *Fundamental research and the universities*. Paris: Organization for Economic Cooperation and Development.

———. 1977. *Centers of learning: Britain, France, Germany, United States*. New York: McGraw-Hill.

Booth, M. Z. 2003. Swaziland. In Teferra and Altbach 2003, 574–82.

Chilundo, A. 2003. Mozambique. In Teferra and Altbach 2003, 462–75.

Chimombo, J. P. G. 2003. Malawi. In Teferra and Altbach 2003, 414–22.

Edee, A. B. K. M. 2003. Togo. In Teferra and Altbach 2003, 595–600.

Effah, P. 2003. Ghana. In Teferra and Altbach 2003, 338–49.

Eisemon, T. O. 1982. *The science profession in the Third World: Studies from India and Kenya*. New York: Praeger.

El-Hawat, A. 2003. Libya. In Teferra and Altbach 2003, 391–402.

Elmahdy, M. 2003. Egypt. In Teferra and Altbach 2003, 285–300.

El Tom, M. E. A. 2003. Sudan. In Teferra and Altbach 2003, 563–73.

Federici, S., and G. Caffentzis. 2000. Chronology of African university students' struggles: 1985–1998. In *A thousand flowers: Social struggles against structural adjustment in African universities*, ed. Silvia Federici, George Caffentzis, and Ousseina Alidou, 115–50. Trenton, NJ: Africa World Press.

Houenou, P. V., and Y. Houenou-Agbo. 2003. Côte d'Ivoire." In Teferra and Altbach 2003, 273–80.

Jibril, M. 2003. Nigeria. In Teferra and Altbach 2003, 492–99.

Kelly, M. J. 2001. *Challenging the challenger: Understanding and expanding the response of universities in Africa to HIV/AIDS.* Lusaka, Zambia: University of Zambia.

Lelo, M. 2003. Democratic Republic of Congo (Zaire). In Teferra and Altbach 2003, 265–72.

Lulat, Y. G-M. 2003. The development of higher education in Africa: A historical survey. In Teferra and Altbach 2003, 15–31.

Maunde, R. 2003. Zimbabwe. In Teferra and Altbach 2003, 636–48.

Mazimhaka, J., and G. F. Daniel. 2003. Rwanda. In Teferra and Altbach 2003, 500–11.

Millot, B., J. Waite, and H. Zaiem. 2003. Tunisia. In Teferra and Altbach 2003, 601–10.

Mkude, D., and B. Cooksey. 2003. Tanzania. In Teferra and Altbach 2003, 583–94.

Musisi, N. B. 2001. A reflection on and taking stock of innovations at Makerere University. A paper presented at the Ford Foundation conference on Innovations in African Higher Education, October 1–3, 2001, Nairobi, Kenya.

———. 2003. Uganda. In Teferra and Altbach 2003, 611–23.

Ndiaye, H-G. 2003. Senegal. In Teferra and Altbach 2003, 516–26.

Ngome, C. 2003. Kenya. In Teferra and Altbach 2003, 359–71.

Ntimo-Makara, M. 2003. Lesotho. In Teferra and Altbach 2003, 372–80.

Ouakrime, M. 2003. Morocco. In Teferra and Altbach 2003, 449–61.

Rule, C. S. 2003. Eritrea. In Teferra and Altbach 2003, 309–15.

Sethi, M. 2000. Return and reintegration of qualified African nationals. In *Brain drain and capacity building in Africa*, ed. Sibry Tapsoba, Sabiou Kassoum, Pascal V. Houenou, Bankole Oni, Meera Sethi, and Joseph Ngu, 38–48. Dakar, Senegal: ECA/IRDC/IOM.

Seyon, P. 2003. Liberia. In Teferra and Altbach 2003, 381–90.

Stiles, J. 2003. Madagascar. In Teferra and Altbach 2003, 403-13.

Subotsky, G. 2003. South Africa. In Teferra and Altbach 2003, 545–62.

Sylla, S., with H. Ez-zaïm, and D. Teferra. 2003. Guinea. In Teferra and Altbach 2003, 350–54.

Task Force on Higher Education and Society. 2000. *Higher education in developing countries: Peril and promise.* Washington, DC: World Bank.

Teferra, D. 2000. Revisiting the doctrine of human capital mobility in the information age. In *Brain drain and capacity building in Africa*, ed. Sibry Tapsoba, Sabiou Kassoum, Pascal V. Houenou, Bankole Oni, Meera Sethi, and Joseph Ngu, 62–77. Dakar, Senegal: ECA/IRDC/IOM.

————. 2002. Scientific communication in African universities: External agencies and national needs. PhD diss., Boston College.

Teferra, D., and P. G. Altbach, eds. 2003. *African higher education: An international reference handbook*. Bloomington: Indiana University Press.

Wondimu, H. 2003. Ethiopia. In Teferra and Altbach 2003, 316–25.

World Bank. 1991. *The African capacity building initiative: Toward improved policy analysis and development management*. Washington, DC: World Bank.

11

Doctoral Education in the United States

octoral education in the United States forms a huge and
diverse enterprise. Seen from the outside, American graduate
education is often hailed as the "gold standard" to which other
nations and academic institutions aspire. From the inside, however,
doctoral education faces many challenges. Examining the current condition and future prospects of doctoral education in the United States
may serve a useful purpose as other countries continue to look to
American research universities for guidelines while coping with the
expansion of doctoral education. As the European Union prepares to
reorganize university degree structures to fit the bachelor's-master's-
doctoral pattern and to implement the European Credit Transfer
scheme, it makes sense to consider the US system, which has included
both of these practices for a century or more. There are several other
reasons why it is relevant to examine US doctoral education. The
United States is the host country for 565,000 students, almost half of
whom study at the graduate level. American doctoral degree recipients
hold key leadership positions around the world, especially in developing countries.

This essay provides some basic information concerning doctoral
education in the United States and will focus attention on the challenges facing doctoral education. While some US analysts would dis-
agree, my basic perspective is that American graduate education in
general and doctoral education in particular is largely successful and
effective. The system of doctoral education as it has evolved in the
United States over the past century and a half serves both the academ-

ic system and society reasonably well (Geiger 1986, 1993). Indeed, many of the problems facing doctoral education are engendered by the system's success. Some of the challenges facing doctoral education relate to broader societal forces while others are internal to the academic system.

Doctoral education needs to be viewed alongside broader trends in American higher education—and especially graduate education. The doctorate, particularly the PhD, is the pinnacle of a large and complex higher education system. This essay focuses mainly on the PhD degree, the research-oriented doctorate, and not on the increasingly important professional doctorates such as the doctor of business administration (DBA), the doctor of law (JD), the doctor of education (EdD), and others, although some attention will be paid to these degrees. Doctoral study also relates to graduate education generally—master's degrees in many fields including the traditional arts and sciences and in numerous professional fields (Conrad, Haworth, and Millar 1993). Postdoctoral study is not examined in detail in this discussion, although in many fields in the physical and biomedical sciences a postdoctoral research appointment is increasingly considered part of research training.

Doctoral education cannot be separated from either the American academic research enterprise or the arrangements for teaching large numbers of undergraduates in the larger research-oriented universities (Graham and Diamond 1997). Doctoral students, especially in the sciences, are an integral part of the research system. They provide the personnel at relatively low cost who do much of the research under the supervision of senior professors. The research grants provided by government agencies such as the National Science Foundation, by private philanthropic foundations, and increasingly by corporations are funding sources for graduate assistants who work on research while studying for their doctorates. In many cases, dissertation topics relate to the funded research. This system of financial support for doctoral study and basic research works well for American higher education. It ensures financial support, faculty mentorship, and supervision for students and creates a steady source of labor for research projects. These research funds are awarded on a competitive basis, and as a result the bulk of financial support for doctoral students in the sciences goes to the prestigious research-oriented universities. Doctoral students in all disciplines, but especially in the social sciences and humanities, serve as teaching assistants and sometimes as lecturers for undergraduate courses. In return for modest stipends and tuition scholarships, doctoral students provide much of the teaching in large undergraduate courses. Typically, they work under the supervision of a senior professor and conduct discussion sections for students as well as helping with grading and evaluation. In the sciences, doctoral students may help with laboratory supervision. Funds for teaching assistants generally come directly from the university.

The United States spends about half of the world's R&D funds, and a significant amount of R&D expenditure is conducted by universities. Basic research, especially, is university based. A significant proportion of applied research, some of it funded by the corporate sector, is also located on university campuses. Thus, the health of doctoral programs in universities is of considerable importance for the entire research enterprise in the United States.

The Size and Shape of the System

In terms of total student enrollments, the American system of higher education is the second largest in the world after that of China, enrolling 14 million students in postsecondary institutions. While no accurate statistics are available on the number of doctoral students in US universities, it is likely that around 400,000 students are working at the doctoral level in all fields.[1] In 2000, 44,808 doctoral degrees and an additional 80,057 postbaccaulearate professional degrees (e.g., medicine, law, theology, and others) were awarded. It is possible that half of the world's doctoral students are studying in the United States.

The size, scope, and diversity of doctoral education make accurate description difficult. A total of 406 universities award doctoral degrees, but 50 of them award half of all degrees (Nerad 2002). The 50 top degree providers consist largely of the most prestigious research-oriented universities—both public and private—although the proportion of doctorates granted by these prestigious universities has declined over the years.[2] People assume that institutions like Harvard and Yale are the largest doctorate-awarding institutions, but in fact of the top 10 providers, 8 are public universities (including the University of California, Berkeley and the University of Wisconsin–Madison, which are the top 2). The only 2 private universities in the top 10 are Nova Southeastern University (a for-profit institution of questionable quality) and Stanford University. Like the rest of the US higher education system, doctorate-granting institutions are highly stratified. While doctoral education continues to be dominated by the most prestigious institutions, much of the growth in the past 30 years has involved less famous public universities seeking to boost their reputations by offering doctoral degrees. In the highly competitive American system, offering graduate and professional degrees is seen as a sign of prestige and of joining the "big leagues" of research universities. Some public university systems, such as California's, limit doctoral degree programs to specific institutions—for example, only the University of California institutions can offer doctoral degrees while the larger number of schools in the California State University system are limited to bachelor's and master's programs. Universities offering the doctoral degree are a reflection of the highly differentiated American system of higher education. Many are among the most prestigious institutions, both public and private, in part because research-oriented universities tend to be at the top of the hierarchy, but others are regional universities offering doctorates in certain fields.

In a small number of cases, specialized institutions offer doctoral degrees. Rockefeller University, for example, offers doctoral degrees in the biomedical sciences only and is one of the most prestigious institutions of its kind in the world. There are a few freestanding law and business schools in this category as well. A small number of specialized institutions are authorized to offer doctoral degrees in psychology or psychotherapy and some other fields. Some well-known universities—such as the California Institute of Technology—are small institutions that concentrate on a small cluster of disciplines. In the past decade, for-profit academic institutions have emerged, and a tiny number offer doctorates. The large majority of doctoral degrees are, however, offered by traditional universities.

Patterns of Doctoral Study
The basic structure of doctoral higher education in the United States has increasingly become the pattern worldwide (Clark 1993, 1995). Aside from some variations, describing the organization of doctoral studies in the United States is a fairly simple task. The traditional pattern of American postsecondary education includes three degrees, the four-year bachelor's degree, a one- or two-year master's degree, and the doctorate.[3] Doctoral study is quite variable in duration. New "executive" doctorates exist in applied fields such as school administration that can be finished in three years, including a dissertation. The "time-to-degree" in the traditional arts and sciences fields has been increasing—to almost nine years in the humanities and six years in the life sciences. In some fields and at some universities, students are admitted to doctoral study directly after completion of the bachelor's degree, while in other cases a master's degree is required for admission to doctoral programs.

Like much else in American higher education, many variations exist in the structure of academic degrees, along with considerable differentiation and competition among institutions and even among academic departments and programs. It should be kept in mind that, at the undergraduate level, the majority of American higher education is uns-elective—community colleges for the most part are "open door" institutions offering entry to anyone with a secondary school qualification. Many four-year colleges and some lower-tier universities admit virtually all students with the appropriate academic qualifications. Doctoral admission is, of course, more selective, even at the less prestigious universities. At the top of the system, admission to doctoral programs is immensely selective, with only the top candidates being admitted; while at institutions lower in the hierarchy, standards for admission are less stringent.

Traditionally, the doctorate was the quintessential research degree, aimed at preparing students for a career in academic or, in some fields, applied research. For years, however, many doctoral recipients have undertaken relatively little research during their careers, having been involved mainly in postsecondary teaching (Rhoades 1991). Virtually everyone who holds a regular academic appointment in a four-year college or university, and many in the community college sector, hold doctoral degrees. The growing disjunction between the traditional purpose of the degree—training for research—and the actual use made of the doctorate has led to some criticism of the pattern of doctoral education but so far little actual change.

The organization of doctoral study varies by discipline, field, and institution. However, in all of American higher education, coursework, a set of examinations, and a dissertation are standard requirements for the doctorate. In contrast to traditional European patterns of doctoral education, the American degree relies heavily on formal courses as an integral part of the process. The standard pattern for doctoral education includes approximately two years of formal coursework, which may require considerable laboratory work in the sciences. Courses typically include basic and advanced material relating to the field and the appropriate methodology for carrying out research and preparing a dissertation. Coursework is followed by a comprehensive examination, aimed at ensuring that the student has in-depth knowledge of the field. These examinations come in many different forms, depending on the discipline, department, and university—including both oral and written parts or just written parts. Some examinations feature extended review essays, while others more directly cover the discipline. If a student fails to pass the examination (several attempts are generally permitted), he or she is dropped from the doctoral program. In such cases, which are not uncommon, the student is often given a master's degree. Upon suc-

cessful completion of the doctoral qualifying or comprehensive examination, the student then prepares a dissertation proposal and engages
in dissertation research. Most universities also stipulate a hearing concerning the dissertation proposal before it is formally approved and the
student has authorization to proceed with the research.

The dissertation is a central element of any doctoral program and is
intended to be a significant piece of original research that makes a new
contribution to science and the discipline. A significant number of students never complete their dissertations, creating the informal category of ABD (all but dissertation). The proportion of ABDs varies by institution and discipline, but it is high and growing. Dissertations differ in
rigor and focus, of course, with major variations by discipline. In the
hard sciences, dissertation topics are often related to the research program of the supervising professor, which may involve a team-based
project. In the humanities and social sciences, dissertations are typically individual projects reflecting the interests of the researcher, often
with some influence from the faculty supervisor. Dissertation supervision is the main responsibility of the "major professor," usually with
the assistance of several other faculty members. The length, scope, and
quality of a doctoral dissertation vary widely, depending on the discipline, the views of the supervisors, the norms of the university, and the
interests and ability of the student. The time it takes for students to
complete dissertations has come under much criticism, especially in
the humanities and, to some extent, in the social sciences as the time-
to-degree has increased for doctoral studies.

The traditional doctorate in the arts and sciences differs from practices in some of the professional fields that offer doctoral degrees. For
example, the doctorate of education (EdD), a degree usually obtained by
people interested in school administration and related education professions, requires a dissertation—but one that is more a description of
a project rather than a product of original research. Other professional
doctorates also have introduced variations on the research-based dissertation. The growing trend toward tailored professional doctorates in
such fields as management studies, and education means that accredited doctoral degrees are now offered that include cohort-based week-
end coursework and dissertations or other research projects that many
would say fall considerably short of traditional doctoral requirements.
While many people have criticized this trend as "cheapening" the traditional doctoral degree, such programs are growing in number, as are
doctoral degrees offered by for-profit academic institutions, usually in
professional fields, that always lack the rigor of a traditional doctoral
degree.

Another aspect of the system of doctoral education is postdoctoral study. In some fields in the sciences, the "postdoc" is becoming a standard part of the doctoral study cycle. A significant number of doctoral degree recipients take postdoctoral positions immediately following completion of their degree studies, spending a year or more affiliated to a laboratory prior to competing on the job market. Postdoctoral study permits a scientist to work closely with a senior researcher and often with a research group. In some fields, postdoctoral experience is a necessary prerequisite to obtaining a regular academic job. This arrangement delays the start of a career in some ways and introduces an additional level of uncertainty. Postdoctoral appointments are largely limited to the sciences and are seldom available in the humanities or social sciences.

Accreditation and Quality Control

Doctoral study takes place mainly at traditional universities in the United States—academic institutions that offer undergraduate and graduate degrees, including the doctorate, in a variety of disciplines and fields. These institutions are accredited by one of the regional agencies responsible for accrediting all postsecondary institutions in the United States. These regional agencies are not government bodies but private organizations controlled by the academic community itself and recognized by government to carry out accrediting activities. Nonaccredited institutions are typically not eligible to receive government loans or grant funds. In some fields of study—such as engineering, business administration, law, and teacher education—additional accrediting bodies controlled by the professional associations must provide authorization for institutions to offer degrees of various kinds. The traditional arts and sciences disciplines have no accrediting beyond the overall institutional accreditation described above. This patchwork of accrediting and authorization, carried out by nongovernmental organizations and agencies, but with government at both state and federal levels recognizing the validity of these accreditors, constitutes the pattern of American accreditation.

Institutional and program accreditation has a long history and is, in general, quite rigorous. Institutions are asked to provide detailed information and self-evaluations of their work—encompassing doctoral programs, extracurricular activities, academic resources such as libraries and laboratories, the qualifications of academic staff, and many other aspects. This information is carefully evaluated by accreditation teams made up of peer committees, and final decisions are made by the accrediting bodies. Institutions and programs are given basic accreditation—they are not ranked in any way. When a university or program specialty is found deficient in some way, it can be given provisional accreditation and asked to remedy the problem or, in rare cases, can be denied accreditation. A denial generally means that the institution or program ceases to function.

In some states, additional authorization from state agencies is required in order to offer specific academic degrees, with some states extending this authority to private as well as public institutions. This authorization is often legally required in order for academic institutions to operate and can apply both to entire colleges or universities or to specific degree programs. In some cases, state authorization is linked to institutional or program quality, but more often it is a matter of appropriately registering with state agencies and providing evidence of adequate academic resources—such as libraries and teaching staff. Some states also take into account the perceived need for additional in-state programs or institutions. There are universally controls over establishing or expanding public institutions or programs. Controls over private institutions vary from state to state and are less rigorous. Accreditation basically provides certification that an institution or program meets the minimum standards of academic quality and holds the minimum resources deemed necessary.

Accreditation does not correspond to quality control or assessment. In fact, there is no systematic quality control over higher education institutions or academic programs at the national level in the United States. A few states execute limited and generally incomplete efforts to measure the academic quality of public institutions and their academic programs. While concerns over quality of academic programs and the cost of providing academic degrees lead to considerable discussion, no comprehensive plans exist to measure quality in any systematic way. One major topic is the perceived need to measure the outcomes of academic programs in addition to the inputs, but there are no agreed standards or programs relating to such measures.

No national or state quality assessment of doctoral programs exist in any discipline. However, several agencies have attempted to rank academic institutions and discipline-based programs. The most influential and widely circulated ranking is the one done by *U.S. News and World Report*, a weekly general interest magazine. The *U.S. News* annual rankings attempt to measure quality based on a number of variables for academic institutions and programs at all levels. Rankings are provided for graduate programs in many but not all academic and professional fields, although there are no specific rankings for doctoral programs alone. The most comprehensive national evaluation of doctoral programs was carried out by the Committee for the Study of Research-Doctorate Programs in the United States and was conducted by the National Research Council (Goldberger, Maher, and Flattau 1995). This study ranked doctoral programs in various academic fields but not in professional areas. Professional organizations, including some that accredit graduate programs, have been connected with quality assessment and assurance as well. For the past 30 years, the Carnegie Foundation for the Advancement of Teaching has provided a categorization of American academic institutions by type—including a category for research and doctoral universities. While not a ranking, this listing helps to identify types of institutions.

The basic fact, however, is that the United States has a complex and highly effective set of accrediting arrangements, sponsored and managed by the academic community. The arrangements provide a basic "floor" concerning academic quality and resources at all levels of the postsecondary system but little in terms of quality assurance or assessment. Indeed, the United States is behind some other countries in examining and implementing programs in this area.

The Funding of Doctoral Study

The pattern of funding for doctoral education in the United States is complex, as with higher education generally, combining a range of sources. For doctoral education, sources include the 50 state governments (mainly through funding of public higher education institutions and systems), the federal government (mainly through research grants to individual professors and occasionally to academic institutions and loan programs), tuition and fees paid by students, university endowments, donations from philanthropic foundations, and investments of businesses. The mix of funding varies by field, type of institution, and even program within a university.

Basic institutional support is provided for public universities by the states, although the proportion of state funding has decreased in many states given the public disinvestment in higher education and current economic difficulties. The federal government traditionally does not provide basic institutional funding, although it does support some university-based laboratories and facilities in areas defined as in the national interest—mainly, although not exclusively, defense related. Neither state nor federal funding is available for essential institutional support for private universities, although some states do provide direct funding to private universities for doctoral education and the federal government funds some research facilities at private institutions. For private institutions, basic funding comes from tuition and fees, the university's own endowment and other funds, and research grants and contracts.

The mix of funding varies by institution as well. The top 50 doctorate-granting universities are granted the bulk of research funding from the federal government. They also receive most of the research funding from foundations and corporations. These universities are typically able to provide funding packages for many or, in some cases, virtually all of their doctoral students. A large proportion of students have research assistantships and work directly on research projects with professors. This pattern is common at both public and private universities. Less prestigious universities have fewer financial resources. More of their students must pay for their studies, and a larger proportion serve as teaching assistants than is the case at top-tier schools.

Other differences are determined by field and discipline. The sciences are generally better funded than the humanities and social sciences. A larger proportion of science doctoral students receive funding packages that permit them to study on a full-time basis; stipends and scholarships are also typically larger in size. There is less external funding available in the humanities and social sciences. As a result, fewer students in these fields receive full financial support, and most study part time. A larger proportion of students obtain loans rather than grants; more take longer to complete their doctorates; and more drop out before completing their degrees. The sciences have more adequate funding, and as a result their noncompletion rates are lower.

Providing funding for doctoral study in the United States is a perennial difficulty. The present situation is especially problematic because of a change in funding patterns in most states and the impact of the economic downturn. State governments, in general, have reduced their overall support to public higher education, and this has had an influence on doctoral education because the decline in general support has meant fewer resources, higher tuition charges, and less funding for academic facilities. At the same time, corporate R&D expenditures in some fields have declined. The federal government has, so far, not significantly reduced funding for research, but the focus on research funding has shifted to some extent. More important, the federal student loan programs have not kept pace with demand or the rising tuition rates at many universities. Funding for doctoral study faces some difficult challenges.

Doctoral Education as an International Enterprise

International students constitute an important element of doctoral study in the United States. Almost half (264,410) of all international students are studying at the graduate level, with a majority of these in doctoral programs. International students constitute 13 percent of all graduate students, significantly higher than the 2.7 percent of all undergraduates who are international students. Just as important, international students tend to be concentrated at the most prestigious universities and in a small number of fields of study. Business management is the most popular field for international students (almost 20 percent of enrollments are international students), followed by engineering, mathematics, and computer science (Open Doors 2005). In these fields, about half of all doctorates are earned by international students. International students from a number of the countries sending the largest numbers to the United States—India, China, South Korea, and several others—tend not to return to their home countries immediately following the completion of their degrees, with half or more remaining in the United States.[4]

In fields such as engineering, computer science, mathematics, and business administration, a significant part of the professoriate is drawn from other countries. International students are especially numerous in doctoral programs at the most prestigious research-oriented universities. Many international students who earn doctorates in the United States do not return to their countries of origin, and significant numbers enter the professoriate (Choi 1995).[5] Those who do return home bring the norms and orientations of their American doctoral training with them.

The model of American doctoral education—the commitment to teaching and research at the same institutions, rather than separating them in specialized research institutions and teaching-oriented universities; coursework as part of doctoral training; a variety of academic institutions of different quality, prestige, and orientations offering doctoral degrees; and a mixture of funding patterns have proved to be quite influential globally. While US universities have not exported doctoral training abroad, as they have done with some undergraduate and especially professional degrees, other countries have looked to the United States as a model for expanding doctoral training. For example, Japan is currently expanding its doctoral training opportunities and is looking mainly to the United States for ideas

Although the United States borrowed the basic concept of doctoral education from Germany in the 19th century, adapting it to meet American conditions, in recent years, the United States has not been much influenced by other countries. The influence flows largely from the United States to the rest of the world.

Challenges to Doctoral Education

Seen from abroad, American doctoral education seems successful and innovative. Unparalleled in size, comprehensiveness, and quality, doctoral education in the United States seems to induce few worries. Yes, major criticisms are raised about doctoral education, and the entire system of doctoral training and research will face some difficult challenges in the early 21st century. The following discussion highlights some of the main points of criticism currently being discussed in the United States.[6]

THE RESEARCH ENTERPRISE

Doctoral education is closely linked to the research enterprise in American higher education, especially regarding basic research. In the sciences, the traditional model of research production is under strain. Greater pressure is applied for research to be linked to applied usage, especially so that income from patents and other innovations can be earned (Bok 2003). There is also demand from private-sector corporations, especially in fields such as biotechnology, to be involved in academic research and to have rights for the results of research undertaken on campus. Traditional funders of basic research, including such government agencies as the National Science Foundation and private philanthropic foundations, have been critical of the traditional patterns of research funding. At present, the level of funding for research has not significantly declined although there is evidence of changes in funding patterns. Moreover, funders are often less willing to provide money for doctoral students, especially when such support cannot be directly justified in terms of research outcomes.

Doctoral education, especially in the sciences and at the most prestigious research-oriented universities, is linked to trends in research funding—both amounts of money available for research and the configuration of research support. These factors introduce significant uncertainty regarding levels of available funding, the areas that will receive external support, and the numbers of student recipients.

The tight link between external research funding and doctoral education in the sciences at the most prestigious universities has always been problematical. So long as funds were available and providers permitted the academic institutions sufficient autonomy, the system worked. Now, with signs that this status quo is changing, it is unclear how basic research or the provision of funds for doctoral students will survive. This situation has never been a major factor in the social sciences or especially in the humanities, since significant research funding has not been available in these fields.

NARROWNESS AND LIMITED RELEVANCE

As knowledge has expanded, doctoral training has become more specialized, producing doctoral-degree holders with limited skills and opportunities for employment as a result (National Academy of Sciences 1995). Employers in industry and many students and recent graduates complain that their training was too narrow and that graduates were ill-prepared for a rapidly changing job market. The curriculum and philosophy of doctoral education are mainly in the hands of professors who are largely insulated from the job market.

A related complaint, perhaps most widespread in the humanities and social sciences, is that doctoral-degree holders are not well trained to teach. This criticism is related to the narrowness of the curriculum, but it also highlights the fact that doctoral programs provide virtually no training in pedagogy and many offer only limited, if any, opportunities to teach.[7] It has been pointed out that a large majority of doctoral-degree recipients in the humanities and social sciences, and a large proportion of the total number in all fields, engage primarily in teaching at the postsecondary level. Critics have advocated that doctoral preparation include training to teach. They point out that even doctoral students who serve as teaching or laboratory assistants during their degree program are often not trained to perform their limited teaching duties. While pedagogical training has never been part of doctoral education in the United States, many advocate it as a necessary reform to meet the changing roles of doctoral-degree holders in many fields.

Doctoral training, many critics argue, has also become overspecialized, creating further problems for degree holders as they enter an increasingly differentiated and complex job market. Increased specialization relates to the expansion of scientific knowledge in all fields and the perceived need to discover new knowledge, albeit in an ever-contracting universe.

GROWING IRRELEVANCE TO THE JOB MARKET

Overspecialization, the changing academic labor market, and the growing employment of PhD-degree holders outside universities have led to criticism that the doctorate has become irrelevant (Altbach 1999). Faculty members responsible for doctoral training still focus on the traditional model of a faculty career. However, even for many persons entering the academic profession, the terms and conditions of the professoriate have changed. Fewer doctoral-degree holders can expect to work at research-oriented universities, while a growing number find themselves at colleges and universities that focus on teaching rather than research. In many fields only a minority of graduates find positions in academe. The job market for doctoral-degree holders has been diversifying as many enter private industry, including entirely new fields such as biotechnology and consulting firms. Government service also increasingly attracts doctoral graduates.

The current market for PhD holders has put pressure on doctoral training to be more flexible and aimed at a wider array of jobs than the traditional academic profession. While fields have made minor changes, there has been little rethinking of the links between doctoral training and the labor market. The Center for Innovation and Research in Graduate Education has done research to show that both the career goals of doctoral students and the actual jobs obtained by graduates are changing.[8] In biochemistry, for example, only 32 percent of doctoral students want to become professors, while in electrical engineering 35 percent aspire to the professoriate. In English, 81 percent desire an academic career, as do 72 percent in political science. In terms of actual employment, a study found that about two-thirds of doctoral-program graduates in English, mathematics, and political science held professorial positions, while half of those in biochemistry and roughly one-third of those in computer science and electrical engineering were in the professoriate (Nerad 2002, 7). A significant and growing number of PhD recipients are employed outside academe.

The transition from doctoral study to work is also increasingly problematical in the United States. Obtaining an academic job, still a goal for doctoral students in many fields, is difficult and ever more complex—especially tenure-track academic jobs. The proliferation of postdocs in the sciences causes it to take longer to obtain a "regular" academic position in those disciplines. There is little relation between doctoral study and the growing number of nonacademic jobs available to PhD holders. Efforts are being made to smooth this degree-to-work transition, but the problems are considerable.

TIME-TO-DEGREE AND DEGREE COMPLETION

Obtaining the doctoral degree is taking longer on average, and this is seen as a problem. It now takes between six and nine years to complete a doctorate—depending on field and institution. The humanities have the longest "time-to-degree," while the life sciences have the shortest. A combination of a carefully organized curriculum, more adequate funding, and dissertation research that is often linked to the work of a laboratory all contribute to the greater efficiency of doctoral study in the sciences. With the expansion of knowledge, it takes more time to impart the necessary skills (including ever more complex methodologies) to doctoral students. As funding has become less available for the growing number of doctoral students, many are forced to study part time or to delay their studies. In the humanities, where funding is most problematical, students often accrue loan obligations of $20,000 to $30,000 during their doctoral studies. Further, the changes in patterns of funding tend to slow doctoral completion as students are asked to serve as teaching or research assistants, often in areas only marginally related to their specialties.

Analysts have pointed out that the increased time-to-degree is not cost-effective either for students or academic institutions. The universities accrue costs from having students remain on campus for an extended period, and the students themselves face inadequate stipends and the continuing expense of study. Increased time-to-degree lowers morale and contributes to a growing rate of noncompletion of studies. This complex nexus of conditions has created a pattern of difficulties that has made doctoral study more difficult.

RECRUITING THE BEST AND THE BRIGHTEST

One of the greatest challenges for American higher education in the coming period will be recruiting top-quality scholars and scientists to staff the postsecondary education system and, especially, to ensure that the research universities have the best-quality staff. Doctoral education plays an essential role in this arena because the academic profession as well as people who staff research laboratories and institutions typically hold doctorates and are trained at research universities that offer doctoral degrees. Postdocs and faculty at the top of the system are trained in the key 20 or 30 American research universities.

Ensuring the future development of scientific and academic leadership is now in question in the United States. Ongoing financial problems are placing strains on the doctoral training system and on higher education. Universities find it hard to compete with the private sector for the best talent. Many of the brightest young minds are unwilling to undergo the long, poorly paid, and often convoluted road to a doctoral degree. The problems encountered by PhD holders during the process of obtaining academic employment are another deterrent.

The United States imports some of the best minds from other countries. In some cases, these people are trained at American universities, and many seek employment in US academe. Other professors are recruited from universities overseas, lured by better salaries and working conditions in the United States. The US practice of poaching talent from other countries is neither fair to those countries, nor is it an assured means of obtaining the best talent.

Conclusion

It may seem paradoxical that the system of doctoral education admired and often replicated in other countries is seen by many people in the United States as having some severe problems. The basic structure of doctoral training in the United States as it has evolved during the past century is an effective system for training creative specialists in the disciplines and in multidisciplinary fields. Doctoral programs have proved to be sufficiently flexible to encourage original scientific research while at the same time adjusting to the development of mass higher education.

The American pattern of combining instruction and research as part of doctoral study has proved to be successful. The "taught doctorate," as opposed to the European-style research doctorate, has been effective in providing the depth of knowledge required by the expanding disciplines (Altbach 2001). Locating doctoral work in universities rather than specialized research-focused institutions has also been useful. The fact that doctoral education exists in a large and highly differentiated academic system is also a major advantage—PhD study is, for the most part, located at the best universities, institutions that can in general afford to provide the facilities needed for quality instruction and research.

The basic structure of American doctoral education does not seem to require dramatic change. However, reforms are needed that will assure that past successes can continue. Of greatest importance, perhaps, is ensuring that sufficient funds are made available to provide high-quality training and to support the research enterprise that is integrally related to doctoral education. It is also necessary to link doctoral programs to changing employment trends, scientific developments, and the needs of doctoral students and faculty.

Notes

1. In 2001, 354,800 students were enrolled in science, engineering, and health fields in academic departments offering the doctoral degree. Some of these are in master's programs, but most are studying for doctorates.

2. The major doctoral institutions are members of the Association of American Universities. This organization, established in 1900, is generally seen as representing the major, research-oriented American and Canadian universities.

3. More than 25 percent of American students attend community colleges, which offer two-year degrees (associate degrees). Study at community colleges may result in a terminal associate degree or students may transfer to a four-year college or university and complete two additional years for the bachelor's degree.

4. Most of these statistics are from *Open Doors 2005*.

5. In many fields, foreigners with US doctorates find it easier to enter the academic profession than to compete for jobs in business or other sectors of the American economy. Americans, on the other hand, are often attracted to private-sector employment, where remuneration is higher than in academe. As a result, foreign degree holders are probably overrepresented in academe.

6. This discussion follows many of the points made by Maresi Nerad (2002) in her paper "The Ph.D. in the U.S.: Criticisms, Facts, and Remedies." The Council of Graduate Schools, which is the main organization representing the interests of graduate programs in the United States, highlights many of these issues in its publications and on its Web site.

7. The Carnegie Foundation for the Advancement of Teaching is currently studying doctoral preparation in the United States and will focus on teaching as an essential part of the process.

8. The Center for Innovation and Research in Graduate Education (CIRGE) is a new agency involved in research and analysis relating to graduate study. Further information can be obtained from CIRGE, Box 353600, University of Washington, Seattle, WA 98195, USA. E-mail: cirge@u.washington.edu.

References

Altbach, Philip G. 1999. Harsh realities: The professoriate faces a new century. In *American higher education in the 21st century: Social, political, and economic challenges*, ed. P. G. Altbach, R. O. Berdahl, and P. J. Gumport, 271–97. Baltimore: Johns Hopkins University Press

———. 2001. The American academic model in comparative perspective. In *In defense of American higher education*, ed. P. G. Altbach, P. J. Gumport, and D. B. Johnstone, 11–37. Baltimore: Johns Hopkins University Press,

Bok, Derek. 2003. *Universities in the marketplace: The commercialization of higher education*. Princeton, NJ: Princeton University Press.

Choi, Hyaeweol. 1995. *An international scientific community: Asian scholars in the United States*. Westport, CT: Praeger.

Clark, Burton R., ed. 1993. *The research foundations of graduate education: Germany, Britain, France, United States, Japan*. Berkeley: University of California Press.

———. 1995. *Places of inquiry: Research and advanced education in modern universities*. Berkeley: University of California Press.

Conrad, Clifton F., Jennifer Grant Haworth, and Susan Bolyard Millar. 1993. *A silent success: Master's education in the United States*. Baltimore: Johns Hopkins University Press.

Geiger, Roger L. 1986. *To advance knowledge: The growth of American research universities, 1900–1940*. New York: Oxford University Press.

———. 1993. *Research and relevant knowledge: American research universities since World War II*. New York: Oxford University Press.

Goldberger, Marvin L., Brendan A. Maher, and Pamela E. Flattau, eds. 1995. *Research-doctoral programs in the United States: Continuity and change*. Washington, DC: National Academy Press.

Graham, Hugh Davis and Nancy Diamond. 1997. *The Rise of American Research Universities: Elites and Challenges in the Postwar Era*. Baltimore: Johns Hopkins University Press.

National Academy of Sciences. 1995. *Reshaping the graduate education of scientists and engineers*. Washington, DC: National Academy Press.

Nerad, Maresi. 2002. *The ph.d. in the US: Criticisms, facts, and remedies*. Paper presented at a conference at the Center for Higher Education Policy Studies, University of Twente, the Netherlands.

Open doors 2005: Report on international education exchange, ed. Hey-Kyung Koh Chin. New York: Institute of International Education.

Rhoades, Gary. 1991. Graduate education. In *International higher education: An encyclopedia*, ed. Philip G. Altbach, 127–46. New York: Garland.

12

Research and Training in Higher Education: The State of the Art

In most countries, higher education has become a large, complex enterprise. As universities and other postsecondary institutions have grown, they acquire elaborate administrative structures in need of major expenditures of public and often private funds.[1] Perhaps most important, postsecondary education is recognized as a central element in modern society. Universities are considered engines of the postindustrial age and of the knowledge economy. Moreover, higher education has become big business. Academic institutions employ thousands of people and educate tens of thousands—or in some cases hundreds of thousands. Degrees in a multiplicity of specialties from ancient history to biotechnology are offered. In 1971 Eric Ashby characterized the American academic system as offering "any person, any study," in describing its diversity and scope (Ashby 1971). Martin Trow analyzed the progression of higher education from elite to mass and finally to universal access (Trow 2006). In industrialized nations, at least, mass access has been achieved, and a few countries—first, the United States and Canada but, recently, South Korea, Finland, Japan, and many others—have moved to semiuniversal access, enrolling half or more of the relevant age group. Many others, mainly in Europe and the Pacific Rim, educate 40 percent or more of the age group. Developing countries lag behind, and the main growth in the coming decades will be in this part of the world (World Bank 2000). China, for example, overtook the United States as the world's largest academic system in 2005, although it enrolls under 20 percent of the relevant age group.

In this context, there is a great need for expertise and data about all aspects of higher education and for a sophisticated understanding of the nature of academic institutions. Academic institutions require thoughtful and competent leadership. Research on higher education and training in the art and science of administration and institutional leadership are critical to the future of the university. Policymakers outside academic institutions, in government and in the private sector, who increasingly wield power over the future of academe, need knowledge and analysis in order to effectively coordinate complex institutions and systems.

An Emerging Field

Higher education research and the preparation of administrative personnel for postsecondary education constitute relatively new and undeveloped fields. Researchers have traditionally been reluctant to study the institutions in which they work. Until the mid-20th century in most countries, academic institutions were small and enjoyed considerable autonomy. Government-mandated systems of higher education did not exist. Universities, though considered to be important, seldom functioned as major social institutions. Except for a few cases, such as the Humboldtian reforms in Germany in the early 19th century where academic institutions became relevant for national development, universities were somewhat peripheral. Social scientists preferred to focus their scholarly attention elsewhere, especially on subjects that might yield more useful theories. Most people interested in pedagogy and education focused on primary and secondary schools and not on higher education. As a result, postsecondary education was ignored by researchers in the field of education as well as by social scientists.

Given their lack of interest in academe, academic institutions and agencies responsible for funding higher education research provided scarce funds or support for research on this topic. The reasons for the paucity of data, research, and analysis concerning higher education tell us something about the origin of the field. Few people claim that the study of higher education is a full-fledged academic discipline. Therefore, the infrastructures that go along with a scientific discipline—academic departments, professorships, and the like—are largely nonexistent (Dressel and Mayhew 1974). In part because higher education lacks a disciplinary base, it has never been inducted into a clear academic home. In the United States, Britain, Canada, Australia—countries with an Anglo-Saxon academic tradition—the study of higher education has been incorporated into the research and teaching activities of universities, mainly in schools of education, where it is often considered peripheral to the main missions of these schools. Recently, in a few additional countries, higher education has been added to the curriculum, again, mainly in education or pedagogical faculties. China is the most notable example; higher education is the subject of research or teaching in at least 400 Chinese academic institutions, with major programs or centers at 20 or more. The Netherlands, Norway, and Finland are other examples of countries that have incorporated higher education into the university curriculum.

Only recently has a perceived need emerged for professionally educated administrators and other staff in postsecondary institutions. The growth of a group of midlevel administrators specifically trained in the field of higher education has occurred mainly in the United States, Canada, and Australia. Senior academic administrators continue to be drawn from the ranks of the professoriate and slowly gravitate to administration as a career. In contrast, in Germany a cadre of senior university managers, appointed by government directly from the civil service, have responsibility for certain elements of university administration and management, especially in finance and nonacademic areas. These top administrative officials have little or no background in higher education. The lack of an institutional base has limited the growth and institutionalization of higher education as an academic specialty, although the growth in the number of professional middle managers in higher education has contributed to the expansion of the field of higher education studies.

The study of higher education is an interdisciplinary endeavor that has been both a strength and a weakness. It is a strength because researchers in many social science disciplines—including but not limited to sociology, political science, psychology, economics, and history—have contributed significantly to the development of research on higher education. Among others, this group includes sociologists Burton Clark, Martin Trow, David Reisman, and Talcott Parsons; political scientist Seymour Martin Lipset; economist Howard Bowen; and many others. Researchers in the field of educational studies have slowly begun to develop an interest in higher education; curriculum specialists, educational planners, and others now work on postsecondary issues. The small number of researchers focusing on higher education obstructed the emergence of a distinctive field. In part because it is an interdisciplinary field, higher education research has no established methodology. It borrows from other fields. Again, this is both a strength and a weakness. Interdisciplinarity has made possible original and quite innovative research, but it has hindered the creation of a permanent research community.

Until recently, there has been relatively little demand for data and analysis of higher education by practitioners. Academic institutions themselves have been governed according to traditional norms and were fairly small, until the post–World War II era. Governments tended to permit academic institutions considerable autonomy, even where state funds largely paid for postsecondary education. When decisions were made, research-based data and analysis were not seen as relevant to decision making.

Funding stimulates research, and little money was available for research on higher education. The few exceptions were short lived and not sustained. For example, major reform efforts in Britain (the Robbins Commission) and in Sweden (the U-68 Report) stimulated some research (Robbins 1966). Both also resulted in significant changes in higher education in those countries. More recently, government initiatives, such as the Thatcher government's abolition of the binary system in the 1980s or the more recent Dearing Commission were not accompanied by major research studies. The Carnegie Foundation for the Advancement of Teaching in the United States and the Leverhulme Trust in Britain sponsored major studies of higher education to understand academic systems undergoing changes and facing considerable challenges in the aftermath of the expansion of the 1960s.[2]

Within the field of higher education, several subject areas do have a fairly strong research base. For example, the economics of higher education has become an especially central topic in a period when the allocation of resources is of great concern. The Institut de recherche sur l'économie de l'éducation in Dijon, France focused on economic issues in higher education beginning in the 1980s as funding became problematic and continues to be active in this area. Funding issues and related themes, such as access, have received attention from commissions in several countries.

Gathering international statistical information concerning higher education has been seen as a priority by UNESCO, which has been engaged in this area for several decades (UNESCO 1993). The Organization for Economic Cooperation and Development (OECD) and the World Bank have also been engaged in compiling statistics. National agencies in many countries collect national statistics, but few efforts exist to link these statistics or to ensure comparability among them (Organization for Economic Cooperation and Development 2003). Consistent and reliable comparative statistical information concerning higher education is currently unavailable. With academic systems worldwide facing similar problems and with international student and staff mobility on the rise, more consistent statistical data are needed.

Comparative studies in higher education are also an identifiable trend in the literature, in part to provide national policymakers with a basis for comparison. This is a growing interest in international bench-marking and comparisons of financial outlays and the like. Several recently published major international analyses of trends are contribut-ing significantly to current discussions of comparative higher educa-tion. The World Bank's 1994 policy review for higher education stimu-lated a good deal of discussion and controversy, including a volume of critiques (World Bank 1994; Buchert and King 1995). UNESCO also completed an overview of higher education trends worldwide (UNESCO 1993). As part of the preparation for the UNESCO study, several reports were prepared. The Task Force on Higher Education and Society issued a useful report on higher education in developing countries in 2000 (World Bank 2000). Truly comparative research is both difficult and expensive, and not surprisingly there are few compar-ative studies. More common are compilations of case studies around a specific theme (Altbach 1996).

Much of the research and data concerning higher education have not been formally published in standard books and journals and may be considered part of a "gray literature" that is difficult to access and often unavailable in libraries or other collections. These data often relate to individual academic institutions and are circulated only with-in the institution. Governmental and other reports are frequently issued only for limited audiences, and there is no effort to disseminate them more widely. Similarly, many of the studies commissioned by the World Bank are kept confidential and are unavailable to the research community. The Internet has proliferated the available data and to some extent analysis concerning higher education worldwide. The problem involves the few guidelines concerning the quality or useful-ness of many items.

After almost a century of intellectual development as a field of research, higher education has, however, built up a sizable literature, a network of communications, and a community of researchers. Those responsible for planning and administering higher education institu-tions and systems are beginning to recognize the need for data and interpretation. Yet, the field has no widely accepted theories. Policymakers and administrators often say that they do not find research produced by the research community directly applicable to "practical" problems of higher education management. Nonetheless, the field has grown and matured.

A Higher Education Research Infrastructure

The field of higher education research has expanded in large part because conditions have created a need for such research and the means with which to conduct it (Sadlak 1981; Altbach 1985). The objective circumstances of higher education have changed: expansion of enrollment, staff, and budgets; a focus on the research mission of the universities; and the value of higher education to postindustrial society have all increased the attention paid to higher education in most societies. The following factors have contributed to the development of higher education research and to the increasingly complex infrastructure of the field.

As academic institutions expand, they need more information about themselves—such as enrollment trends, indicators of student achievement, and data concerning faculty and staff. This data gathering is referred to as "institutional research" and is focused on a single institution but may be relevant to a wider audience.[3] Institutional research offices exist at thousands of academic institutions worldwide—they are common in larger universities in countries such as the United States, Britain, Australia, and Canada and are of growing importance in Europe and Japan. In China, there are more than 400 higher education centers attached to universities—many mainly focused on institutional research and planning. Elsewhere, institutional research is less well organized and is commonly carried out as part of the administrative work of universities. Networks of researchers in this field are well organized in North America and Europe. The output of the institutional research offices of individual universities probably constitutes the largest part of research on higher education. However, much of this research is only of local interest, and little of it is made available to a wider audience.

University-based centers or departments with a focus on higher education have been established in a small number of countries to educate higher education professionals and researchers. These departments and academic programs, located mainly in academic institutions in Anglo-Saxon countries, have also been the source of a considerable amount of research. There are probably more than 500 university-based programs worldwide. In the United States, close to 100 universities have programs in higher education, mostly located in schools of education that provide postbaccalaureate degrees. While many of these US programs are small and without a research emphasis, several have contributed significantly to research in the field. The larger and more research-oriented programs include the University of California, at Los Angeles, the University of Southern California, Pennsylvania State

University, the University of Michigan, Michigan State University, the University of Pennsylvania, and several others. Prominent European examples are the Center for Higher Education and Work at the University of Kassel in Germany, the Center for Higher Education Policy Studies (CHEPS) at the University of Twente in the Netherlands, and the Institute for Higher Education Studies at the University of London—all of which have a strong research focus but also offer graduate-level degrees and certificates in higher education. The centers in Kassel and Twente, for example, have conducted significant research for the European Union and a number of agencies and have published many research studies.

A recently established EU-sponsored higher education master's program is headquartered at the University of Oslo in Norway and involves other universities in Finland and Portugal. The Research Institute for Higher Education at Hiroshima University, along with a similar center at Tsukuba University in Tokyo, and newer efforts at Nagoya and Kyoto universities, and Waseda and Obirin universities among the private institutions are Japanese examples. All of these Japanese institutions offer degree study as well as working on research projects. China may have the largest number of higher education programs and centers of any country. Among the prominent Chinese institutions are the Institute for Higher Education at Peking University, Huazhong University of Science and Technology, and the Institute of Higher Education at Xiamen University, although there are more than 400 higher education research institutes around the country. Some of these university-based centers focus mainly on research, others on teaching.

Governments require national data and research for planning in higher education, the allocation of funds, and related purposes. In some countries, national research institutes have been established with funding made available for higher education research and data collection.[4] In some places, government-sponsored agencies assist with higher education reform and innovation. These agencies have responsibility for collecting statistical information on higher education, and some have a research mission as well. Research institutes vary greatly in size, purpose, and orientation. Some are linked with academic institutions, while others are attached to ministries of education. In Japan, for example, the Hiroshima University center is funded by the national government for the purpose of data collection and analysis regarding Japanese higher education as well as overseas trends.

State planning and coordinating agencies have been established in many countries, and these organizations sometimes sponsor research and collect statistics to assist their work. Some of these agencies were established in the 1960s and others more recently—during the period of expansion of higher education—to meet the need for relevant information and analysis. Not surprisingly, the former "socialist" countries of Central and Eastern Europe and the former Soviet Union, with their centrally planned economies, established large higher education research agencies to provide the data needed for planning and development, as well as for coordination with other economic and political entities; these agencies have either been scaled back or abolished. The Higher Education Funding Council for England is the governmental body responsible in that country for allocating funds to academic institutions and also conducts limited research. Scotland has a similar agency. In the United States, most state governments have coordinating bodies for state-supported higher education, and in some cases, these agencies collect and publish research as well. The US federal government, through such agencies as the National Center for Educational Statistics, collects data, publishes analyses of higher education developments, and commissions some research.

The Indian University Grants Commission has a research function and a responsibility for allocating research and other funds from the national government to higher educational institutions. The semigovernmental Korean Council on University Education has funding and coordinating responsibilities and also sponsors some research. ANUIES, the Mexican federation of universities, publishes a journal as well as other publications. The Center for University Studies at the National Autonomous University of Mexico also produced research studies and a journal. Other countries have similar agencies and organizations. The arrangements for the collection of national statistical information and the allocation of public funds to higher education vary considerably around the world—the expansion of the higher education enterprise has led to the growth of agencies responsible for coordination, the allocation of funds, and to some extent research.

University associations in many countries engage in research domestically and to some extent internationally. In the United States, the American Council on Education, the National Association of State Universities and Land Grant Colleges, the Council of Graduate Schools, and many other entities have made research and the dissemination of information a part of their missions.[5] The German Hochschulrektorenkonferenz sponsors publications and supports some research. The Association of Indian Universities publishes books and journals and funds some research. These are just a few examples of university-sponsored organizations that conduct research and analysis as well as representing the interests of academic institutions to government and the public. On a regional basis, the Association of African Universities and the European Universities Association disseminate information and occasionally conduct research. Globally, the International Association of Universities has promoted research and its dissemination at an international level; its journal, *Higher Education Policy*, is the source of useful research.

International and regional organizations are among the most effective in bringing together specialists on higher education as well as providing a forum for discussing higher education issues. UNESCO, established in 1946, has from the beginning been involved with postsecondary education—sponsoring many conferences, stimulating research, and publishing books and reports. It has also established regional offices that concentrate on higher education—such as the UNESCO European Center for Higher Education (CEPES), based in Bucharest, Romania, which focuses on Central and Eastern Europe; and the Center for Higher Education in Latin America and the Caribbean.[6] In recent years, the World Bank has sponsored research and issued publications concerning higher education. While much of its research concerns World Bank loans and projects and thus is unavailable to the public, a growing number of studies have been published and now constitute some of the best sources for research on higher education on developing countries (Saint 1992; Salmi and Verspoor 1994). OECD, an agency representing the industrialized nations, has long been involved with higher education research and related activities and has produced a series of country-based studies that provide useful analysis. The OECD also sponsors the Institutional Management in Higher Education initiative and a journal, *Higher Education Management*. Some parts of the world, such as Southeast Asia, do not have active regional organizations, while others, such as Latin America, have a range of research-based groups.

A large number of private nongovernmental organizations have emerged in recent years to provide research and policy perspectives on higher education. Some of these organizations have an international focus, while many serve national needs. The Program for Research on Private Higher Education (PROPHE), based at the State University of New York at Albany in the United States, focuses on private higher education internationally—one of the fastest growing sectors of postsecondary education. The Center for Higher Education Policy Studies (CHEPS) in the Netherlands has a special interest in higher education policy, but its research and publications have a broader focus. The Institute for Higher Education Policy, based in Washington, DC, is an example of an organization that does research, mainly with a US focus, on policy but also has an advisory role. The Center for Higher Education Transformation (CHET) in South Africa provides advice on higher education to government and universities and also has an active research and publication program. These are only a few examples of many national, regional, and a few international organizations focusing on higher education.

The perceived need for data and analysis has spurred a plethora of organizations and agencies to provide information. Many are new, reflecting the emerging nature of the field, and they exist at institutional, national, regional, and international levels. There is relatively little interaction or cooperation among them. Almost the entire infrastructure of higher education research is a post–World War II phenomenon—a product of expansion in the 1960s and of the emphasis on accountability and assessment as postsecondary education experienced financial problems in the 1980s and 1990s.

The Information Infrastructure in Higher Education

With the proliferation of research centers and agencies concerned with higher education administration, coordination, and policy, a network of publications and other means of communicating the knowledge base in higher education have developed. In many countries, journals relating to higher education have been launched that are aimed at researchers and other professionals in the field. While their circulation is usually limited, these journals do provide access to relevant research, current data, and analysis on the field. There are also many publishers who consistently publish books and monographs in the field of higher education. The Internet has stimulated the development of Web sites devoted to higher education, which are now significant sources of data and analysis. Many journals are now available online to subscribers as well, although there do not yet seem to be any solely electronic journals in higher education.

It is not possible, in the context of this essay, to discuss all of the national, regional, and international publications in the field. However, it is useful to focus on selected sources of information. As noted earlier, much of the higher education research base is not easily accessible either because it has not been published or has been issued by institutions only in limited editions. These informal publications ("gray literature") is generally not included in standard indexes or reference sources. Much of the material deals only with specific academic institutions, but some are institutional planning documents and studies, reform reports, and similar policy-related materials with wider relevance. Unfortunately, there is no clearinghouse or data center for gray literature in higher education. The ERIC (Educational Resources Information Center) bibliographies and database, which was sponsored by the US Department of Education, was the single largest source of bibliographical information; it included some of this below-the-radar literature. ERIC mainly collected American material and is of limited relevance to the rest of the world. Several years ago, the US government stopped funding ERIC—its work was decentralized—and it is no longer a prominent agency collecting research information.

Several bibliographical sources in higher education exist. *Contents Pages in Education* (a journal that covers scholarly and research periodicals in education, including higher education) is an important worldwide resource, although it is limited to publications in English. Several abstracting journals dealing with higher education publications in Britain and the United States have good coverage of their respective countries. However, as pointed out earlier, these publications include only material published in journals or, in some cases, books.

Additional contributions to the research literature can be found in two encyclopedias on higher education in an international context (Clark and Neave 1992, Forest and Altbach 2006). These reference volumes provide not only worldwide coverage of higher education but also include "state-of-the-art" essays on key topics in the research literature. They are benchmarks for the field, showing that the study of higher education has come of age and has produced a coherent and reasonably comprehensive body of research. There are also several national encyclopedias or handbooks focusing on higher education. An important resource is the annual *Higher Education: Handbook of Theory and Research*, edited by John C. Smart and published by Springer. Now in its 22nd year, this largely US-focused publication features lengthy essays on aspects of research on higher education.

The number of research-based and other journals focusing on higher education has expanded in the past several decades. Most of the internationally circulated journals in the field have started since the 1960s. In the past decade, new internationally focused specialized journals dealing with assessment, quality issues, technology, and teaching in higher education have been founded, reflecting important new trends in the field. A number of successful more broadly focused internationally circulated magazines and newspapers relating to higher education provide news, commentary, and reporting on research and policy initiatives. The most important of these are the *Chronicle of Higher Education* in the United States, the *Times Higher Education Supplement (The Higher)* in Britain, and *Le monde d'éducation* in France. All of these publications have an international circulation, and all report on international developments as well as national news. There are also many national periodicals with similar aims—for example, *University News* in India, *China Education Daily (Zhongguo Jiaoyu Bao)* in China, *Das Hochschulwesen* in Germany, *Universitas* in Italy, and *Universidades 2000* and *Campus Milenio* in Mexico.

There are a small number of internationally circulated research journals in higher education. These publications set the standard internationally for research and disseminate key scholarship in the field. Most are published in English, and are edited and published in the United States, Western Europe, or Australia. *Higher Education, Higher Education Management, Minerva,* and *Higher Education Policy* are the most explicitly international of the journals. Other periodicals include *Studies in Higher Education* and *Higher Education Review* (Britain); and the *Journal of Higher Education, Review of Higher Education,* and *Research in Higher Education* (United States). *Higher Education in Europe* and the *European Journal of Education* focus on higher education from a mainly European perspective.

Hundreds of national journals also exist. In general, these do not circulate outside the countries of origin. Among the most important of these journals are the *IDE Journal* in Japan, *Universidad Futura* in Mexico, the *Canadian Journal of Higher Education*, and *Change* in the United States. Others, such as the *South African Journal of Higher Education* are less well known internationally but publish valuable material. There are approximately 400 journals devoted to higher education in China alone—all but a half dozen published by individual universities and seldom circulated outside the sponsoring institution.

The publication of books on higher education has also increased significantly. Several publishers now specialize in books on higher education. Multinational publishers such as Springer (formerly Kluwer) publish many higher education books and journals. Others include the Open University Press in Britain; RoutledgeFalmer Publishers, Jossey-Bass, Greenwood, Praeger, and the Johns Hopkins University Press in the United States; Tamagawa University Press in Japan; Campus Verlag in Germany; and Lemmons Publishers in the Netherlands. Research institutions and other organizations also publish books and monographs in the field—these include the Research Institute on Higher Education at Hiroshima University in Japan, the Russian Research Institute on Higher Education in Moscow, the American Council on Education in the United States, and others. The Society for Research into Higher Education in the United Kingdom has perhaps the largest series of books in the field of higher education, published in cooperation with the Open University Press.

A Map of the Field

Although the field of higher education studies did not exist until after World War II, a small but insightful literature on higher education predates the field and helped to shape thinking about the nature of higher education. For example, Hastings Rashdall's history of the medieval university remains a classic of scholarship (Rashdall 1895). The Arab scholars who established the Al-Azhar University in Cairo thought about higher education, as did those responsible for the establishment of universities in medieval Europe (Makdisi 1981). Philosophers such as John Henry Newman (Newman 1899), and sociologist Max Weber (Shils 1974) analyzed higher education. Psychologist G. Stanley Hall is said to have taught the first academic course on higher education, at Clark University, in 1893 (Goodchild 1996). Visionary academic leaders, from Alexander von Humboldt to Robert M. Hutchins, have articulated their views on the development of the university. Plato and Aristotle discussed advanced education in their writings, and Confucius had a profound impact on the nature of higher education in China and East Asia.

One of the first formal policy-focused studies was Abraham Flexner's influential report on American medical education, which inspired significant policy reforms in the training of physicians (Flexner 1910). Later, Flexner wrote one of the first books to use a comparative approach to study higher education and recommend policy. His *Universities: American, English, German* was aimed at stimulating reforms in American higher education (Flexner 1930). One of the first government-sponsored reports on higher education was conducted as part of a reform effort in 1911 at the University of Calcutta in India. This document, and several others commissioned to shape higher education policies in colonial areas, influenced the later use of official reports on higher education in India. There is a rich literature in many countries concerning the history of higher education, focusing especially on the history of individual universities (Rüegg 2004).

This brief review indicates that although the research has been scattered and lacking in focus, influential work of high quality had been produced in the century or more prior to the emergence of a field of higher education studies in the mid-20th century. Scholars and researchers worked within the confines of their disciplines, although with little if any communication across fields of study. Thus, higher education was hardly a neglected subject, although it did not emerge as a field of scholarly and research analysis until the past half-century.

At approximately the same time that higher education was developing as an interdisciplinary field, researchers in other subspecialties were dealing with topics relating to the higher education enterprise. For example, the sociology of science grew dramatically as researchers turned to analyzing how research networks in the scientific disciplines work, how research is carried out, and how scientists and researchers measure productivity and influence in science. This subfield established its own journals and other infrastructures. The sociology of science and the history of science relate only indirectly to higher education studies (Ben-David 1991). Researchers in the two disciplines rarely come into contact, and the science studies literature is seldom used by higher education scholars. Similarly, the subfield of bibliometrics, which examines the impact of research and the diffusion of scholarly work, is not generally consulted by researchers in the field of higher education.

The links are closer between the field of higher education and that of science policy studies. The journal *Minerva*, especially during the editorship of Edward Shils, straddled both fields and attempted to contact the concerns of researchers in both areas. Others, such as *Technology and Society*, cover this intersection of fields. However, there has been little cross-fertilization, and only a limited number of researchers pay attention to both fields. Science policy is central to higher education now because it seeks to examine research networks that extend beyond the universities—for example, to university-industry linkages.

More integrally related to higher education is the community of researchers involved with planning for college and universities. This field has its own professional organizations and a small research network. The Society for College and University Planning in the United States is the main organization. Higher education management has also emerged quite recently as a distinct subspecialty, but in this case there are strong links with higher education research. The OECD's *Higher Education Management* journal provides an international perspective on this topic. Because of the increasing complexity of academic institutions and the growing professionalization of university administration, there is a growing interest in management issues. So far, there seem to be few links between the broader field of management studies and higher education (Cohen and March 1986). Management studies and business administration actually have a special relevance to higher education.

Another strand of research relates to globalization and internationalization in higher education. With the growth of international study— about 2.5 million students study outside of the borders of their own countries—and a concern about how academe is being globalized, there has been an expansion of interest in this field. The *Journal of Studies in International Education* was established in 1996 to reflect this interest. Hans de Wit has analyzed internationalization trends in the United States and Europe (de Wit 2002; de Wit, Jaramillo, Gacel-Avila, and Knight 2005). The globalization of higher education—defined by the increasing use of English for communication and teaching world-wide, academic institutions from one country being established in another nation, the role of the World Trade Organization and the General Agreement on Trade in Services (GATS) in higher education, and other factors—have concerned higher education as well (Altbach 2004). The European Union's Bologna Accord is the most important European initiative in internationalization and will harmonize European academic systems and increase intra-European mobility, international study, and international students (Reinalda and Kulesza 2005). International student exchange remains a key theme of internationalization (Davis 2003; Altbach, Kelly, and Lulat 1985). Organizations such as NAFSA: Association of International Educators in the United States, the European Association for International Education, and the Canadian Bureau of International Education sponsor research—much of it applied and intended to improve international education programs and exchanges.[7] The Institute of International Education's *Open Doors* provides annual statistics concerning international study in the United States.

The internationally prominent higher education programs and centers, mostly located in North America and Europe, control most of the publications. The major research paradigms originate mainly in the major English-speaking nations, which play a central role in defining the field. Other parts of the world are to a considerable extent peripheral. Approximately 75 percent of the world's internationally circulated research in the field of higher education emanates from the United States, Britain, and Australia. In the 1990s, the research communities in such countries as Japan, the Netherlands, China, and Germany did, however, grow in size and scope. Initiatives on the Pacific Rim and, to a lesser extent, in Latin America are indications of growth of higher education research and analysis and the establishment of centers and institutes. While the major English-speaking countries continue to dominate the research networks, the balance is changing as other countries build up research capacity in higher education. The field of higher education displays the same geographical inequality as most scientific disciplines, although probably to a lesser extent than in many fields.

Institutional Research

Institutional research, the collection of data concerning all aspects of a specific academic institution, is in great demand as academic institutions expand and as accountability becomes a more central part of governmental agendas worldwide. Institutional and systemwide planning also increases the salience of institutional research. Although rarely reported or released outside the institution, and of limited relevance to a wider audience, institutional research data are increasingly essential assets. Institutional research on enrollments, student achievement, and fiscal arrangements has become of central importance for planning, accountability, benchmarking, and other purposes and is increasingly used in higher education research.

The institutional research community appears well organized in only a few countries; outside of Europe and North America, few national or international links exist. Outlets for publication and analysis of data based on institutional research have grown in recent years, although they remain to some extent outside the mainstream of higher education research. In the United States, the Association for Institutional Research provides a professional forum for the research community, although there is still only limited coordination between the institutional research community and the wider higher education research community. The European Association for Institutional Research recently altered its mission to encompass broader higher education research as well as traditional institutional research. There are no international journals focusing on institutional research and few forums for international discussion in this field other than at conferences held in the United States or Europe. Despite these problems, institutional research is coming into its own as a subfield of higher education research and is increasingly part of the mainstream.

The Education of the Administrative Estate

Academic administration worldwide has become increasingly complex. As institutions have become larger and provide many more services and specialties, the need to provide skilled management and administration has grown as well. It is no longer possible for amateurs without training or a serious interest in administration to run modern universities.

Senior academic leaders everywhere, including presidents, rectors, vice chancellors, and deans still come from the ranks of the senior professoriate. They typically have no specific training for the administrative roles they perform, and most individuals who assume these offices return to teaching and research after serving one or two terms. The

United States is somewhat unique in that many senior academic administrators enter into administrative careers, going from one senior post to another, often at different institutions, and do not return to the professoriate.

Most midlevel managers in higher education have not been faculty members. The United States, with the largest and most diverse academic system, initiated this new professionalized administrative cadre. These personnel typically require training for their jobs. The field of higher education administration developed after World War II, and by 2000, more than 100 American universities offered graduate-level specialties in higher education. Among the largest subspecialities in higher education is student personnel administration—providing training for those responsible for counseling and guidance, student extracurricular activities, and administering dormitories and other student facilities. Training for general academic administration and the development of such subspecialties as financial management and university legal affairs evolved. Special areas such as leadership studies, institutional research, community college administration, fund raising, and others are also part of many administrative training programs.

Today, higher education programs are offered as graduate (postbaccalaureate) degrees at both the master's and doctoral levels and serve both entry-level students seeking administrative careers as well as experienced administrators wishing to upgrade their skills and qualify for higher office. Traditionally, higher education graduates were hired for lower- and midlevel management positions at colleges and universities, as well as posts in government agencies dealing with higher education, think tanks, and related jobs. Institutional researchers often hold graduate degrees in higher education. In recent years, higher education graduates have assumed presidencies and other upper-management positions, especially in the community college sector and in lower-ranking four-year institutions.

Higher education administration has become a well-established field in a few countries, most notably the United States and, to some extent, China. The programs are typically located in schools of education in many of the top universities in the United States. Faculty members in these programs provide much of the published research on higher education and are often called on to serve as consultants and advisers for postsecondary institutions.

Similar programs have been introduced in several other countries, although growth has been surprisingly slow given the expansion in the number of administrators worldwide. The major English-speaking countries of the United Kingdom, Canada, and Australia now have university-based programs that provide training for academic administrators. A few other countries, such as China and Japan, are beginning to provide training for administrators, and others are beginning to think about it. It is likely that this field will continue to grow in response to the need for career-level administrators informed about higher education and schooled in the application of management theory, legal issues, student psychological development, and other social science–based disciplines.

A rapidly growing field of in-service or pre-service training for higher education administrative personnel has emerged. Short training programs, provided by professional organizations, higher education graduate programs, specific universities, or other groups are offered to provide some basic training. Programs, especially in the United States, exist for new presidents, department chairs, provosts, student affairs vice presidents, legal officers, fund raisers, and many others. The programs last from a few days to two weeks. As the complexity of academic administration and leadership is recognized worldwide, efforts to provide training for administrative positions will expand.

Future Trends

Higher education research is recognized as analyzing the challenges facing higher education institutions. Yet, critics in government and in academic administration feel that higher education research does not directly address the day-to-day problems faced by managers in postsecondary education. This is probably an inevitable and unresolvable tension in the field. Some of the research produced by higher education scholars examines fundamental issues such as the relationship of academe to government. Another purpose involves building up the methodologies or knowledge base in the field. This type of research is thus largely irrelevant to the search for immediate solutions to problems faced by academic institutions or systems. Practitioners and the public are often impatient for results. At the same time, at least some of this broadly based work is a necessary underpinning for more applied research. In fact, the tension between the two poles in the field is, in many ways, a strength. Those in control of research funding are insufficiently committed to the work of building a solid knowledge base, methodological rigor, and theoretical perspectives in the field. At the same time, there is often an unnecessary distance between university-based researchers and the consumers of research in academic administration or government agencies.

The following trends may characterize the future development of the field of higher education studies:

1. The field will expand into countries and regions where it is now either weak or nonexistent. Recognition of the value of information and analysis about postsecondary education will stimulate continued growth in the field. There will be a related expansion of the sources of information—journals, books, Internet sites, and newsletters—in these new research communities.

2. The Internet has become a key source for research, statistical information, and analysis and commentary in higher education, in common with other fields of knowledge. National, regional, and international agencies are paying increasing attention to it.

3. There is a growing focus on the process of teaching, learning, and assessment in higher education. Instruction, the central element in higher education, is imperfectly understood. In part to improve learning and create better ways to measure the results of higher education, there has been increased interest in the evaluation of teaching, measurement of instructional results, and assessment.

4. The gulf between institutional research and other research on higher education remains considerable. The field would benefit from better links between institutional research and the broader research community. The tension between basic and applied research in higher education will continue, with some confusion regarding the audience for research in the field.

5. Higher education is an interdisciplinary field of inquiry. It will not emerge as a separate scientific discipline.

6. The recognition that academic institutions require a trained cadre of administrators will lead to the expansion worldwide of university-based training programs in higher education. Some programs may offer academic degrees and require a rigorous curriculum of studies. Others may consist of shorter courses, seminars, or other academic experiences. This will contribute to a larger research community, since many of the faculty members appointed to teaching positions in these programs may also engage in research.

7. Large-scale research, either within one country or internationally, will be limited due to lack of funds.

8. A better balance between the research agenda of higher education researchers and the users of that research will strengthen the research community. There is a tendency for funding agencies to provide support for research that will yield specific answers to questions of immediate concern. In the long run, this approach weakens the knowledge base. This conflict between "basic" and "applied" research is by no means limited to the field of higher education.

9. Strengthening regional and international networks for reporting

data and research will improve communication and build up the field. Organizations, databases, and publications that bring together researchers from different countries will also expand. In short, there is a need to build better networks in the higher education research community. Regionally based publications, both journals and books, require additional support.

10. Comprehensive, comparable, and accurate international data concerning higher education are central for both research and policy development. Stronger international organizations can provide a basis for improved data collection.

11. Inclusion of currently peripheral research communities, such as those in smaller countries or in regions without any tradition of research in the field, into the international mainstream is a key priority.

12. Better integration of the institutional research community as well as institutional research into the higher education research system will help this largely ignored part of the higher education research community become part of the mainstream. In Europe, the European Association for Institutional Research has linked the two streams in the field.

13. Improvement of links between the higher education research community with researchers in the social sciences will strengthen the field of higher education by adding more interdisciplinary work.

Conclusion

Higher education research and training have expanded over the past four decades. The organized infrastructures of a research community have emerged in government, academe, and research organizations—with geographical scope and increasing sophistication. The field has developed a broader concept of higher education, the value of the university, and the diversities of academe in a period of expansion. It has also contributed insights into the specific policy needs of academic administrators and political authorities. Higher education has legitimized itself as a research area within educational studies, gaining acceptance among the leadership of higher education. A small but growing number of social scientists have taken on higher education as an area of research. This, too, has improved the literature and has helped to provide an analytical base.

In a number of countries, university-based training programs for academic administrators have been established. These programs have contributed to the expansion and legitimization of higher education research. Some of the graduates of these programs become researchers in the field, although most go into academic administration or policy-making positions, where they make use of research results. This trend is likely to extend to other countries, where professionally trained administrators are needed for large postsecondary institutions and systems.

The research output in the field ranges from what the social scientists would call "middle-range theory" to the most applied data gathering pertaining to a specific problem at a single university. Social scientists from a number of disciplines have attempted to theorize about the university, about the dynamic of leadership in higher education, and about teaching and learning. Few theories are accepted as applying overall to postsecondary institutions. The quality of the research is also mixed, as is probably inevitable for a field in its early stages of development.

The field of higher education research is poised for change. It is gaining importance and legitimacy in parts of the world traditionally underserved. Expansion will be slower in the traditional centers as resources have become limited although research is still needed. The field has achieved a measure of legitimacy in the academic community, and it is now accepted as important by policymakers in national as well as regional and international organizations.

Notes

1. This essay is a revised and updated version of Altbach (1997). See also Teichler and Sadlak (2000).
2. In the early 1970s, under the leadership of Clark Kerr, the Carnegie Commission on Higher Education sponsored more than 50 volumes that provided an impressive research base for American higher education. The commission also issued a number of policy-oriented reports. At the end of the decade, again under Kerr's leadership, the Carnegie Council on Policy Studies in Higher Education sponsored additional studies and reports. These impressive efforts were funded by the Carnegie Foundation for the Advancement of Teaching. The foundation continues to be actively involved in sponsoring research and has a special interest in policy-oriented studies. At about the same time, the Leverhulme Trust in Britain sponsored a dozen or more volumes relating to British higher education in the aftermath of the Robbins Report.
3. Institutional researchers have organized themselves into several national and regional groups. The Association for Institutional Research in the United States is one of the largest research-oriented organizations in the world. In Europe, the European Association for Institutional Research has expanded its focus beyond institutional research to broader higher education issues.
4. Examples of national organizations focused on higher education research and information are, among many others, the Hochschul-Information-System (HIS) in Germany, the Research Institute on Higher Education in Russia, and the National Center for Educational Statistics in the United States.
5. The National Center for Higher Education, located at 1 Dupont Circle in Washington, DC is well known as the headquarters of many of the Washington-based associations representing the higher education community—many of which sponsor research. The American Council on Education, representing the presidents of a large number of American universities, is the leading organization.
6. CEPES has been particularly active in stimulating research. Its journal, *Higher Education in Europe,* has focused on key issues in higher education, and its publication program has sponsored research on European higher education themes.
7. Similar organizations exist in Japan and in several other countries.

References

Altbach, Philip G. 1985. Perspectives on comparative higher education: A survey of research and literature. In *Higher education in international perspective: A survey and bibliography,* ed. Philip G. Altbach and David Kelly, 3–54. London: Mansell.

———, ed. 1996. *The International academic profession: Portraits from 14 countries.* Princeton, NJ: Carnegie Foundation for the Advancement of Teaching.

———. 1997. Research on higher education: Global perspectives. In *Higher education research at the turn of the new century: Structures, issues and trends,* ed. Jan Sadlak and Philip G. Altbach, 3–24. New York: Garland.

———. 2004. Globalization and the university: Myths and realities in an unequal world. *Tertiary Education and Management* 10 (1): 3–25.

Altbach, Philip G., David H. Kelly, and Y. Lulat. 1985. *Research on foreign students and international study: An overview and bibliography.* New York: Praeger.

Ashby, Eric. 1971. *Any person, any study: An essay on higher education in the United States.* New York: McGraw-Hill.

Ben-David, Joseph. 1991. *Scientific growth: Essays on the social organization and ethos of science.* Berkeley: University of California Press.

Buchert, Lene, and King, Kenneth, eds. 1995. *Learning from experience: Policy and practice in aid to higher education.* The Hague: Center for the Study of Education in Developing Countries.

Clark, Burton, and Guy Neave, eds. 1992. *The encyclopedia of higher education.* 4 vols. Oxford: Pergamon.

Cohen, Michael D., and James D. March. 1986. *Leadership and ambiguity: The American college president.* Boston: Harvard Business School Press.

Davis, Todd M. 2003. *Atlas of student mobilitity.* New York: Institute of International Education.

de Wit, Hans. 2002. *Internationalizxation of higher education in the United States of America and Europe: A historical, comparative, and conceptual analysis.* Westport, CT: Greenwood.

de Wit, Hans, I. C. Jaramillo, K. Gacel-Avila, and J. Knight, eds. 2005. *Higher education in Latin America: The international dimension.* Washington, DC: World Bank.

Dressel, Paul L., and Lewis B. Mayhew. 1974. *Higher education as a field of study.* San Francisco: Jossey Bass.

Flexner, Abraham. 1910. *Medical education in the United States and Canada.* New York: Carnegie Foundation for the Advancement of Teaching.

————. 1930. *Universities: American, English, German*. New York: Oxford University Press.

Forest, James J.F., and Philip G. Altbach, eds. 2006. *International handbook of higher education*. Dordrecht, Netherlands: Springer.

Goodchild, Lester. 1996. G. Stanley Hall and the study of higher education. *Review of Higher Education* 20:69–100.

Makdisi, George. 1981. *The rise of colleges: Institutions of learning in Islam and the West*. Edinburgh: Edinburgh University Press.

Newman, John Henry. 1899. *The idea of a university*. London: Longman, Green.

Organization for Economic Cooperation and Development. 2003. *Education at a glance: OECD indicators*. Paris: OECD.

Rashdall, Hastings. 1895. *The Universities of Europe in the Middle Ages*. 3 vols. Oxford: Oxford University Press.

Reinalda, Bob, and Ewa Kulesza. 2005. *The Bologna process: Harmonizing Europe's higher education*. Opladen, Germany: Barbara Budrich.

Robbins, Lord. 1966. *The university in the modern world*. London: Macmillan.

Rüegg, Walter, ed. 2004. *A history of the university in Europe*. Cambridge: Cambridge University Press.

Sadlak, Jan, ed. 1981. *Directory of institutes and organizations in research on higher education*. Geneva: International Bureau of Education.

Saint, William S. 1992. *Universities in Africa: Strategies for stabilization and revitalization* Washington, DC: World Bank.

Salmi, Jamil, and Adriaan M. Verspoor, eds. 1994. *Revitalizing higher education*. Oxford: Pergamon.

Shils, Edward, ed. 1974. *Max Weber on universities: The power of the state and the dignity of the academic calling in imperial Germany*. Chicago: University of Chicago Press.

Teichler, Ulrich, and Jan Sadlak, eds. 2000. *Higher education research: Its relationship to policy and practice*. Oxford: Pergamon.

Trow, Martin. 2006. Reflections on the transition from elite to mass to universal access: Forms and phases of higher education in modern societies since WWII. In *International handbook of higher education*, ed. James J.F. Forest and Philip G. Altbach, 243–80. Dordrecht, Netherlands: Springer.

UNESCO. 1993. *World education report, 1993*. Paris: UNESCO.

World Bank. 1994. *Higher education: The lessons of experience*. Washington, DC: World Bank.

World Bank. 2000. Higher education in developing countries: Peril and promise. Washington, DC: World Bank.

About the Author

Philip G. Altbach is J. Donald Monan, S.J. professor of higher education and director of the Center for International Higher Education in the Lynch School of Education at Boston College. He has been a senior associate of the Carnegie Foundation for the Advancement of Teaching, and served as editor of the *Review of Higher Education, Comparative Education Review*, and as an editor of *Educational Policy*. Philip G. Altbach is author of *Comparative Higher Education, Student Politics in America*, and other books, and co-edited the *International Handbook of Higher Education*. Dr. Altbach holds the B.A., M.A. and Ph.D degrees from the University of Chicago. He has taught the University of Wisconsin-Madison and the State University of New York at Buffalo, where he directed the Comparative Education Center, and chaired the Department of Educational Organization, Administration and Policy, and was a post-doctoral fellow and lecturer on education at Harvard University. He is a Guest Professor at the Institute of Higher Education at Peking University in the Peoples Republic of China, and as been a visiting professor at Stanford University, the Institut de Sciences Politique in Paris, and at the University of Bombay in India. Dr. Altbach has been a Fulbright scholar in India, and in Malaysia and Singapore. He has had awards from the Japan Society for the Promotion of Science and the German Academic Exchange Service (DAAD), has been Onwell Fellow at the University of Hong Kong, and a senior scholar of the Taiwan Government. He is listed in *Who's Who in America* and other major biographical volumes. He was the 2004-2006 Distinguished Scholar Leader of the New Century Scholars initiative of the Fulbright program.